Penguin Education

Economics of Busines
Bryan Carsberg

Industrial Economics
Editor: H. Townsend

Penguin Modern Economics
General Editor: B. J. McCormick

Bryan Carsberg

Economics of
Business Decisions

Penguin Books

Penguin Books Ltd,
Harmondsworth, Middlesex, England
Penguin Books, 625 Madison Avenue,
New York, New York 10022, U.S.A.
Penguin Books Australia Ltd,
Ringwood, Victoria, Australia
Penguin Books Canada Ltd, 2801 John Street,
Markham, Ontario, Canada L3R 1B4
Penguin Books Books (N.Z.) Ltd,
182–190 Wairau Road, Auckland 10, New Zealand

First published 1975
Reprinted 1977

Made and printed in Great Britain by
Richard Clay (The Chaucer Press) Ltd,
Bungay, Suffolk
Set in Monotype Times

Penguin Modern Economics Texts

This volume is one in a series of unit texts designed to reduce the price of knowledge for students of economics in universities and colleges of higher education. The units may be used singly or in combination with other units to form attractive and unusual teaching programmes. The volumes will cover the major teaching areas but they will differ from conventional books in their attempt to chart and explore new directions in economic thinking. The traditional divisions of theory and applied, of positive and normative and of micro and macro will tend to be blurred as authors impose new and arresting ideas on the traditional corpus of economics. Some units will fall into conventional patterns of thought but many will transgress established beliefs.

Penguin Modern Economic Texts are published in units in order to achieve certain objectives. First, a large range of short texts at inexpensive prices gives the teacher flexibility in planning his course and recommending texts for it. Secondly, the pace at which important new work is published requires the project to be adaptable. Our plan allows a unit to be revised or a fresh unit to be added with maximum speed and minimal cost to the reader.

The international range of authorship will, it is hoped, bring out the richness and diversity in economic analysis and thinking.

B.J.MCC.

For Debbie and Sarah, who have played many different games since this book was started and have often played them quietly because they wanted to help.

Contents

Editorial Foreword

This volume is of value to economists, accountants and management scientists. It is perhaps unfair to suggest that accounting is practice without theory and economics theory without practice, but the two disciplines with complementary interests have pursued separate lines of development for a surprisingly long time. The double exclusiveness is now disappearing, as this book makes plain. Professor Carsberg explores the borderline between economics and accounting, and in doing so provides a theoretical structure for the use of accounting in decision-making, and at the same time provides a fresh viewpoint from which to see the practicability of microeconomic theory. At each stage he takes care to show how problems may be set out for solution by computer. His book is inter-disciplinary in the best sense of the word: it is concerned with the interface of two subjects and increases understanding of both.

Bryan Carsberg teaches accounting at Manchester. He has a background of study of both economics and accounting, and so writes in both subjects with equal ease and authority.

H.T.

Preface

One often hears methods used to reach business decisions described as 'pragmatic' or 'theoretical'. Such descriptions are often intended to be critical. A pragmatic approach is often characterized as a method which fails to consider carefully and systematically all the consequences of a decision and hence is unlikely to achieve the best results. A theoretical approach is often characterized as likely to yield impracticable decisions; it implies a method that appears impressive on paper but will not work in the 'real world'. In my view such a dichotomy is unfortunate. The aim of theory is to improve practice. A theory which will not work in practice is a bad theory. Equally, I would argue, practice is generally capable of improvement – by good theories. Essentially, in business, this involves reaching a clear view of the objectives of decisions; analysing carefully the likely effects of various alternative decisions and collecting evidence about the effects wherever possible; and choosing one alternative by logical argument relating likely effects to objectives.

The first aim of this book is to analyse modern theory dealing with short-term business decisions. Some of the ideas, mainly those concerned with risk and uncertainty, are still in the development stage and not yet refined to the point at which they can become a part of routine practice. Nevertheless, the structure of the analysis seems to provide useful insights. The major part of the analysis is, however, directly applicable in practice. Indeed it is already being applied in some leading firms though much less widely than seems possible or desirable. A subsidiary aim of the book is to bring together methods of accountants, economists and operational researchers and show how each can complement the other.

This aim has not required the use of advanced mathematical techniques.

The book deals with material which I have developed in teaching managerial accounting to undergraduates and postgraduates at the University of Manchester, and in giving seminars to practising managers. I hope that it will be useful for courses in accounting and industrial economics at Universities, Polytechnics and other Colleges of Further Education; and also that it will be useful for accountants and other practising managers. I should like to thank my former students collectively for the help they have given me by their constructive criticism and enthusiastic interest. I owe a particular debt to my colleagues in the Department of Accounting and Business Finance at the University of Manchester for the stimulus they have given to my work and to Professor Michael Bromwich and Mr Leslie Falk who have read a draft of the manuscript and made many helpful suggestions. The views I express may not be shared by those who have helped me. I should also like to thank Colette White and Maureen Scapens for their extraordinary patience and proficiency in typing the manuscript. Finally and most importantly, I should like to thank my wife Margaret. She has not distracted me from my work more than was optimal, and any merit that my work may have is due in large measure to her support and encouragement.

1 The Nature of Management

Introduction

The management accountant has been recognized as an important member of the management team in business and public undertakings for several years. He has contributed to decisions by providing numerical calculations and qualitative judgements of the consequences of various courses of action. The basic technique of his discipline emerged originally from modifications of traditional book-keeping practice and often comprised rules of thumb methods, the rationale of which had not been clearly thought out.

Since the end of the Second World War, however, there has been a remarkable development of techniques available to the management accountant. His original methods have been augmented by techniques developed by mathematicians, notably operational researchers. They have been reshaped by the rigorous analysis of the economist – and they have emerged with a clearer rationale. Indeed the well-trained management accountant is now aptly described as a business economist and managerial accounting may be seen to be a branch of applied economics.

The attainable level of sophistication in management decision-taking, as evidenced by the current literature, is a good deal above the level normally achieved in practice. The divergence may have arisen, in part, because managers have studied the available techniques and doubted their practical relevance. It may also have arisen because many modern techniques have not been described adequately to those who might use them. New methods have been developed by specialists who have described their ideas in the technical language of their profession, obscure to the uninitiated.

Members of many different professions approach particular business problems from different points of view – each valuable in its own way. Important progress might be made if a free exchange of ideas were undertaken. But free exchange has been inhibited by difficulties of communication. Accountants, mathematicians, economists, engineers and others have been reluctant or unable to talk to each other; each has tended to defend his special territory as best he could – and the contribution of each has, arguably, suffered in consequence.

This book will attempt to bring together some of the different approaches to management problems. It is hoped that it may be useful both to managers who wish to obtain a general view of modern techniques and to students of economics and accounting. Its main purpose is to describe the use and rationale of methods available for the analysis of short-term decisions, such as the choice of volume and mix of production. The exposition will be couched mainly in terms of the problems of managing a firm in the private sector of the economy. Many of the arguments used may, however, be applied to the public sector with little adaptation, for the problems of the public sector are often similar in principle to those of firms. The fundamental approach of the book will be that of the accountant; however, traditional accounting techniques will be examined critically and emphasis will be given to methods of analysis used in economics and to mathematical techniques where appropriate.

A knowledge of advanced mathematics is not required for the understanding of this book. We shall attempt, by using simple numerical illustrations, to identify problems which can best be analysed by mathematical methods; we shall discuss the rationale of such methods and the interpretation of the solutions which they produce. We shall not, however, attempt the solution of complex problems which require a technical sophistication in mathematics.

Management accounting is still today in a state of rapid development. New techniques seem to raise almost as many difficulties as they solve. They may require information, estimation of the consequences of present actions, in a form more detailed than that required by the old techniques. Such information may not be readily available. In consequence, the emphasis in research may shift from the development of techniques of analysis to problems of measurement and prediction. Progress in dealing with such problems would represent a revolution in management techniques, comparable in its significance for society to the revolutions which have taken place in technology and natural science during the last few centuries. A beginning has been made by adopting the approaches to problem-solving used in economics and operational research. Management has thus adopted a scientific method, a method which holds out hope of progress with the most intractable problems. Management has, perhaps, already started its Copernican revolution. The use of scientific method in analysing management problems seems to be of such fundamental significance that it will be made a cornerstone of our analysis. Its nature and its advantages will be discussed in chapter 3.

A related modern development is the study of the effects of business decisions and accounting systems on human behaviour. This involves the attempt to specify the desired flows of financial information in a business enterprise, taking account of the effects of the system in motivating employees as well as other economic effects. Such considerations were substantially neglected in early work on management methods; but they seem to hold great promise of progress and will be referred to in this book whenever appropriate.

The nature of the management process

It will help to put the scope of this book further in perspective if we identify the main activities of managers in so far as they are relevant to the matters which we shall discuss.

We may view the management of an enterprise as the undertaking of a sequence of activities which are repeated in a cyclical manner. The process is described in a simplified manner in Figure 1.

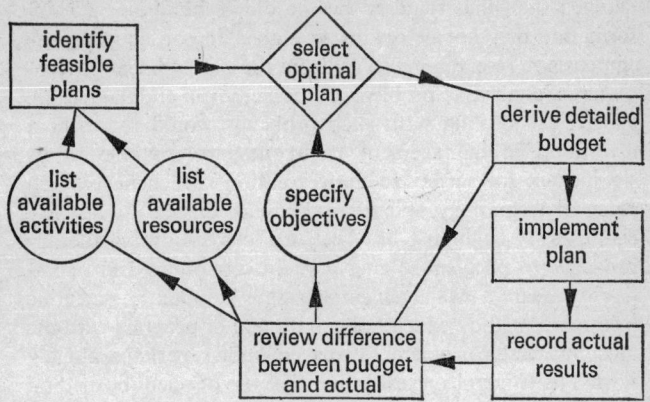

Figure 1 A simplified management cycle

The selection of activities

We begin our description by breaking into the cycle at the point at which a new enterprise would start. Its managers might first settle on some objective for their operations. Then, having decided what period is to be covered by their initial plan, they would consider details of activities which might be undertaken during that period, products which might be manufactured, investments undertaken (including different means of production) and so on. They would also need to assess what resources were available for carrying out the activities, how big a labour force could be employed, how much capital could be raised and so on. The components of these two initial inventories, of activities and resources, may be combined in various ways to yield a number of feasible plans, i.e. groups of activities which can be carried out with the resources available.

The next task is to choose from the various feasible alternatives the optimal plan, i.e., the plan which best satisfies the objectives of the enterprise. The advance specification of objectives gives a yardstick by which the various plans may be compared. The above steps in the management cycle involve the choice of activities.

Control of the plan

There follows what may be called a control phase. The detailed consequences of the chosen plan are predicted in the form of budgets (estimated statements) showing the quantities of resources required and corresponding income and expenditure. Actual results are recorded in a similar form and compared with the estimates in order to identify differences and assess the reasons for them. The differences may be due to poor prediction or faulty execution of the plan. For example, if actual man-hours used in production exceed the estimate, the difference may be attributable to wasted time or to unrealistic estimation of the time required. In either event managers obtain information which may help them in the formulation or implementation of the next plan.

Some modifications of the simple process

In practice, the process of management is not so straightforward as the above description suggests. The first specification of available activities and resources may not identify any satisfactory plan, judged by the objectives. Managers must then attempt to locate better activities or more efficient resources or else modify their objectives (or possibly abandon the enterprise). In either event, the selection of the optimal plan may be viewed as an iterative process rather than a simple sequence of actions as described above. The timing of the actions also deserves some comment. The length of period for which plans of a given amount of detail should be made may well vary from one type of enterprise to another. The choice will depend on the costs and benefits of different possibilities. For example, it may not be equally easy to predict the nature and amount of output required over a long period for a firm with a standard product line and for a firm which undertakes special contracts; furthermore products are subject to higher rates of obsolescence in some industries than in others.

In consequence the costs and benefits of long-term budgets

may differ from industry to industry. Any enterprise, however, should normally draw up several descriptions of its plans, covering different lengths of time and giving different amounts of detail; it might prepare (a) a long-run budget including estimates of major investment projects and general indications of output levels, (b) a budget covering one year and describing predictions of output and resources required in considerable detail and (c) a weekly or monthly budget used as a basis for monitoring actual progress. Such procedures would make it possible to plan for consistency between investment and production whilst also being able to take corrective action quickly to remedy operating inefficiency revealed by the short-term budget.

Furthermore, actual practice does not see the sequence of actions in one whole decision-cycle completed before the next one begins. The search for activities and resources and the consideration of objectives may, for example, be carried on more or less continuously; and information revealed by comparing a weekly budget with actual results may lead to adjustment of an annual plan long before the year is elapsed. Nevertheless, the idea given in Figure 1 of management as a learning process involving an indefinite sequence of activity selection and control is an important one.

The main focus of this book will be on the means of selecting an optimal plan, given information about the available activities and resources. Some attention will also be given to the means of identifying the characteristics of the various activities available. A detailed discussion of the control phase is beyond the scope of this book.

The contribution of various disciplines

As already noted, this book will attempt to bring together the approaches to managerial problems adopted in several different disciplines, notably accounting, economics and applied mathematics. It is characteristic of many fields of study today that subject boundaries are becoming blurred and it is hard to say which subject embraces a particular problem area. Just as, in the natural sciences, some problems are of mutual interest to biologists, chemists and physicists, so are managerial problems open to investigation by specialists in several different subjects.

Accounting

Accounting literature has a history extending over some five hundred years and accounting practice is doubtless much older. The most distinctive characteristic of accounting is perhaps that it is concerned with the collection of data of a financial nature. The earliest accounting records were probably intended to list rights and possessions to prevent their loss by fraud or oversight; such records might, for example, deal with the explanation by a servant (employee) of how he had dealt with resources entrusted to him by his master (employer). Gradually the accounting records evolved into elaborate systems recording all the financial transactions of a firm.

In early times, managerial decisions would be taken without much formal analysis; they reflected the result of a judgement more artistic than scientific in nature. As business activities became more complex, however, managers felt the need to base their decisions explicitly on financial information about their likely consequences. It was natural that they should turn to accountants for such information, since accountants were already engaged in the recording of information about ongoing activities. As we shall see later, however, the seeking of information for decisions from accountants was not without dangers. Accountants' preoccupation with the recording of information about past events might lead them to assume, uncritically, that the same information was a good guide for decisions concerning the future.

Economics

Although accounting may aptly be regarded as a branch of applied economics, its methods developed for many years without any link with the formal methods of analysis developed in the literature on economics. More recently, however, recognition has been given to the idea that a grounding in economics can contribute greatly to the understanding of the issues involved in management problems – although the acceptance of this idea is not yet as general as seems desirable. Traditionally economists have been concerned to develop descriptions and predictions of the aggregate behaviour of industries and the national economy – and this may explain the delay in applying economics to managerial problems of the firm. These descriptions have been built on assumptions concerning the behaviour of firms and people, both individually and collectively. A good deal of work remains to be done to establish the validity of many of the assumptions. To the extent that the assumptions are generally accepted, however, it is a natural further step to apply those that are relevant to decision-taking problems within the firm. The relevance of economics to managerial problems is illustrated by the following propositions of economic analysis:

1 Value depends on relative scarcity and relative wants. A change in the tastes of consumers or in the available techniques of production can negate the expected benefits of long-established methods and expensive plant and equipment.

2 All costing problems reduce in essence to a choice between alternative courses of action. If resources available are scarce in relation to their possible uses, the cost of using the resource on one activity will be the benefit from the alternative use that therefore has to be sacrificed.

3 A plan is only the best available if no small changes would effect an improvement. The estimation of the effects of various small changes in a plan may give some indication of whether it is close to the best possible, and will indicate the direction of changes that would at least improve the plan even if they would not make it optimal.

4 Events in the past are not directly relevant to current choices; for example, the cost of a resource, purchased in the past and subsequently held in stock, is not a relevant measure of the cost of using it on a current activity. Nevertheless, past events determine, in part, the spectrum of opportunities available now, and they also provide a basis for estimating the outcomes of similar future events.

Operational research

An even more recent development in the study of managerial problems has been the application of mathematical and statistical techniques. An important branch of such applications grew out of studies undertaken during World War II. It seems that a pioneering study took place when a team of scientists was called in to advise military leaders on the best deployment of planes and pilots. The results of the assignment were judged to be successful and several operational research teams (as they came to be called) were subsequently employed in the investigation of other military problems.

After the war, the team members returned to civilian life and came to see the possibilities of applying similar methods to the solution of business problems. The method is essentially that which is commonplace in investigations in the natural sciences; its application in business has given rise to the movement which is often described as 'scientific management'.

The model-building approach

The essence of scientific method is well captured in the expression 'the model-building approach'. A firm applies the model-building approach if it firstly decides what it wants to achieve, and then devises an expression for the relationship between these things and matters which can be influenced directly by its decisions. Such an expression is known as a model. A firm may, for example, wish to make its income as large as possible. Its business decisions, however, do not relate to income as a *primary* variable; they must deal with such intermediaries as how many output units are to be produced, men employed and machines purchased. A model is required to predict the relationship between income on the one hand and output and employment levels on the other in order that estimates may be made of the best decisions. Such a model would incorporate assumptions about the productivity of the resources, their prices and the selling price of the output.

We shall discuss later, detailed considerations in the application of scientific method in business. In view of its fundamental importance in this book, however, it seems appropriate to say a little more here about the justification for using some form of quantitative analysis. It is admitted that some factors influencing business decisions cannot readily be expressed in numerical terms. Quantitative analysis is limited by the difficulty in deriving an accurate and complete model and the difficulty in analysing some models by the mathematical techniques available at the present time. And although the development of electronic computers has greatly expanded the available computational capacity, that capacity may still be too small or its use too costly for some practical cases. Furthermore some managers achieve notable success by a sort of artistic flair.

However, the case must be argued generally and not merely in relation to exceptional managers; and it is argued that the model-building approach has generally a number of advantages. It involves making explicit assumptions about the relationships governing the effect of business decisions; the assumptions may then be examined critically and perhaps tested by statistical means in order to consider whether they may be improved. Whenever a decision is taken some relationship must be assumed at least implicitly. Only if the assumptions are made explicit, however, can a consensus be reached as to whether they are the best possible. Even then the assumptions must often remain the subject of considerable uncertainty. In that case a decision need not and normally should not be made on the basis of one set of assumptions. The model-building approach provides a good basis for exploring the effect for a particular decision of different assumptions. It makes it possible to ask the question: If such a relationship prevailed or such conditions held, what would be the consequences for the decision? Such an approach is likely to lead to much better considered decisions than a more intuitive one. It should also be emphasized that the consequences of business decisions depend on the complex interaction of a number of forces. A careful logical analysis, based on a decision model, may reveal the likely consequences of a given action to be quite different from ones predicted intuitively.

The fundamental justification, however, for basing a discussion of decision-taking on a model-building approach, is a practical one. Many managers have used the approach in their firms and believe that they have achieved worthwhile results. The literature describing successful applications has grown rapidly; and there is an expectation that the future will see that growth continue.

None of this implies that decisions can normally be taken solely according to a quantitative analysis. Many actions will have effects which defy the assignment of numerical values. The model-building approach is only a sound basis for decision taking, that is, it provides a rigorous framework within which managers may exercise their judgement. The relationship between quantitative and qualitative analysis will be explored further in chapter 4.

2 The Objectives of the Firm

One primary activity in the process of managing a firm is the specification of business objectives. We noted the need for this step in chapter 1. We shall now discuss in more detail the desirability of specifying objectives explicitly and independently of the other processes in the selection of a plan; we shall also consider some of the difficulties in settling what the objectives of a firm should be.

It would be possible for managers to take decisions by studying details of a selection of possible plans and simply choosing the one that they liked best without formulating reasons for their choice. That would be a haphazard procedure, however. If a firm had no explicit objective, the plans selected from year to year might well lack consistent direction and the implications of the decisions would probably be unclear to those who took them. Moreover, senior managers cannot consider all possible plans personally – there would be too many. An explicit statement of objectives will be useful to assistants in selecting the plans to put on a short-list.

It may also be argued to be important in principle that the objectives should be settled independently of the selection of the plan. In this way it is possible to minimize the danger that the expression of objectives might be biased by an irrational desire to accept a particular plan.

Controversy concerning the choice of objectives

Questions concerning what business objectives are normally sought by a firm and what objectives should be sought are matters of considerable controversy. It seems to be impossible to demonstrate that some particular objective is the only proper one for a firm. Managers are in a position to influence the well-being of various classes of people, those who provide the firm's capital (shareholders and others), various groups of employees (including the managers themselves), the customers of the firm, society at large and so on. The traditional view has been that managers should aim to secure the best position possible for the owners, the providers of the equity capital, and to meet only the minimum obligations to others. Writers have argued that this view is supported by the law relating to limited liability companies; for this law seems to recognize the interests of shareholders as predominant by giving them certain fundamental rights of control, e.g. the right to remove directors whose policy they dislike – by resolution in general meeting of the company.

However, a more modern view has suggested that managers may reasonably serve the interests of other groups by providing for them something over their minimum contractual reward. Such a policy is likely to be feasible – shareholders rarely exercise their right to remove managers who serve interests other than their own, either because they do not know the nature of the managers' policy, or because they admit the reasonableness of the policy, or because the exercise of their legal rights is too difficult. And there is no logical argument by which the advancing of interests of groups other than shareholders can be shown to be improper. We must content ourselves with concluding that everyone who has some influence on decisions in a firm should consider the possibilities and make his own choice. Firm policy will then be set by whatever consensus emerges; indeed it may happen that different decisions under the control of different managers are taken according to different objectives if the system of the firm allows it. Our analysis of decisions will assume that objectives have been set and ask how they are most likely to be achieved.

Profit maximization

In the following chapters, we shall normally assume acceptance of the traditional business objective which may be described, loosely, as the maximization of profit for the owners of the firm (the ordinary shareholders of a limited company), or more aptly, as the maximization of their wealth. As we shall see later, this objective does not necessarily imply making the accounting measure of profit as large as possible (because of the unsatisfactory nature of measurement conventions which may be used in accounting). The implications of the objective of wealth maximization have been considered in the literature concerned with the appraisal of investment projects; their detailed discussion is beyond the scope of this book, concerned, as it is, with short-term decisions. However, short-term decisions should be consistent with long-run objectives. A short discussion of the objectives assumed for investment appraisal is therefore necessary for our purpose.

The starting point of the modern theory of investment appraisal is that an individual has the main economic objective of achieving the best possible distribution of consumption over his lifetime. He buys goods for consumption with cash or its equivalent – and he derives his basic supply of cash from wage or salary earnings possibly supplemented by legacies, gifts and so on. However, he may not wish to spend cash on consumption when he receives it, and he can alter the time pattern of cash available for consumption by borrowing or investing. An investment normally involves setting aside some cash at one time in return for the expectation of the receipt of a larger amount of cash at a later time, i.e. it involves the postponement of consumption in return for the earning of interest. Similarly, borrowing involves an increase in cash available at an early time in return for the payment of an interest cost. (An individual may borrow and invest concurrently if he expects to be able to earn a return on the investment in excess of the cost of borrowing.)

Suppose that the least profitable investment accepted by an individual earns interest of 5 per cent per annum (we assume this return to be constant for all time periods). We may deduce that he attaches an approximately equal value to £1 spent on extra consumption now, £1.05 in one year's time, $£(1.05)^2$ in two years' time and so on. If he attached a higher relative value to present consumption, he would not have been willing to accept an investment yielding only 5 per cent per annum; if he attached a lower value to present consumption, an investment yielding only, say, 4 per cent would have seemed worthwhile.

If the individual is behaving rationally, his most expensive borrowing in any year will have an interest cost of 5 per cent per annum. Borrowing at a higher rate would not be worthwhile in comparison with the earning on the least profitable investment (it would be better to give both up); if cheaper borrowing is available but unused, our individual would improve his position by accepting additional loans and accepting additional investments yielding a little less than 5 per cent per annum (assuming such investments to be available).

The best position for the individual will involve equality between the return on the least remunerative investment and the most expensive source of borrowing. This 'marginal' rate of interest (5 per cent per annum in our example) is known in economics as the marginal rate of time preference. It may be used to form a rate of exchange at which we may convert small changes in cash available for consumption at different times in order to compare their worth. Our hypothetical decision-taker values equally £1 now and £1.05 a year later; hence, given a choice, he would prefer an extra receipt of £100 now to an extra receipt of, say, £103 a year later; the converted value of £103 is £103/1.05 = £98 approximately – he values the sum of £103 equally with only £98 now. In making a choice we should not compare the absolute amounts, £100 and £103; that would involve ignoring the influence of the timing of the receipts on their value. We may generalize this example by letting $£A_0$ be an immediate receipt, $£A_1$ a receipt in one year's time and i the marginal rate of time preference expressed as a decimal. Given a choice, an individual would prefer the immediate receipt if, and only if, $£A_0$ was greater than $£A_1/(1+i)$. Similarly, an individual would value a receipt of $£A_2$ in two years time at $£A_2/(1+i)^2$ and so on.

If an individual buys shares in a limited company he is making an investment which will yield a return in the form of dividends (and possibly later sales proceeds). Let us assume that he would hold the investment for an indefinitely long period of time and that he expects the shareholding to yield dividends of £d_j at time j (i.e. £d_0 immediately, £d_1 after one year, £d_j after j years and so on). The value of the holding, the aggregate of the values attached to the consumption derived from each dividend, may be represented as:

$$V = d_0 + \frac{d_1}{1+i} + \frac{d_2}{(1+i)^2} + \frac{d_3}{(1+i)^3} + \ldots + \frac{d_J}{(1+i)^j} + \ldots$$

Now suppose the firm has an alternative plan which will yield a different stream of dividends, D_j at time j. The value of the consumption associated with this plan may, consistently, be said to be

$$V = D_0 + \frac{D_1}{1+i} + \frac{D_2}{(1+i)^2} + \frac{D_3}{(1+i)^3} + \ldots + \frac{D_J}{(1+i)^j} + \ldots$$

Hence, if the company wishes to choose between the two plans according to which would be preferred by the shareholder, it should select the one for which V is the greater.

This argument depends on a number of assumptions concerning the nature of individual behaviour and the characteristics of available borrowing and investment opportunities; furthermore we have avoided the difficult question of how a value may be found for i, the rate of interest, in practice. Such questions are not wholly resolved in the literature but they are not central to problems of short-term decisions and limitations of space prevent their discussion here. It must suffice for our purposes to note that the approach described is generally accepted in investment appraisal literature as the best available at the present time.

Short-run objectives

The exclusion of investment projects from consideration in this book means, in effect, that we are restricting ourselves to projects which may be assumed to have no direct effect on cash receipts and payments after the current decision period. At most, our decisions will influence cash receipts and payments over the span of a few months and, over so short a period, it is a reasonable approximation to ignore any adjustment to the values of receipts and payments which might be made because they arise at different times. Our short-term decisions will be consistent with the long-run objective of maximizing the value of a firm's dividend stream, therefore, if we adopt the plan which yields the largest possible excess of cash receipts over cash payments. It does not follow that all this cash surplus would be distributed to shareholders. Some might be retained for reinvestment in the firm but this decision would be the subject of additional studies.

We assume that our decisions are taken in the context of a broader system of plans which have already set the best levels of reinvestment in premises, plant and machinery and other long-lived assets. We also assume as an approximation that our decisions do not have any *long-term* effect on such matters as the amount of stock which has to be carried or the amount of credit which a firm gives or receives; for such effects would imply that the project in question had a delayed impact on cash receipts or payments and that it should be treated as an investment project.

Risk and uncertainty

The above discussion has suggested that a choice of plan could be made by predicting what cash would be generated by each available plan. This implies that the outcome of each plan can be predicted with considerable confidence. If it is thought that the outcome might vary within a wide range, a decision should, perhaps, be based on a prediction of a single representative value for the outcome and an estimation of a range of likely values to indicate the level of uncertainty in the plan. The effect of a plan on the well-being of an individual may depend both on the representative value and on the level of uncertainty, because he may like or dislike bearing uncertainty.

In order to simplify the exposition, we shall introduce the analysis of decisions ignoring risk and assuming that it is permissible to consider only a single estimate of the outcome of each activity. We shall discuss explicit allowance for risk and uncertainty in chapters 13, 14 and 15.

Multiple objectives

Some firms may select a set of objectives comprising various different purposes each of which is valued as an end in itself. As noted above, a firm may decide that it does not wish to secure the maximum well-being of the ordinary shareholders whilst paying other groups merely the minimum needed to retain their association with the firm. It may wish to pay additional rewards to other groups, to managers and other employees for example.

Multiple objectives of this nature do not pose a special problem for the choice of activities, at least in the short-run. It remains appropriate, as a first step, to choose a plan which will maximize net cash receipts after allowing for basic contractual payments over the planning period. This pool of surplus resources would be divided between several groups of people instead of being earmarked for the ordinary shareholders alone.

If a firm has multiple objectives, there is clearly a conflict of interest between the different groups; the larger the share of one group, the less is available for others with interest in a firm's surplus. Planning the division of the surplus, indeed, may present considerable difficulty; in practice it may be effected by an informal bargaining process over the year. It is also possible that a division will be imposed by some dominant group (such as the managers).

When a firm professes to have multiple objectives, it is hard to know whether each objective is really valued and pursued as an end in itself or whether some objectives really fulfil the role of proxies. It might well be the case that the payment of some surplus remuneration – say to employees – would so improve the motivation and hence the operating efficiency of the group that the action would be entirely consistent with profit maximization for the ordinary shareholders. Proxy objectives will be discussed further in chapter 4.

Another goal which sometimes features in a company's statement of its objectives is some variant of 'to sell goods of excellent quality at reasonable prices'. This kind of statement often included in the annual statement by the chairman of a limited company, may be no more than an attempt to foster good public relations, a form of advertising. If it is to be taken seriously, however, it is hard to interpret. It seems to imply that the managers are charging less than the maximum possible prices given the volume of output. It is hard to understand why they should want to do this although it may equally be impossible to convince them of its wrongness by logical argument.

Perhaps the most likely explanation is that their policy is really another example of a proxy objective for profit maximization, the rationale being that the charging of moderate prices now will protect the firm's market share in the long-run.

Satisfactory performance versus optimal performance

Before concluding our discussion of business objectives, we should note that some writers believe that businessmen are content to find a plan that is satisfactory, judged by various criteria, rather than try to maximize some single value. It may be that firms are 'satisficers' rather than 'maximizers'. One study of actual practice has observed that firms, when confronted with a particular type of problem, consider various possible solutions in sequence until one which offers a satisfactory level of performance is found; the search for solutions is abandoned when the first satisfactory solution is found and little or no attempt is made to find an even better solution. This approach has been supported by the argument that, in practice, business planning is too complicated for a strictly optimal plan to be identified (except by chance).

It may be readily conceded that a firm cannot demonstrate its plan to be the best of all the plans it could possibly have undertaken; the number of possible plans would be too large. Hence the plan chosen will be, at best, the preferred selection from a small set of plans and subject to more or less arbitrary limits in terms of the activities considered for inclusion, e.g. the type of product in which the firm is willing to deal and so on. Nevertheless, it seems feasible and strongly desirable that a firm should make a real effort to consider some alternative plans and not just accept the first feasible plan discovered; and if this is acknowledged, a firm will presumably wish to select the best possible plan from the limited set considered. Such a procedure might be regarded as 'satisficing' and less than optimizing but the distinction hardly seems justified. Restriction of the possible plans considered to a relatively small number is presumably optimal because it reflects the view that the cost of analysing further plans would be likely to outweigh the benefits in terms of increases in the value of the plans.

3 Scientific Method in Business

The primary purpose of this book is to study business decision taking in the framework of the model-building approach, based on the application of scientific method. We identified in chapter 1 the following main steps in the process of choosing an optimal plan:

1 The specification of the objectives of the firm.

2 The description of decision alternatives (projects and other activities available to the firm) and of resources available to carry them out.

3 The formulation of a model expressing relationships between the fundamental variables (the immediate subjects of decisions, e.g. output levels) and values reflected in the objectives.

4 The use of the model to study the implications of different decisions for the firm's objectives and the choice of the best set of decision alternatives judged in terms of the objectives.

We considered the specification of the objectives of the firm in chapter 2. We now discuss the role of scientific method in the other parts of the decision-taking cycle. Firstly, however, we will consider the nature of the method employed in investigations in the natural sciences, in order to understand what it has to contribute to business problems.

Methodology in the natural sciences

A large part of scientific enquiry is given to a study of the relationships between natural phenomena. When a scientist studies certain types of events, he tries to establish a model – a simplified picture in words or mathematical symbols – which explains the event in terms of its relationship with more basic factors – the variables. For example, a scientist studying gravity might be interested in the time taken by various objects to reach the ground when rolled down a slope or dropped freely. He might therefore develop a model explaining the time taken in terms of such variables as the steepness and length of the slope, the weight of the objects, the density of the atmosphere and so on. The first step in the study of a problem is to seek a trial model – a hypothesis – which expresses his view of the underlying relationships involved. A tentative hypothesis will be useful if it helps in predicting the characteristics of future events of a similar nature.

In order to establish confidence in the usefulness of a hypothesis, the scientist subjects it to a series of tests in which the results predicted by the hypothesis are compared with observed results. He may often be able to conduct the tests as controlled experiments in a laboratory, experiments in which he can hold some variables constant whilst varying others in a desired way so as to study the overall consequences. The student of gravity might, like Galileo, measure the time taken by balls of different weight to descend slopes of different length and steepness in order to establish which variables influence the time taken and in what manner. A student with more modern facilities might attempt to vary the density of air and investigate whether weight makes any difference to the time taken by an object to descend in a vacuum (or an approximation to a vacuum). A diligent investigator does not simply study situations in which his hypothesis seems most likely to be correct. He seeks situations in which it seems less likely to hold good – thereby making a deliberate effort to refute it. Only if his hypothesis withstands such tests can he have considerable confidence in it. The more tests a hypothesis has withstood the better may be the confidence placed in it; but a hypothesis can never be proved to be correct – one can never be sure that the next experiment will not show an inconsistency which will call for its revision or even abandonment.

Formulation of the business decision model

Business models are similarly concerned to explain results in terms of fundamental variables. In studying short-term decision problems, we assume, consistently with the discussion in chapter 2, that a firm wishes to maximize the net cash receipts from current activities. However, decisions are not expressed directly in terms of effects on cash receipts and payments; they are concerned with more fundamental variables such as methods of technology employed in production and the output volumes and prices of different products. In order to select an optimal set of decisions, we need to describe the relationship between the fundamental variables and the resulting net cash receipts, i.e. we need to formulate a model. Its role is the same as that of the model in scientific investigations.

The form of business models

A business decision model may be expressed in words, in pictures (e.g. as a graph) or in mathematical symbols. The mathematical form is often most useful because it lends itself to further analysis. The following expression is an example of a mathematical model for a firm which manufactures three products:

$$F = 18a + 23b + 14c - 20\,000$$

where a, b, c, are the numbers of units manufactured and sold of products A, B and C, and F is the associated net cash inflow.

The assumptions underlying the model are that (a) the parameters £18, £23 and £14 measure the contribution (the selling price less the manufacturing and selling costs) per unit of each product and (b) the fixed costs of the firm are £20 000, i.e. this cost is incurred at the given level whatever combination of products is manufactured.

It is important to recognize that the equation is not a statement which must hold true by definition. It is an expression of one of many possible relationships which might hold and it must therefore be considered critically before it is accepted as a basis for decision. The model implies, for example, that each additional unit manufactured of product A adds £18 to the value of the plan. It is possible, however, that successive units may add more or less than £18; as volume increases it may be necessary to accept a lower selling price in order to dispose of the whole output and larger outputs may make possible economies which reduce the unit costs.

The variables included in the above model are of a type known as controllable variables. Such things as the volume of production can be controlled, at least within certain limits, by decisions in the firm. It may sometimes be useful for a firm's model to include non-controllable variables as well. For example, the prices charged by a competitor may influence a firm's volume of sales and hence its cash receipts; it may be desirable to include the competitor's prices in the model in an attempt to predict their effect on the firm's own results even though those prices are not controllable by the firm itself.

Constraints on the variables

The optimal plan of action for a firm may be found by considering different values for the controllable variables to find which lead to the best cash flow as predicted by the model. In practice there will normally be restrictions on the values that can be given to the variables and these should also be reflected in the model. In this section, we consider some of the main types of restriction (constraint) which may have to be included in a model.

In the production process, a firm uses various resources or inputs; for example, different grades of labour, various types of material and component, managerial time, various administrative services, the services of various types of machine and so on. One type of restriction on the values that may be given to the variables may arise because some of these resources are in limited supply.

Consider again the model used as an illustration above and suppose that the firm in question uses only one grade of skilled labour in production and that it can hire, at most, 22 500 hours of that labour during the year; products A, B and C require six, ten and eleven hours of labour per unit for their production. The limit to the supply of labour imposes a limit on the production that is possible. This limit may be represented in the model by adding the expression

$$6a+10b+11c \leqslant 22\ 500;$$

this expresses the requirement that the total number of hours used in making a, b, c units of products A, B and C (the left hand side of the expression) must be equal to or less than 22 500, the number of hours available. (Readers who are not familiar with this form of algebraic notation will notice that the symbol $\leqslant$ means 'equal to or less than'; similarly the sign $\geqslant$ means 'equal to or greater than'.)

A second type of constraint in a model may be needed to deal with market demand factors. The quantity that can be sold of any product will normally be related to the price at which it is sold. In the simplest type of formulation, the price is taken as fixed and the maximum volume that can be sold at that price is estimated and included in the model as a restriction, for example, the addition to the model of the expression $a \leqslant 400$ would indicate that we expected not to be able to sell more than 400 units of product A at the chosen price. The adequacy and extension of this simple type of formulation will be discussed in later chapters.

There may, thirdly, be restrictions of a technological nature on the variables. Some products may, for example, be the output of a joint process and hence necessarily manufactured in a fixed ratio. The requirement $a \leqslant 2b$ might indicate the need to produce one unit of product B for each two units of product A.

Finally, the model should also include a set of rather obvious requirements of the form $a \geqslant 0$, i.e. that negative production (or whatever) is impossible. Even obvious requirements have to be included in a formulation of this kind. The calculation of the optimal solution may be made on an electronic computer which would use mechanically whatever information it is given; it would consider any values which might be given to the variables, including negative values, unless given instructions to the contrary. The above description of various types of constraint is by no means exhaustive but it gives a sufficient illustration for present purposes of the main situations which call for the inclusion of constraints in a model.

Testing the model

The form of business model required may vary considerably according to the precise situation in a firm. It is important that a good deal of effort should be devoted to a critical appraisal of a model in order to form a view on whether it is the best possible description of the relationships involved.

In testing the model, the business manager has a harder task than the natural scientist. Consider, for example, the model which an astronomer uses to describe the motions of planets in the solar system. He can use the model to predict the positions of the planets in the solar system at different times and then make observations to check his predictions. He can be reasonably confident that the main forces which determine the behaviour of the planets remain constant from time to time so that he is conducting a valid test in the sense that the same model is applicable at various times. Moreover, as we have already noted, the natural scientist can sometimes test his model by controlled experiments in a laboratory.

It may be possible to conduct somewhat similar tests of a business model. For example, it may be possible to obtain details of actual costs incurred by a firm in past periods for various output plans and discover by statistical means whether these are consistent with the predictions of the model. However, one can never be sure that a model is stable over the period studied; the relationships investigated may change over time and information about costs at different times may properly be regarded as information associated with different models. Technologies may change rapidly as may the general economic environment affecting levels of prices and demand. Furthermore, past results will normally indicate the consequences of giving only a narrow range of values to the decision variables and hence fail to provide a test of the predictions of the model for all the output levels which may be considered;

and it is normally impracticable to conduct controlled experiments which indicate cost levels for a large number of output combinations.

In testing business models one has to use a less direct approach than in the natural sciences and one normally has correspondingly less confidence in their accuracy.

The role of managerial judgement

The difficulties of testing business models are sometimes cited in criticisms of the model-building approach to business decisions. The critics argue that the method gives a spurious impression of exactness to the decision process and that, since exactness is really unattainable, it is preferable to leave business decisions to the skill of managers in judgement, a sort of artistic skill unaided by scientific method.

The scientific approach has, indeed, not displaced the role of managers' judgement. There is ample need for judgement in such matters as discovering and identifying the characteristics of activities available to a firm, in formulating the model, in specifying objectives and so on. The argument attributed to the critics rests on a misunderstanding of the case for the model-building approach. Any method of decision taking must at least imply some assumed relationship between the decision variables and values sought in the firm's objectives – unless it is merely random. An important merit of the model-building approach is in making the assumptions explicit so that they may be examined critically and perhaps improved. We can have little confidence in the reasonableness of assumptions which are not made explicit. Furthermore, we need not take a decision supposing that one set of assumptions is uniquely correct. We may consider various models reflecting a range of different assumptions about the relationships so as to discover which relationships are vital for a particular problem – which ones lead to materially different decisions when they are varied; evidence as to those relationships may be examined with particular care. A series of trial investigations on these lines will give a manager a good feel for the structure of a problem.

The impact of the model-building approach on a firm's decisions is unlikely to be a trivial one. The relationships between variables are often quite complex and hence the overall effect of certain decisions may not be obvious in the context of intuitive judgement – indeed it may be quite surprising. Several wrongs do not make a right. The difficulty of establishing a reliable model is no argument for neglecting to use such information as is available in a methodical way.

The search for the optimal plan

The choice of plan requires, in principle, the feeding into the model of predicted values for non-controllable variables and of every possible combination of values for the controllable variables in order to derive predictions for the overall result of each possible plan. Some plans might have to be discarded as failing to satisfy the constraints. The plan which yields the best value, judged by the objectives of the company, will be selected from those remaining.

Such a procedure is easier to describe than to implement. For most practical situations the number of possible plans would be astronomically large – so large that it would be impracticable to examine them all even using an electronic computer. If the model comprises simple mathematical relationships, it may be possible to overcome this difficulty by using some mathematical method of calculation. The essence of such methods is that they involve the examination of a relatively small number of possible plans whilst guaranteeing that those plans not considered have worse results than the ones that are. Linear programming is one example of such a method.

In some cases, the models which give the best predictions may have a form which is too complex for rigorous mathematical analysis. It may then be desirable to use another model that has a convenient form, as an approximation. It would be difficult or impossible to estimate what such an approximation costs in terms of shortfall of value. It is at least possible, however, to compare the results predicted for such a plan with the results predicted for plans selected by more traditional methods. An improvement over alternative methods is all that is required to justify the use of a model.

Even if no model of a simple mathematical form is regarded as a sufficiently good approximation, it is still possible to investigate several possible plans by substituting various values for controllable variables in the complex model using trial and error rather than rigorous analysis. This method, known as simulation, may yield a better plan than any other method even though it may fall short of the best possible.

4 Business Strategy

The scope of scientific method in business

It is possible to specify conditions under which the scientific approach described in the last chapter could be guaranteed to produce optimal business decisions. These conditions are:

1 That an objective has been determined, dealing only with results which can be measured and valued precisely.

2 That managers know for certain details of all actions which can possibly be taken by the firm, including precise numerical measures of all their consequences.

3 That a definitive model is available, relating the outcomes of possible actions of the firm to the overall results sought under its objectives and describing all the constraints on decisions.

4 That the model has a sufficiently simple form that mathematical analysis can be applied to yield the optimal set of actions, judged by the objectives.

If all these conditions could be met, there would be no doubt about our ability to select optimal decisions. However, any actual situation will inevitably fall short of this ideal.

The structure of problems

We may think of the various activities available to a firm as falling on a spectrum measuring the degree to which the conditions for guaranteeing strict optimality of decisions can be met. At one end is the 'well-structured' decision problem. This category comprises decisions which have simple effects in terms of the objectives, e.g. if a given output may be obtained in various ways, the method which involves minimum cost will normally be accepted as best with little controversy; it also comprises decisions, the outcomes from which can be predicted with considerable confidence using simple mathematical models.

The classical problems of operational research fall in this category. An example is the transportation problem; a firm has a given supply of goods at various warehouses and a requirement for specified quantities to be delivered to various selling outlets; it is desired to calculate the best plan for moving the goods – what quantity of goods should be despatched from each warehouse to each outlet? In formulating a problem of this type, it is probably possible to describe all ways of effecting the transportation (which are worth consideration) and to give a good estimate of the cost of each. Furthermore, a plan which minimizes the cost of transportation is likely to be in substantial accord with any objectives the firm may have. Such problems are not free from remote effects, which are hard to measure – a delay in supplying a particular outlet may lead to a loss of sales, the long-term effect of which is hard to assess. However in many cases the remote effects may be assumed to be so small that they may be neglected as a first approximation.

A great majority of business decisions relate to situations which are less well-structured than those described in the last paragraph. There is then a greater chance that the application of the model-building approach will fail to select the best possible plan. One can never know for certain whether a set of decision procedures has produced the best results because it is impossible to know what would have happened had a different set of decisions been taken. Confidence in the optimality of decisions is likely to diminish, however, as the level of uncertainty increases. The level of uncertainty will vary widely from project to project. It will normally be smaller for short-term projects than for long-term ones, smaller for established products and services than the development of new ones and smaller for activities which have few interactions with other aspects of a plan than for those which have many.

This is not to say that the model-building approach should not be used when there are important uncertainties in a decision situation. On the contrary, this method seems more likely to yield optimal decisions than any alternative method, for the reasons given in chapter 3. In some cases the uncertainty can be expressed quantitatively (in the form of probability distributions) and dealt with explicitly in the analysis; such cases are discussed in chapter 13. It is desirable that, in a financial analysis for decision purposes, remote effects of an activity should not be ignored or handled in a haphazard manner. The difficulties posed by the ill-structure of decision problems should, if possible, be studied in a logical framework. Otherwise the benefits of any analysis undertaken may be offset by factors omitted from consideration. Confidence in the decision-taking process may be increased by strategic analysis, in the manner described in this chapter.

At the other end of the spectrum of uncertainty from the well-structured problem is the 'ill-structured' problem, calling for a decision on an activity with effects which are predominantly remote and difficult to measure. Examples of ill-structured problems are decisions on what level of welfare facilities – sports ground, staff canteen and so on – a firm should provide for its employees. Such decisions may have important implications for a firm's level of net cash receipts; the influence on employee morale may well affect both productivity and staff turnover and hence training costs. The measurement of these effects, however, would be a matter of considerable difficulty.

There are three main respects in which actual decision situations commonly fail to meet the ideal conditions described at the beginning of this chapter: there is difficulty in (a) identifying a sufficiently wide range of available activities, (b) measuring all the costs and benefits of the activities identified and (c) computing the optimal plan, given the measurement of costs and benefits.

First, as already noted in chapter 3, the number of different activities available to a firm may be astronomically large. To appreciate this one has merely to consider how many different lines of business are available, how many different services or products might be offered in each, how many different ways each basic product might be designed and manufactured, advertised and priced and so on; every possible combination of these individual considerations represents a different plan that the firm might adopt. It will normally be impossible to consider them all and considerations of cost may reduce the set actually considered a long way below what is theoretically possible.

Secondly, some effects of an activity may be so obscure that they virtually defy any attempt at measurement. The worthwhileness of introducing a new product will depend, *inter alia*, on the following factors: the volume of sales which could be made at various prices (and this would depend in part on the products offered, and pricing policies adopted by competitors), the costs of production (which may depend on untried technological developments), the effect on output of other products, arising because the new product would make demands on scarce resources, the effect on the demand for the firm's other products (which may be complementary to the new one or in competition with it) and the effect on the efficiency of resources (e.g. the effect on the general productivity of manufacturing labour from considerations of morale). The last two effects are 'remote' from the product itself and, though no less relevant, may be harder to measure than the first two; and we can never be sure that all the relevant effects of an activity have been described, let alone measured adequately.

Thirdly, the model which best expresses the relationships between the qualities sought under the objectives and the results of available activities may be complex – so complex that mathematical analysis cannot determine a strict optimum. Let us consider some aspects of these three types of difficulty in more detail.

The structure of the search for activities

One of the first questions which a firm has to face in setting its strategy for taking decisions is how it is to identify available activities. There is little guidance available in the literature.

A firm must restrict, in some way, the range of activities which it investigates as possibilities for adoption. The larger the set of activities considered, the larger the cost of the search; and if the search is extended too widely the extra cost of considering more activities may well outweigh any likely benefits in the form of increased earnings. In an extreme situation, managers might spend all their time in search for activities and none in actually implementing some of those discovered. It is hard to assess the worthwhileness of particular search policies by quantitative analysis. One cannot estimate whether the cost of a search is likely to be justified without making some assumption about the characteristics of the projects which would be identified. Most firms, though not all, begin the definition of the area of search for activities by restricting themselves to some particular industry, i.e. they ask the question 'What business are we in?' Presumably they adopt this policy because they believe that the economies of search costs associated with the restriction to one industry make it consistent with achieving their objectives.

The area of a firm's search for activities is not completely identified by the assumption that it is normally restricted to a particular industry, however. There are other considerations. A firm may restrict its search further by considering new activities only if they are complementary to each other or to existing activities. Thus a firm may consider its particular strengths, for example, what resources it has available with excess capacity, including technical know-how, and seek new activities which will enable it to exploit these facilities. Similarly a firm's objective may include a desire to limit risk and uncertainty; in consequence it may seek projects which are complementary in the sense of reducing uncertainty.

There is some evidence that, in practice, a firm's search for new activities is prompted primarily by some danger signal associated with existing activities, and that the search is abandoned as soon as some way is found of effecting a tolerable improvement. If, for example, a particular production process is producing a large number of defective units of a particular product, a search for an improved process may be provoked, but the firm may abandon the search as soon as a satisfactory process is found rather than continue it in an attempt to discover a process that is even better.

One cannot have much confidence in the achievements of a firm which follows such a practice. It seems that it would be better to search for some new activities independently of existing problems; for example, a firm should, perhaps, consider the desirability of introducing new or redesigned products and new production processes from time to time even if existing ones have not yet manifested signs of failure. Furthermore, a firm should perhaps not consider one new activity at a time but rather make a deliberate attempt to consider alternatives. Hence one project would be accepted only after competition with other projects and a firm might claim with some justification that it has something approaching the best possible solution and not just any satisfactory solution.

Heuristic method

Let us now consider the difficulties of analysis when some of the cash effects of activities are hard to measure. We will consider, firstly, the method used to reach decisions on ill-structured problems, a decision, for example, on whether or not to build a sports centre for employees. As a preliminary, estimates will be made of the costs of providing various types of facility. The benefits, however, will probably defy estimation in money terms. The method used will be the so-called heuristic method. A manager, preferably with experience of similar problems, will steep himself in the problem, consider all its aspects qualitatively and give his advice. He will presumably draw on his previous experience but the logical relationship between the present situation and previous ones will remain implicit. He will no doubt consider what evidence he can find about the present state of morale (level of staff turnover, productivity, absenteeism and so on) and he may attempt to discover the wishes of employees by direct questioning. He may also attempt to discover what experience other firms have had following the establishment of sports centres.

The final report will probably relate different levels of cost to benefits described qualitatively. Questions such as 'Are the benefits from providing playing fields and a pavilion likely to exceed the cost of £40 000?' and 'Are the extra benefits from building squash courts likely to exceed the extra cost of £15 000?' at least represent a step forward compared to the more primitive question 'Should we provide a sports centre?' The analysis may go further and indicate that 'If the provision of a sports centre reduced staff turnover by 1 per cent per annum, it would yield a saving of £3 000 per annum in training costs' and thereby direct attention to judgement of the likelihood of such a reduction. Almost certainly, however, the final report will present more qualitative arguments than quantitative.

It is hard to see how decisions on this type of problem will become well-structured in the near future. It is possible to conceive of experiments which might lead to more precise estimates of remote costs and benefits; the techniques of cost–benefit analysis, used to evaluate benefits of projects in the public sector (e.g. the building of a new road) hold out some hopes; but until substantial technical advances are made, many of these experiments must be ruled out on grounds of practicability.

Meanwhile we must content ourselves with noting that useful perspective on such problems may be gained by evaluating them systematically in relation to other similar projects so that they are subjected to the obstacle of competition with other possibilities even though the ranking may be mainly subjective. Moreover a project with material costs and benefits of a remote nature is likely to be subjected to judgement by a top-level committee – the precaution may be taken of weighing the judgements of several individuals in debate instead of relying substantially on a financial report prepared by one person.

The nature of remote costs and benefits

We now turn to consider projects in the middle of the spectrum, i.e. projects with substantial direct effects and also important remote effects. Suppose that a firm has the main short-term objective of maximizing net cash inflow. It may seem to its managers that the current level of cash receipts could be increased by eliminating products with low 'profitability' from the range offered and using the limited capacity set free to expand output of the most profitable products. Such a course may not be optimal, however. The less profitable products may attract customers for the others and their elimination may cause a greatly reduced volume of business in future years.

More generally there may be dependencies between different activities not reflected in simple cash flow measures. The volume of sales of one product may affect the volume which can be sold of another product at the same time because buyers like to buy all their supplies of goods from one firm. Hence the volume of sales of a product may be important not only for its direct contribution to cash flows but also because of its filling out of the range of products offered. Similarly, activities may be dependent over time – the market share which a firm obtains now may affect the volume of sales which it can achieve in the future (at a given price). These factors are examples of remote costs and benefits which may influence the appraisal of an activity which also has costs and benefits of a more direct nature.

Proxy goals

One method of weighing the indirect effects of activities is in the use of 'proxy' goals. Instead of specifying a single primary objective, such as the maximization of cash inflows, a firm may specify a set of goals concerned with the level of cash earnings, the market share attained, the product range offered, opportunities for employee career development and so on. Such things as product range and market share are included not because they are desired as ends in themselves but rather because they are thought to be consistent with, indeed prerequisites for, cash flow maximization in the long-run. It may be best to accept a relatively low level of cash in the current year, if this is the price of increasing the market share, because this course of action may lead to the largest cash flows in later years. In view of the difficulty of measuring the effect of market shares on future cash flows, it may be preferable to express the objective and corresponding estimates of the results of activities in terms of (say) a combination of current cash flows and market share, i.e. to use market share as a proxy for long-run cash flows. Judgement on the relative value of current cash flows and market share could then be postponed to a late stage of the analysis.

The quasi-analytic method

The use of proxy objectives provides a framework for appraising decision' problems which are not well-structured. The method may be regarded as intermediate between the approach of operational research and that of the heuristic method; it has been called the quasi-analytic method.

The use of a system of proxy objectives does not solve the measurement problems discussed. The loose structure described does not provide us with definitive decisions. If we could specify some relationship between the various goals, e.g. if we could specify what increase in future cash flow would be gained from a percentage increase in current market share, we should have a determinate basis for decision. However such a specification would represent a measurement of the indirect effects of market share and the problem is that managers may be unwilling to commit themselves to such a measurement.

Under the quasi-analytic method we recognize this difficulty and deliberately leave the relationship between the various goals unspecified. The method is better structured than the heuristic method, however, because we do study the problems in a particular numerical framework. We consider the various sets of activities that a firm might undertake and form a view of the consequences of each in terms of the goals of the firm. We make what calculations we can of the consequences of each set for the firm's cash surplus and we also assess the effect of each one on features of other goals, e.g. the effect on market share. The decision-maker explores the consequences of different strategies and in doing so gets a good understanding of the inter-relationships between the various goals and the various plans. He discards some plans which he feels to be unsatisfactory and seeks additional possibilities which may dominate some of those already tried, i.e. be superior in terms of all goals. His final decision will involve a choice between a relatively small group of superior plans; it will involve a trade-off between different goals and hence probably contain some element of the heuristic. In choosing one particular plan he will imply a judgement of the relative importance of different goals, for it is inconceivable that one plan will be best judged against all goals (market share can almost always be increased if a large enough fall in cash inflows is accepted).

The strategy of diversification

The level of uncertainty borne by a firm is determined by its choice of activities but this is another effect that is hard to deal with by precise numerical calculations. Some analysis is both possible and useful, as we shall argue in chapter 13. Meanwhile, it is worth noting that some aspects of a firm's attitudes towards uncertainty can conveniently be dealt with in the framework of the quasi-analytic method.

A study of business history suggests that, whereas most technological changes have taken place steadily over time, there have been some which brought about drastic changes in a short time; the invention of the internal combustion engine and the development of plastics are two examples.

If a company concentrates all its efforts in a narrow range of activities and these are affected by some dramatic new development, it may find itself forced into bankruptcy. A business which concentrates on a narrow area is not headed for certain disaster but it is bearing a larger risk than the firm having wide ranging interests.

Various types of diversification

A firm which wishes to reduce the uncertainty that it bears may consider various diversification strategies. Essentially this means that it will seek to undertake a range of activities which are subject to different external influences. Hence, if some new situation destroys the profitability of one line of business, the chances are that other lines and the stability of the firm overall will be unaffected.

By adopting a strategy of diversification, a firm may also

achieve flexibility – it may acquire footholds in a number of areas of activity and be in a position to develop in any area if particularly worthwhile opportunities should become available. At the same time, diversification may impose a cost – it may involve the acceptance of lower levels of cash inflows.

There are various degrees of diversification which may be undertaken and they have different net effects on cash flows and convey different degrees of protection against uncertainty. A firm may attempt a relatively modest diversification in expanding the range of its customers for a given range of products; or it may diversify into new products in the same industry either vertically, by making components previously purchased, or horizontally, by dealing in additional products. Alternatively it may diversify into activities in a different industry but one which involves the use of similar resources to those already at the firm's disposal. The choice may be made by a quasi-analytic method on the lines described above.

Sub-optimization

We have now discussed the first two main reasons described above why a firm may fail to select an optimal plan. It may fail to consider a wide range of activities, and it may be unable to assess adequately the activities considered because of difficulty in measuring all their costs and benefits. We conclude this chapter with a note about the third difficulty, one which is essentially computational. There are two types of problem. First, the mathematical form of the model may be so complex that mathematical techniques are not yet able to compute a strict optimum; at present, mathematical techniques depend on the use of a reasonably simple model. The second difficulty is associated with the size of the required computations.

Strictly, a firm should choose a plan by considering activities in all parts of its business at one time. For activities in different parts may be mutually dependent – they may compete for limited resources, or for market outlets and so on. Quite apart from the difficulties in measuring the interdependences of such activities there is a computational problem in dealing with the vast calculations needed to guide decisions in the whole of one large firm. In consequence, it may prove necessary to deal with one part of a firm at a time, possibly by delegating the decision-taking to sectional managers.

This raises the problem known as sub-optimization. If several sections of a firm each choose the best plan for themselves independently, ignoring their inter-relationships with other sections, the overall result for the whole firm may be less than the best possible. One section may, for example, have and be able to keep the use of a scarce resource which could be used more profitably in another section.

To some extent these difficulties are probably inevitable, even though the occasions on which they arise are being reduced by the power of modern computational techniques. The difficulties do suggest that care should be taken in defining the size of unit which is given decision-taking autonomy. The divisions of a firm should be chosen so that there are as few interdependences between the decisions of different divisions as possible, having regard to the limitations of practicability.

5 Relevant Costs

The discussion in the previous chapters suggests the conclusion that some quantitative analysis should be an important part of almost all business decisions although it will often require supplementation to deal with remote effects which are not readily quantifiable. We now turn to a discussion of the principles on which the quantitative analysis may be based.

We shall restrict our discussion to 'short-term' projects, i.e. activities having results in the current period which may reasonably be considered independently of the results of similar activities in future periods. We therefore exclude projects requiring material investment – the purchase of equipment, the undertaking of development and so on – producing benefits beyond the current period. We do not, however, exclude activities of the current period simply on the grounds that they may be repeated next period with broadly similar results provided they are undertaken successfully now, e.g. annual contracts. For the reasons given in chapter 2, we shall assume that the objective of the firm may be taken to be the acceptance of projects which will yield the largest possible net cash inflow in the short term.

We shall consider, in this chapter, the appraisal of projects or activities that call for accept/reject decisions, i.e. projects which have to be either accepted as whole units or rejected (in contrast to the manufacture of products which can be undertaken at various output levels). In the simplest situation we have merely to decide whether to accept or reject a project independently. On other occasions, we may have to decide which, if any, of a set of projects should be accepted. It may be impossible to accept them all (a) because they are mutually exclusive – the firm is unwilling or unable to accept more than one (e.g. project *A* may be to employ someone to make cups of tea, project *B* the hire of a tea-vending machine – only one source of supply is wanted) – or (b) because the firm is unable to obtain a sufficient supply of resources to accept them all.

We shall consider, in later chapters, decisions concerned with setting the best volume of activities, where volume may be varied over a range of values.

The cost of resources

It is convenient to estimate cash outlays – costs – associated with a project by estimating what resources it would require and assigning a cost to those resources. Inputs required for a project are classified as separate resources if they are not perfect substitutes for each other. For example, labour is a resource which may be used on a project and different grades of labour would be classified as different resources; for even if different grades of labour could be used on the same work, the cost would not be the same. Other examples of resources are raw materials, components, various administrative facilities, machine time and so on.

The appraisal of projects when there are no resource constraints
No resources already owned
Let us begin by assuming that there are no resource constraints, i.e. no resources are so limited in supply that it is necessary to reject projects which would otherwise be judged worthwhile. A simple accept/reject decision merely calls for an estimation of the effect of acceptance of the project on the cash receipts and payments of the firm. The project would be accepted if it were expected to yield a positive net cash inflow. If a set of mutually exclusive projects is under consideration, a firm would select the one project expected to have the largest positive net cash inflow or reject them all if none have positive cash inflows.

The cash payments included in the analysis would reflect the costs of using resources that have not yet been purchased or are not the subject of a firm commitment; they would merely be the amounts that would have to be paid in acquisition, the purchase price, wage rate or whatever.

It would be necessary to take into account all extra payments caused by the project. If acceptance would cause increases in administration costs, these are none the less relevant because they are remote and difficult to estimate. The relevant cost of a project is the difference between the total costs to the firm if the project is accepted and the total costs if it is rejected.

Some resources already owned

If the firm has already purchased some units of a resource required for a project – e.g. a supply of raw material – or entered a binding contract to purchase some, the original purchase price is no longer directly relevant. It has been incurred (or will be incurred) regardless of whether any particular project is undertaken and is not a cash payment caused by acceptance of the project. The cash effect of accepting the project can best be assessed by considering the use to which the resource would be put if the project were not accepted. There are two main possibilities:

1 The resource may be sold because there is no other use for it within the firm. The sacrifice involved in accepting the project is the amount of sale proceeds foregone, net of any selling costs.

Example: Mercury Ltd has a stock of several tons of copper purchased at a price of £30 per ton. It is appraising a project which would require the conversion at a cost of £74 of five tons of copper and yield a receipt of £260. Because of changes in the firm's product range, no other uses for copper within the firm are anticipated; the stocks could be sold, however, at a net price of £45 per ton. The effect of accepting the project would run as follows:

Receipt from project	£260
less conversion costs	74
Net cash inflow	186
Sales proceeds of copper – five tons at £45	225
Net cash deficit from accepting project	39

The project should be rejected even though it more than covers the original cost price of the copper (provided that the project has no indirect effects sufficient to tip the balance).

2 If other worthwhile uses for the resources are expected to become available within the firm, their use on the project under consideration will make it necessary to purchase a larger supply in the future. It is this extra cost – the replacement cost – which is the relevant outlay. Total cash payments will be increased by the amount of the replacement cost if the project is accepted.

Example: Venus Ltd has a stock of eighty-five components of type SP, a component in common use. It has to decide whether to accept an order which would require the use of twelve components; selling price of the output would be £78 and other costs, £32. The components originally cost £3.50 each, but the market price has subsequently increased to £4. The effect of accepting the project would be:

Selling price		£78
less: extra payment arising from the use		
of components: twelve at £4	£48	
other costs	32	80
Deficit		£2

The project is not worth accepting even though (again) receipts would cover the original cost of resources.

A mathematical model of the selection process
No resources already owned

The ideas explained above do not, perhaps, require further justification. We may, however, make the exposition a little more rigorous and pave the way for some of our later discussion by developing a simple mathematical model. Consider a firm that has no resources in stock. The objective of the firm is to maximize the value of its net cash flow C, where

$$C = a_1 x_1 + a_2 x_2 + \ldots + a_n x_n - F \qquad \qquad 1$$

and $x_1, ..., x_n$ are variables which represent the acceptance or rejection of projects 1 to n; $x_1, ..., x_n$ may take the value 1, signifying acceptance, or 0, signifying rejection, but no other value.

$a_1, ..., a_n$ represent the net cash surplus on projects $x_1, ..., x_n$ (they may be negative, implying that the project yields a deficit).

F represents cash outflows which arise at a fixed level, independently of what projects are accepted (and hence are irrelevant to any decision).

C will be maximized by giving the value 1 to those of the variables for which the coefficient a_j is positive and 0 to the variables for which a_j is negative (x_j is shorthand for all the variables $x_1, ..., x_n$ and a_j represents $a_1, ..., a_n$). If some projects are mutually exclusive, we shall maximize C by finding which, if any, of the projects in the mutually exclusive set has the highest positive value a_j and giving the value 1 to the corresponding x_j. We may express the fact that projects 1, 2 and 3 are mutually exclusive by adding to the model the expression $x_1 + x_2 + x_3 \leqslant 1$, i.e. the requirement that the sum of the values of x_1, x_2 and x_3 must be equal to or less than 1; since each variable can have only the values 0 and 1, one at most can then have the value 1.

It may help to make the above formulation clear if we consider a numerical example. Suppose Mars Ltd is considering the undertaking of ten jobs during the next period. Each job requires the use of one special component which would have to be purchased at a cost of £90 (none of these components are held in stock). The firm will incur fixed costs of £110, i.e. costs of this amount will arise regardless of what combination of jobs is accepted. Jobs 1, 2 and 3 are mutually exclusive. Full details of the available jobs are given in Table 1.

The model describing the opportunities open to Mars Ltd might be expressed as follows:

Maximize $C = 80x_1 + 90x_2 + 70x_3 + 30x_4 - 50x_5 + 40x_6 -$
$$- 60x_7 - 30x_8 + 10x_9 - 30x_{10} - 110, \qquad 2$$

with the restriction that

$$x_1+x_2+x_3 \leqslant 1,\qquad\qquad 3$$

and each variable of the type x_j may be given only the value 0, indicating rejection of the job j, or 1, indicating acceptance.

Table 1 Cash flows for jobs available to Mars Ltd (£)

Job number	1	2	3	4	5	6	7	8	9	10
receipts	290	260	240	310	280	190	120	220	150	190
sundry costs of jobs	120	80	80	190	240	60	90	160	50	130
gross surplus	170	180	160	120	40	130	30	60	100	60
cost of components	90	90	90	90	90	90	90	90	90	90
net surplus	+80	+90	+70	+30	−50	+40	−60	−30	+10	−30

The optimal plan for the firm is to accept jobs 2, 4, 6 and 9 (this implies giving the value 1 to each of x_2, x_4, x_6 and x_9) and reject the others. The cash flow, C, will then have the value £60 {i.e. $(80\times0)+(90\times1)+(70\times0)+(30\times1)-(50\times0)+(40\times1)-(60\times0)-(30\times0)+(10\times1)-(30\times0)-110$, substituting in equation 2}. The optimal solution involves accepting all jobs which have a surplus except jobs 1 and 3, these being rejected because they are part of a mutually exclusive set with job 2 and earn less than job 2.

The optimal solution in this case is trivial. However, it may be established to be correct formally by considering whether any possible alteration would increase the value of C. Suppose, for example, that we evaluate the effect of altering x_1 from 0 to 1; the restriction expressed in equation 3 requires us to reduce x_2 to 0 at the same time; the net effect on C is therefore $+£80-£90 = -£10$; this alteration is not desirable. We should get the same conclusion for any other possible alteration. This procedure for investigating the optimality of a plan, although trivially simple here, is of considerable usefulness for more complex problems.

It is important to notice the role of the fixed costs in the analysis. Such costs are not altered by the acceptance of an individual job and hence do not influence the appraisal of the worthwhileness of individual jobs. They are relevant in a final stage of the analysis however. We must ensure that the jobs which are worthwhile individually generate a sufficient surplus to cover fixed costs; if this condition is not met, the firm would have to question whether continuance of business was worthwhile – an analysis which would involve long-term considerations.

Some resources already owned

It will be instructive to consider the extension of this model-building technique to the choice of plan for a firm which already holds some resources in stock; we will consider here the simplest case in which only one type of resource is held. We meet the difficulty that we cannot specify in advance a general rule on how the surplus on each job should be calculated. The use of units of resources already in stock might have an effective cost equal to realizable value or replacement cost according to whether the firm would wish to sell or buy in more units of the resource in question; and the decision on this can only be settled at the same time as the decision on the acceptability of the various jobs. We can avoid this difficulty, however, by adopting the following revised formulation:

Maximize $\quad C = A_1 x_1 + A_2 x_2 + \ldots + A_n x_n + S y_s - R y_r - F,$ 　4

subject to the restriction

$$b_1 x_1 + b_2 x_2 + \ldots + b_n x_n + Y_s - Y_r \leqslant K, \qquad\qquad 5$$

where $x_1, \ldots, x_n$ must have the values 1 or 0; $A_1, \ldots, A_n$ represent the cash surplus earned on jobs 1 to n, calculated without any deduction for the cost of using resources of the type held in stock; S and R are the prices at which units of the resources in stock could be sold (net realizable value) and at which additional units could be purchased (replacement cost); Y_s and Y_r are variables representing the numbers of units of the resource sold and purchased: they can be given any positive whole number value; $b_1, \ldots, b_n$ represent the numbers of units of the resource required to be used on each job $1, \ldots, N$; K is the number of units of the resource already owned by the firm; and other symbols have the same meaning as previously.

The expression for C again represents the total cash earned by the firm during the planning period; it comprises the surplus from each job undertaken plus any proceeds from selling units of the resource in stock, less any cost of buying extra resource units and less fixed costs. The restriction **5** specifies the physical constraint that total resource units used on jobs undertaken (b_1x_1 and so on) plus units sold, less any units provided by purchase, may not exceed the number of units in stock.

It is important that as many jobs as practicable should be included in the formulation. We assume, in order to demonstrate principles, that it is possible to describe enough available jobs to indicate whether the firm will be a net buyer or seller of the resource which is stocked; this implies that, if the firm will be a net buyer, at least enough jobs are included to account for the use of existing stocks.

Let us adapt the example of Mars Ltd to provide a numerical illustration of the use of this formulation. Suppose that the components have a purchase price of £90 each (as before) but (because of their specialized nature) they can be realized for only £50 each; we shall consider the alternative possibilities (a) that the firm has three components in stock and (b) that it has twenty components in stock. The formulation should run as follows:

Maximize $\quad C = 170x_1 + 180x_2 + 160x_3 + 120x_4 + 40x_5 +$
$$+ 130x_6 + 30x_7 + 60x_8 + 100x_9 + 60x_{10} +$$
$$+ 50y_s - 90y_r - 110 \qquad\qquad \textbf{6}$$

with the restrictions that

$x_1 + x_2 + x_3 + x_4 + x_5 + x_6 + x_7 + x_8 + x_9 + x_{10} + y_s - y_r$ must not exceed (a) 3 or (b) 20, $\qquad\qquad\qquad\qquad\qquad$ **7**

that $x_1 + x_2 + x_3$ must not exceed 1, that $x_1, \ldots, x_{10}$ must each have the value 1 or 0 and that y_s and y_r must have the value zero or some positive whole number.

Expression **6**, representing the total net cash flow, comprises the surplus on each job before deducting the cost of components (see Table 1) times the variables representing acceptance or rejection of each job plus proceeds of sale of components ($50y_s$) less the cost of buying additional components ($90y_r$) and less fixed costs. Expression **7** describes the use of components; it has the same form as expression **5** with $b_J = 1$ reflecting the information that each job requires only one component.

In case (a), the optimal solution, as before, involves accepting jobs 2, 4, 6 and 9; the firm has to purchase one extra component to supplement the three held in stock and the value of the cash surplus earned is £330, made up from the surpluses on jobs, £180+120+130+100, less £90, the cost of purchasing one extra component and less £110 for fixed costs. We establish the optimality of the plan, in the manner discussed above, by considering all possible alterations which might improve it. For example, any of the jobs 2, 4, 6 and 9 might be rejected and the purchase of the extra component would then be avoided. The effect of this change would be to reduce the overall surplus by the amount contributed by the job concerned and increase it by £90, the cost of the extra component saved. The change would make results worse provided that the cash contributed by the chosen job exceeded £90, and this is the case for all of jobs 2, 4, 6 and 9. This line of reasoning indicates that each job may be appraised separately by costing components at £90, the current buying (replacement) cost.

In case (b), however, the stock of components exceeds any possible need (i.e. it is more than would be required for the acceptance of all ten jobs); and we assume that the components would not be required for any jobs at later times; some, clearly, should be sold. The best plan is to accept jobs 2, 4, 6, 8, 9 and 10. The surplus earned will be £1240, i.e. £650 from the six jobs accepted (£180+120+130+60+100+60) plus £700 from the sale of components (14 at £50) less fixed costs (£110). Again the optimality of the plan is demonstrated by showing that no possible alteration would increase the surplus. One type of alteration would be to reject one of the jobs 2, 4, 6, 8, 9 or 10 and sell the extra component set free. The result would be to reduce cash earnings by the amount contributed by the job chosen and to increase them by £50, the selling price of the component. Total cash inflow would be reduced provided that the amount contributed by the job chosen exceeds £50 – as is the case for all selected jobs. Hence we could have chosen the optimal plan by appraising each job separately and pricing the components at £50, their realizable value.

In this example, the choice between the mutually exclusive projects is not affected by the varying cost attributed to components, because each project uses one component only. If the jobs required different numbers of components their ranking might change according to whether the buying or selling price was the relevant cost of using components.

We have seen, from the use of the simple mathematical model in this section, confirmation of the analysis given earlier; that if a resource is already owned (or ordered) it should be priced for decision purposes at:

1 Replacement cost, if extra purchases will be required for use in the firm on other activities, *or*

2 Realizable value, if the best alternative to use on a particular project is external sale.

The formulation could readily be extended to yield similar conclusions where a firm has several different resources already in stock.

Selection from interdependent projects

The simplest decision situation which may face a firm arises when it has to select from a number of activities which are completely independent in their effects on the firm's cash surplus, i.e. the worthwhileness of undertaking an activity is the same, regardless of what set of other projects is undertaken. In such a case, a decision on whether to accept each project may be taken without reference to the characteristics of any other (assuming that the worthwhileness of continuing in business is established).

In this chapter, we have considered two types of situation in which projects are not independent; (a) the case of mutually exclusive projects and (b) the case in which some resources were in stock so that their relevant cost depended on the alternative uses available for them. We now consider a more general case of interdependence in which the costs associated with any particular project depend upon what other projects have already been accepted.

Table 2 Cash surpluses on jobs available to Jupiter Ltd

Project	1	2	3	4	5	6	7	8	9	10
cash surplus	£550	£50	£400	£250	£500	£100	£750	£150	£200	£450

Suppose, for example, that Jupiter Ltd has available the ten projects described in Table 2, cash surpluses being calculated after deducting all independent costs. In addition, the firm

Table 3 Administration costs of Jupiter Ltd

Number of projects accepted	1, 2 or 3	4, 5 or 6	7 or 8	9	10
administrative costs	£1100	£1900	£2350	£2600	£2750

would incur administrative costs at a level which depended on the volume of projects accepted, as described in Table 3. There are no mutually exclusive projects.

Table 4 Calculation of the optimal plan for Jupiter Ltd

Number of projects accepted	Optimal set	Gross surplus	Administrative costs	Net surplus
1	7 only	750	1100	−350
2	7 and 1	1300	1100	+200
3	7, 1 and 5	1800	1100	+700
4	7, 1, 5 and 10	2250	1900	+350
5	7, 1, 5, 10 and 3	2650	1900	+750
6	7, 1, 5, 10, 3 and 4	2900	1900	+1000
7	7, 1, 5, 10, 3, 4 and 9	3100	2350	+750
8	all except 2 and 6	3250	2350	+900
9	all except 2	3350	2600	+750
10	all	3400	2750	+650

This type of problem does not lend itself to a neat mathematical formulation. The choice of optimal plan may be made by considering in turn each possible number of projects accepted, starting with one project, two projects and so on, calculating the largest cash surplus attainable in each case and then choosing the largest surplus overall. This process is described in Table 4. The largest surplus, £1000, can be earned if the best six projects are accepted as could be seen virtually at a glance in this simple case. The optimal solution is by no means obvious, however, for more complicated cases of interdependence.

The appraisal of projects when there are resource constraints

We have supposed up to now that the number of projects which a firm can accept is not restricted because of a limitation in the supply of some resource. If such a limitation exists, the criterion for acceptance of a project becomes more stringent. To feature in the optimal plan a project must not only yield a cash surplus – it must yield a higher cash surplus than any feasible *alternative* project or combination of projects. The existence of such resource constraints therefore represents another case in which projects should not be appraised independently.

In this chapter, we shall consider only the situation in which there is one simple resource constraint. The more general treatment of resource constraints will be discussed in chapter 11.

A general formulation for the situation in which a single resource is in limited supply might run as follows:

Maximize $\quad C = A_1 x_1 + A_2 x_2 + \ldots + A_n x_n + S y_s - R y_r - F,\quad$ **8**

subject to the restrictions

$$b_1 x_1 + b_2 x_2 + \ldots + b_n x_n + y_s - y_r \leqslant K, \qquad\qquad \textbf{9}$$
$$y_r \leqslant T.$$

$$x_1, \ldots, x_{10} = 0 \text{ or } 1, \qquad\qquad\qquad\qquad\qquad \textbf{10}$$

$$y_s, y_r \geqslant 0.$$

This formulation is the same as that used above (expressions **4** and **5**) with the added restriction that the number of resource units purchased may not exceed T, the number supposed to be available. (There may be considerable uncertainty in practice about the number of resource units available, just as in the estimation of cash flows, but this does not affect the principles demonstrated.)

Let us consider a numerical example. Saturn Ltd is considering its optimal plan with the restriction that components are subject to limited supply; three components are already owned and a maximum of four more may be purchased during the planning period. The components originally cost £80 but the current replacement cost is £90; they may be resold for £50. Saturn Ltd has ten jobs available; each requires the use of one component and they yield the following cash surpluses, before allowing for the cost of components: £180; £170; £120; £210; £150; £220; £100; £80; £140; £190. Fixed costs are £250. The problem may be formulated as follows:

Maximize $\quad 180x_1 + 170x_2 + 120x_3 + 210x_4 + 150x_5 + 220x_6 +$
$$+ 100x_7 + 80x_8 + 140x_9 + 190x_{10} + 50y_s - 90y_r - 250, \qquad \textbf{11}$$

subject to the restrictions

$$x_1 + x_2 + x_3 + x_4 + x_5 + x_6 + x_7 + x_8 + x_9 + x_{10} + y_s - y_r \leqslant 3, \qquad \textbf{12}$$

$$y_r \leqslant 4, \qquad \textbf{13}$$

$$x_1, \ldots, x_{10} = 0 \text{ or } 1 \qquad \textbf{14}$$

$$y_s, y_r \geqslant 0. \qquad \textbf{15}$$

Since nine of the projects have surpluses large enough to cover the cost of components at £90, the best plan will be to use all seven components available – there will be no advantage in selling any. If the firm is to obtain a maximum cash surplus and since it will use a fixed number of components, it must obtain the maximum net cash inflow per component. The optimal plan is to accept projects 1, 2, 4, 5, 6, 9 and 10; these projects have the largest surpluses and, since each uses one component, they also have the largest surpluses per component. This plan will yield £(180+170+210+150+220+140 +190)−(90×4)−250 = £650.

We may again test the optimality of our plan by seeking alterations which will improve it. We might think of accepting project 3, with a cash yield of £120. However a spare component would be needed for the acceptance of project 3 and none is available – a component could be made available only by abandoning one of the projects previously chosen for acceptance. Project 9 (surplus £140) might be given up with the net result that cash earned would fall by £20. Moreover, project 3 is the best of the projects rejected and project 9 is the least rewarding of the projects accepted. Hence any other alteration would reduce the cash surplus by a larger sum and the plan chosen is shown to be optimal.

Opportunity cost

The procedure by which we selected the optimal plan in the last example was to rank projects in the order of their earning rate per component: in this way, we made sure that all the uses of components included in the plan were more worthwhile than the uses rejected. We could have achieved the same result by regarding the cost of a component as £120, the surplus on project 3, and accepting only those projects which had a surplus after deducting that cost, i.e. the projects accepted would be those which earned more than project 3. Such a concept of cost is known in economics as opportunity cost. It may be defined as the amount of cash earned by applying a unit of the resource under consideration in the best available use apart from uses included in the optimal plan. Alternatively, but consistently, opportunity cost may be regarded as the amount by which the value of the optimal plan could be increased if one more unit of the resource were to become available, free of cost. If the opportunity cost of a resource, defined in this way, is less than the current buying price of the resource, any limitation of supply is irrelevant to the analysis; the firm would not want to use more units anyway. For example, in the problem of Saturn Ltd, if projects 3 and 7 had both offered surpluses of £80, the opportunity cost of components would have been £80; Saturn would not have wanted to accept the projects, however, since they would not cover the buying price of £90 – the price of £90 would have been relevant for the analysis.

The opportunity cost of a resource in limited supply may be viewed as the purchase price of the resource (or the sales proceeds if that is the relevant measure of sacrifice) plus a surplus which could be earned in an alternative use; e.g. in the problem of Saturn Ltd, the opportunity cost of a component comprises the purchase price of £90 plus a surplus of £30.

We shall discuss the usefulness of the concept of opportunity cost later. One limitation may be noted immediately, however. We cannot use opportunity cost precisely in appraising the worthwhileness of available activities. For we have to identify the optimal plan *before* we can identify opportunity cost – the best alternative – and once we have the optimal plan our need to know the opportunity cost is reduced.

Summary

The main conclusion of this chapter is that if we are appraising activities for inclusion in the plan of a firm, and there are no interdependences between projects apart from those arising from limitations in the supply of resources, the optimal plan will include those activities, and only those activities, which yield a surplus when resources are valued as follows:

1 If they are not owned or ordered already and not in limited supply – at cost price.

2 If they are owned already or ordered, but not in limited supply – at their replacement cost or at realizable value if there is no alternative worthwhile use for them within the firm.

3 If they are in limited supply, at the higher of their opportunity cost and the value in 1 and 2 above.

6 Patterns of Cost Variation

In chapter 5, we considered some basic principles of cost identification for the appraisal of projects which could be only wholly accepted or rejected. We turn now to the identification of costs in another common business situation, the situation in which it is desired to estimate the best level of output of a product when any one of a wide range of different levels is possible.

It is convenient to begin with a general description of the main models which may be used to describe the types of relationship between total costs and output levels. Most possibilities fall into one of a few main categories: costs may be 'fixed', 'step-functions' or 'variable'. In addition, some cost patterns may be viewed as combinations of the basic types; for example a combination of fixed and variable costs may yield a pattern that is 'semi-variable'.

Fixed costs

There are two senses in which costs may be said to be fixed. They may be unavoidable in the sense that no decision of the firm will alter them or they may be invariant with respect to the level of output (or other measure of activity).

An example of an unavoidable cost is the rent of a factory under a lease which excludes the possibility of sub-letting (and hence of offsetting the cost by rent received). A cost which is strictly unavoidable is not relevant for any decision purposes – by definition it will be the same whatever decision is taken. A cost is normally unavoidable, however, only for a quite short period of time – its fixedness would arise out of some contract which will expire sooner or later.

Costs are described as fixed in relation to output if they

would not be altered by changes in the volume of output. A manufacturing firm may have a factory fully equipped with machinery and providing a certain potential productive capacity. Some costs, such as the factory rent and perhaps the foreman's wages, are likely to be unaltered by changes in volume of output within the limit set by capacity. If the firm rules out the possibility of increasing capacity, such costs would be regarded as fixed in setting the level of production.

Few costs, if any, are fixed with reference to all alternative plans that might be considered by a firm. Factory rent would no longer be fixed if the possibility of expanding capacity were to be considered. Or consider, as another example, a firm which manufactures scientific instruments which are tested on special equipment before sale. An increase in volume of a given product range may not cause any increase in the costs of testing equipment; such costs would be classified as fixed for decisions concerned with such changes in volume. However, if a similar increase in volume measured in some convenient unit were to be achieved by the introduction of new products, a new dimension would be introduced to the problem. The costs of testing equipment might no longer be fixed. It is therefore important to keep in mind the particular decision problem which sets the frame of reference when defining fixed costs.

Costs as 'step-functions'

A more general way of regarding the behaviour of this type of cost is as a 'step-function', so called because of the step-like appearance of the cost–volume relationship when plotted on a graph (Figure 2). The characteristic of a step-function cost is that it remains constant over a range of output levels, but increases suddenly as volume is increased over certain critical levels. Figure 2 pictures the relationship between output and the annual cost of factory rent and supervisory labour for a single-product firm. The factory, rented at a cost of £10 000 per annum, provides capacity for 5000 units, and, if capacity were to be increased, the best plan would be to acquire another, similar, building; supervisors earn a wage of some

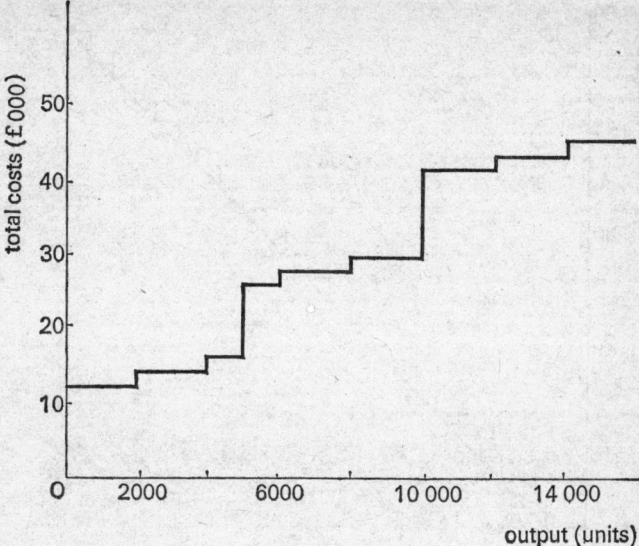

Figure 2 Total costs as a step-function of output

£2000 per annum, and each can control the output of 2000 units per annum.

The smaller the height and depth of each step, the more closely the cost relationship can be approximated by a straight line, representing a directly variable cost. Figure 3 describes the relationship between manufacturing wages and volume of output for a firm which, as matters of policy, hires and fires employees to match its production needs and has each employee work exactly 2000 hours per annum. (There is no overtime and no short time.) Each employee is paid £2000 per annum and takes one hour to produce a product unit. In practice manufacturing wages are usually regarded as a directly variable cost. Figure 3 shows the cost of wages as a step-function and (in the broken line) as a variable cost; the variable cost line can be seen to be a fairly close approximation of the step-function.

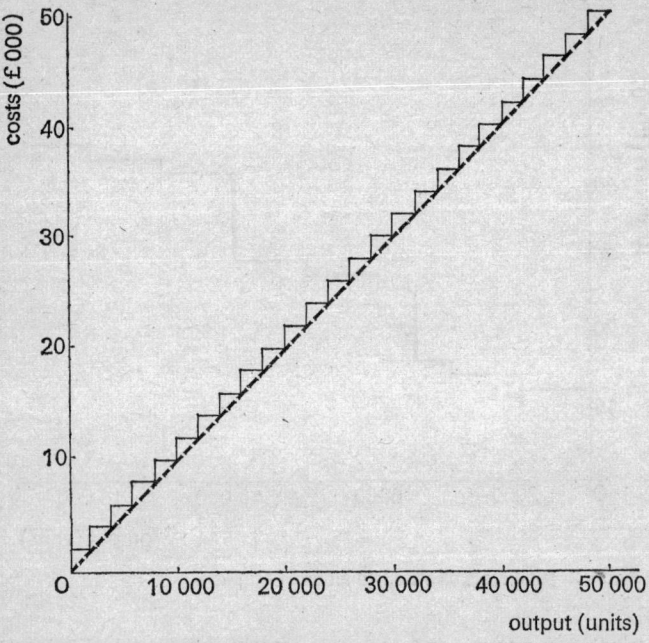

Figure 3 Labour costs regarded as step-function and as variable cost

Variable costs

This leads us to consider a third type of cost, that which is variable. The main characteristic of such a cost is that it tends to increase steadily rather than in steps as output increases. The simplest type of relationship is the linear one, illustrated in Figure 3, so-called because it is represented as a straight line on a graph. In this situation the amount added to total cost for each unit added to output is a constant, e.g. the cost of the hundredth unit is the same as the cost of the thousandth unit. The relationship between variable costs and output may also be more complicated in nature, i.e. non-linear. Figure 4 illustrates such a relationship for a case in which each unit added to volume yields successively smaller increases in total

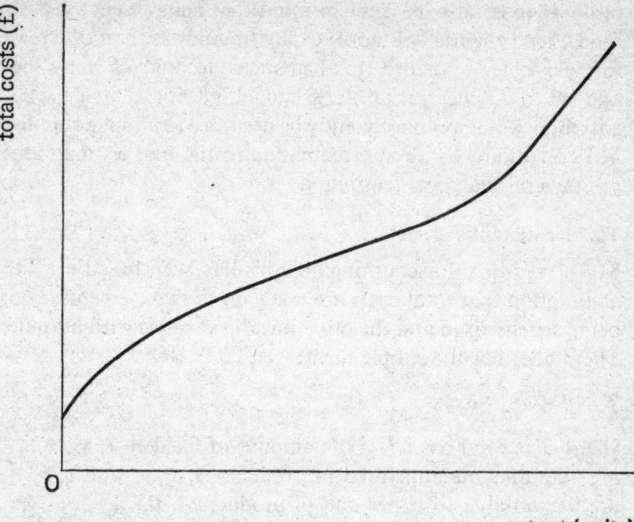

Figure 4 Non-linear variable costs

cost up to some critical level beyond which added units have increasing costs.

The identification of actual cost relationships

In practice, the identification of how total costs are likely to move as output varies is an important part of the analysis required for any decision. It should not be assumed that some particular type of cost relationship is likely to have general applicability. A special study would normally be required to estimate what model would best describe the pattern of costs for each decision situation.

The pattern of total costs associated with various output levels of a particular product may well comprise a combination of the different types of cost relationship described above. Fuel costs, for example, may be best viewed as part fixed and part variable, e.g. in the case of electricity charged on a two-part tariff. It must also be kept in mind that some types of cost model lend themselves more readily to analysis than others – for example, standard mathematical techniques may be applied to a linear variable cost model but not to a step-type cost model. It may consequently be desirable to adopt a simplified cost model as an approximation to the best estimate on grounds of analytical feasibility.

The accountant's model

Much traditional accounting analysis has been based on the assumption that total costs are made up of two elements, one being strictly fixed and the other linearly variable with output. The model has the simple form:

$$T = F + ax_a + bx_b + \dots,$$

where T is total cost, F is the amount of fixed cost, $x_a, x_b, \dots$ are the units manufactured of products $A, B, \dots$, and $a, b, \dots$ are the variable costs per unit of products $A, B, \dots$.

At first sight, this model seems quite plausible. Some costs will normally be unaffected by changes in output, at least within a certain range. Other costs will be linearly variable if a simple aggregation rule applies – if the cost for the manufacture of two product units is equal to the sum of the costs for two separate units. It seems quite reasonable to assume the applicability of this rule – to suppose, for example, that if one unit of output requires the use of twenty labour hours at a cost of 75p per hour (total cost £15), then two units will require forty labour hours at a cost of 75p per head (total cost £30).

The economist's model

However, the accountant's model of cost behaviour rests on certain assumptions which may be false. The assumptions are, in essence, that the efficiency of the use of variable resources and their prices are independent of the volume of activity. Economists have tended to take a different view from that of accountants and to admit the general possibility that cost may vary in a non-linear relationship with output. They have seen, for example, that the labour cost of a product unit may diminish as volume increases up to a certain point because employees may become more skilled in an operation with constant practice, and it may become feasible to organize output in a more efficient way given a large volume (e.g. by having employees specialize in particular operations). Another possibility is that the labour cost per unit may increase once volume exceeds a certain level; this may be caused, for example, because it is possible to achieve further increases in the volume of output only by pressing into service employees who are unskilled in the required operations. Another influence which may negate the assumption of linearity of cost is the possibility of buying supplies at lower prices when a certain minimum quantity is ordered.

Learning curves

Several studies have been undertaken of ways of measuring changes in the labour time required in production, taking account of economies resulting from increased familiarity with the operation. As a result, some standard models for predicting costs have been developed; they are known as learning curves. One such relationship is illustrated in the following example.

Example: Helios Ltd has been offered a contract for the manufacture of one thousand widgets and it wishes to estimate the total labour cost involved. All employees used would earn £0.75 per hour. Widgets would be manufactured in batches of fifty and it has been discovered in a trial run that the first widget would take fifty hours to manufacture, but the fiftieth widget would require only slightly over forty-seven and a half hours. The total time required for the first batch would be 2425 hours. It is decided, on the basis of this information and a detailed study of the operations, to assume that (a) the time required for the manufacture of the first unit of the second batch would be forty-seven and a half hours, i.e. 95 per cent of the time required for the corresponding unit of the first batch and (b) the proportionate time saving for subsequent units and batches would be similar, i.e. that a unit of output in any batch would require 95 per cent of the time for the corresponding unit of the previous batch.

It follows that the total time required for the second batch would be 2425×0.95 hours, that for the third batch 2425×0.95^2 and that for the 20th (and last batch) 2425×0.95^{19}. Hence total labour time would be:

$$L = 2425 + 2425(0.95) + 2425(0.95)^2 + \ldots + 2425(0.95)^{19}$$

$$= \frac{2425(1 - 0.95^{20})}{1 - 0.95} \quad \text{(using the formula for summation of a geometric progression)}$$

$$= 31\,114 \text{ hours,}$$

and the total cost would be

$$£31\,114 \times 0.75 = £23\,336.$$

The model assumed in this example – the so-called learning curve – is illustrated in Figure 5. This figure depicts the relationship between total labour cost and volume of output and shows that although labour is a variable cost, the relationship is non-linear (the broken line in Figure 5 represents a linear variable cost for purposes of comparison). The situation assumed in this example is a simple one. Total labour cost is represented by the model

$$T = \frac{wt(1 - p^n)}{1 - p},$$

where t is the number of hours required for the first batch (which might comprise only one item), w is the wage rate per hour, $1 - p$ is the percentage time saved from one batch to the next and n is the number of batches.

The assumption that the time taken on any batch is a constant proportion of time taken on the previous batch is not the only reasonable assumption and it may not be the one which best fits a particular situation. Models can, however, be formulated for the prediction of labour costs in situations in which there is some other standard pattern of time saving.

Decision variables

The discussion of this chapter has concentrated attention on the relationship between total cost and the level of output. It is

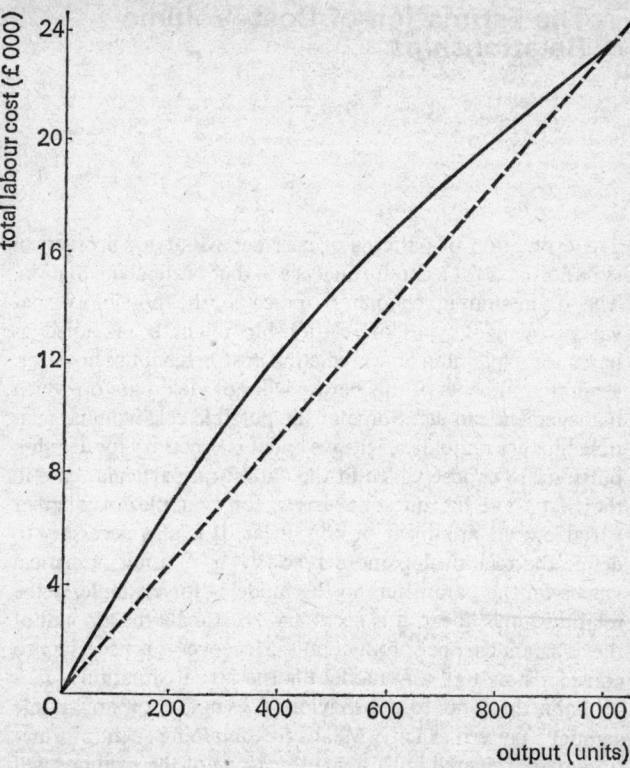

Figure 5 Learning curve

worth noting that total cost may be influenced by other variables within the control of the decision taker, for example the number of items manufactured in one production run (there may be an economy in long runs) and the technology used in production. An overall optimal decision must consider all these variables. It will involve the estimation of total costs for different output levels for each technology, production run size and so on.

7 The Estimation of Cost–Volume Relationships

The estimation of patterns of cost behaviour for a practical situation calls for a careful analysis of that particular situation. The discussion in chapter 6 indicated the possibility that various general types of relationship might be assumed as bases for explaining and predicting cost behaviour; however, general arguments of this nature will not yield data on which management can act. Some of the possible cost–volume relationships are mutually exclusive and it is necessary for decision purposes to choose which fit the data for a particular case in the best way; the question arises, for example, of whether variable costs are linear or non-linear. It is also necessary to define the relationship more precisely by putting numerical values on the parameters in the model – for example, if the relationship is linear, it is necessary to estimate the amount of the constant cost per product unit. Moreover it is necessary to consider how well any model fits the actual situation – it is probable that actual cost behaviour does not follow any simple standard pattern exactly. Means for obtaining such information are considered in this chapter. None of the methods will give a guaranteed correct answer; but taken together, they may provide the best available basis for decisions.

Work study

One method used for estimating a model for the prediction of costs for different output levels is known as work study. It involves undertaking trial manufacturing runs under carefully controlled conditions. Measurements are made of resources used in the manufacture, e.g. time of different grades of labour, machine time, quantities of various materials; the resources are then costed at estimated prices to yield a total cost estimate.

Although it may yield helpful insights into cost relationships, work study has serious limitations, some of which are typical of difficulties in using controlled experiments in business and the social sciences generally. Employees involved in the production will inevitably be aware that their work is the subject of special study and this knowledge may affect their behaviour. Work study practitioners will be aware of this difficulty and will try to adjust for it – the availability of routine records, time records of employees, stock records and so on, may provide helpful indications; however such adjustments are necessarily speculative in estimating the best performance that is reasonably possible. Moreover, it will normally be practicable to undertake the study only for a relatively small volume of output and the extrapolation of the results may not give good cost predictions for large volumes. The work study method is not designed to detect the effect of volume changes on costs that are remote from output, such as administrative overheads – it is essentially confined to cases where direct physical measurements are possible both of resources used and related output, most commonly labour.

The analysis of financial results for estimating cost models

Alternative methods for estimating cost models involve the analysis of actual financial results recorded for past periods. Such methods are not directly relevant in assessing the desirability of introducing new products. They may, however, be useful in obtaining cost information for setting the optimal price and output level for existing products. The methods in use range from crude rules of thumb to quite sophisticated statistical methods. A detailed discussion of these methods, and in particular of the mathematical refinements of the statistical methods, is beyond the scope of this book. An indication of their nature and rationale can be provided, however, by considering a simple situation in which a firm is involved in the manufacture of a single product and it is assumed that the only independent influence on cost is exerted by changes in volume of activity.

Rule of thumb methods of analysis

A simple first approach to the estimation of a cost model is provided by the analysis of each type of expenditure for a particular period according to whether it seems to have the characteristic of being fixed or variable. It is normally assumed that the variable element bears a linear relationship to output. Table 5 gives details of expenditure for one year for an imaginary, single product, firm. The first column gives total costs by main cost classifications, as they might be extracted

Table 5 An accounting analysis of cost

	Total costs (£)	Fixed costs (£)	Variable costs (£)	Notes
materials	97 280	—	97 280	quantity varies directly with output level
direct labour	78 350	—	78 350	quantity varies directly with output level
supervisory labour	12 600	2 100	10 500	six men employed. One required for overall control – others added as output expands
factory rent	20 000	20 000	—	fixed by contract
cost of using machinery (depreciation)	56 000	—	56 000	machines have to be added as output expands
fuel and power	12 590	2 000	10 590	contract for fixed sum plus amount which varies with output
general administration	33 490	33 490	—	establishment can cope with capacity output and no savings possible at lower output
	310 310	57 590	252 720	

from the firm's accounting records and the other columns give an analysis between fixed and variable costs with notes on the rationale of the division. Assuming output for the year to be 8000 units, the variable cost per unit would be estimated at

$$\frac{£252\ 720}{8000} = £31.59,$$

and the assumed cost relationship would be represented by the model:

$$T = 57\,590 + 31.59q, \qquad \textbf{1}$$

where T is the total cost, and q is the number of units produced. This method of cost estimation is aptly described as 'rule of thumb'. Since the cost model is derived by referring to cost data for only one year, it amounts to the analyst's forcing his view of a plausible cost relationship on the data. The division of costs between fixed and variable is more or less arbitrary. The model is not subjected to the critical test of discovering whether it would yield a good prediction of total cost in another period when output was different. Such a test is required before we can have confidence in our model. Ideally we should like to have details of output and total cost for several periods as a basis for identifying the cost relationship. However we should probably then fail to find any model which accounted for all the results *exactly* and we should require some means of judging what model provided the best estimate of total costs overall.

Statistical cost analysis
Cost determination using simultaneous equations

Statistical methods are designed to deal with this question. Their application involves making some preliminary assumption about the general nature of the cost relationship as do the rule of thumb methods; a common assumption is again that total cost comprises a fixed element and a linearly variable element. However, the data for several periods may be examined to estimate the value of the parameters – the amount of fixed cost and variable cost per unit – and systematic methods are used for judging what model best fits the data.

Let us give ourselves a degree of omniscience in order to examine the basic ideas; let us imagine that we are dealing with a firm (which we will call Selene Ltd) for which we know the cost–output relationship to be

$$T = 100\,000 + 45q. \qquad \textbf{2}$$

On the basis of this knowledge, we could predict the total cost for different levels of output as in Table 6. The relationship is illustrated in Figure 5, the output levels given in Figure 6 being indicated by crosses.

Table 6 Costs and output levels of Selene under omniscience

Output (q)	Fixed cost (£)	Variable cost (45x) (£)	Total cost (T) (£)
500	100 000	22 500	122 500
1000	100 000	45 000	145 000
2000	100 000	90 000	190 000
3000	100 000	135 000	235 000
5000	100 000	225 000	325 000

Let us now return to earth and suppose that we have no advance knowledge of the cost–volume relationship for Selene Ltd; however, let us assume the relationship to be of the general form

$$T = a + bq,\qquad\qquad 3$$

where a and b are unknown constants; suppose also that we have the data for output and total costs given in Table 6 – obtained from past financial records of the firm. In this situation, it would be a simple matter to infer the cost–volume relationship. We could use a graphical method, plotting the known values for costs and output and drawing a straight line through them. Alternatively, the relationship could be inferred algebraically from any two pairs of observations of output and cost. From the data we know

$122\,500 = a + 500b$ (substituting $T = 122\,500$ and $q = 500$ in equation 3)

and $325\,000 = a + 5000b$ (substituting $T = 325\,000$ and $q = 5000$ in equation 3).

Solving these equations we find $a = 100\,000$ and $b = 45$ and we can readily verify that the other cost and output data satisfy the derived relationship; i.e. we can infer exactly equation 2 from which the figures were actually derived.

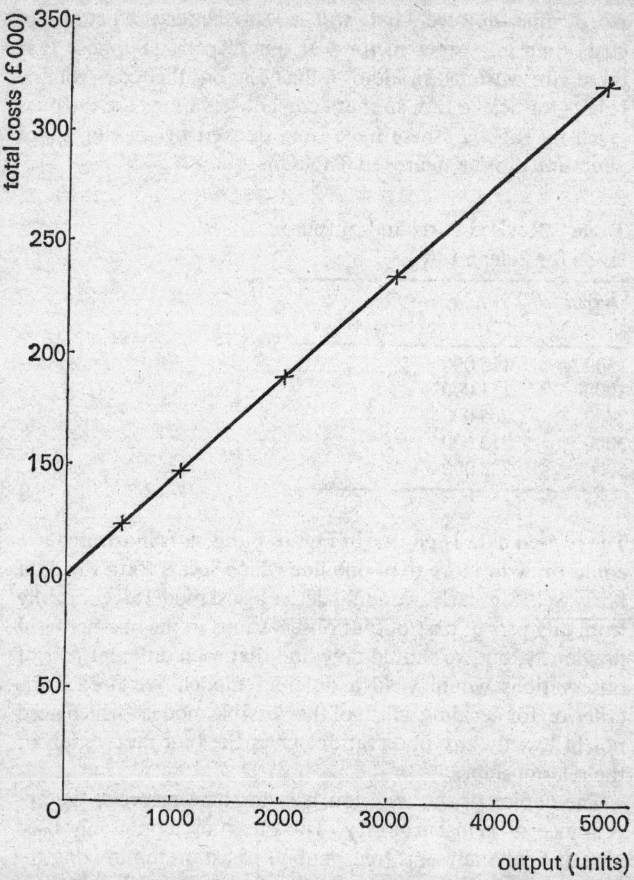

Figure 6 An omniscient view of the cost–volume relationships

'Least-squares' analysis

In practice, however, as we have already noted, it is very un-likely that any equation will predict an actual cost–volume relationship exactly. Various random effects are likely to cause the actual costs to differ somewhat from the predictions of any simple model. The search for a numerical relationship is still worthwhile, however, if it will lead to better predictions of costs than any other method at our disposal. Suppose that there are various random influences on the cost–volume results for Selene Ltd, so that actual observations are the ones given in Table 7 (these have been derived by making slight alterations to the figures in Table 6).

Table 7 Revised costs and output levels for Selene Ltd

Output (q)	Total cost (T) (£)
500	115 000
1000	151 000
2000	205 000
3000	212 000
5000	328 000

The revised data is plotted in Figure 7 and, as is illustrated, we could draw in more than one line which seems to fit the data fairly well. Similarly, we could derive a cost model algebraically from any pair of cost/output observations in the manner used previously, but we should now find that each different pair of observations would yield a different model. We need some criterion for deciding which of the possible models (which need not fit exactly any observation) gives the best description of the relationship.

The choice of the criterion has, in some respects, the appearance of being arbitrary. The one most commonly used in statistical analysis is (reasonably) based on minimizing the differences between costs as predicted by the model and actual cost observations. Because of its convenience in more sophisticated statistical analysis, the actual criterion is that the model chosen should minimize the sum of the squares of differences between actual and predicted costs. One result of using squares of differences is that since a squared number is always positive, the values for each observation can be added to obtain a measure of overall difference – the sum of simple differences

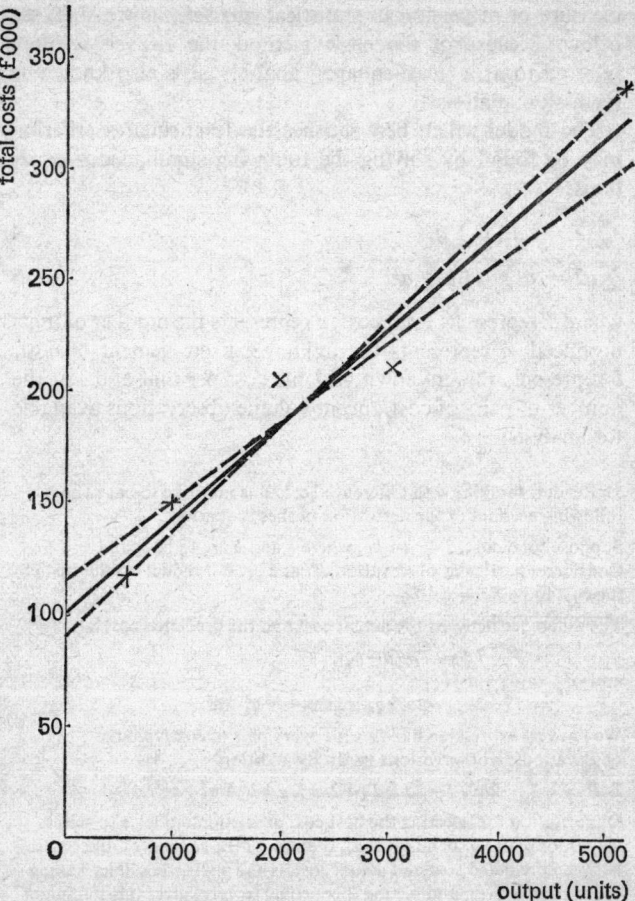

Figure 7 The actual cost–volume relationship for Selene Ltd

might be very low for a quite poor model if positive differences for some observations cancelled with negative differences for others. A more important result is that the analysis can be related to the calculation of the variance, an important measure of dispersion in statistical analysis, as we shall see below. Because of the basic method, the analysis is often referred to as a 'least-squares' analysis; it is also known as regression analysis.

The model which best satisfies the least-squares criterion may be found by solving the following simultaneous equations:[1]

$$\sum T = na + b \sum q, \qquad\qquad\qquad\qquad\qquad\textbf{4}$$

$$\sum qT = a \sum q + b \sum q^2 \qquad\qquad\qquad\qquad\textbf{5}$$

where T represents total cost, q represents the number of units produced, a represents the unknown fixed element of cost, b represents the unknown variable cost per unit and n is the number of pairs of cost/output volume observations available for analysis.

1. Readers familiar with differential calculus may like to have the following account of the derivation of these equations.

Suppose total cost, $T = a + bq$, where a and b are to be found. Consider a particular observation, T_1 and q_1; our model would predict the cost to be $T^* = a + bq_1$.

The difference between the actual cost and the predicted cost is

$$d_1 = T_1 - T^* = T_1 - a - bq_1,$$
$$\text{and} \quad d_1^2 = (T_1 - a - bq_1)^2$$
$$= T_1^2 - 2aT_1 - 2bT_1 q_1 + 2abq_1 + b^2 q_1^2 + a^2.$$

We have an expression like this for every pair of cost/volume observations, n observations in all. By addition

$$\Sigma d^2 = \Sigma T^2 - 2a \Sigma T - 2b \Sigma Tq + 2ab \Sigma q + b^2 \Sigma q_1^2 + na^2.$$

Our criterion for selecting the best cost prediction model is to select values for a and b such that Σd^2, the sum of the squares of differences between predicted cost and actual cost, is as small as possible. Taking partial derivatives, and setting them equal to zero, gives this minimum value and the following conditions:

$$\frac{\partial(\Sigma d^2)}{\partial a} = -2 \Sigma T + 2b \Sigma q + 2na = 0,$$

thus $\qquad \Sigma T = na + b \Sigma q;$ \qquad\qquad\qquad\qquad **4**

and $\quad \dfrac{\partial(\Sigma d^2)}{\partial b} = -2 \Sigma Tq + 2a \Sigma q + 2b \Sigma q^2 = 0$

thus $\qquad \Sigma qT = a \Sigma q + b \Sigma q^2.$ \qquad\qquad\qquad **5**

Readers who are not familiar with mathematical notation should note that Σ (the Greek letter sigma) stands for the sum of the group of items described by the symbol which follows it. Hence ΣT stands for the sum of all the observations of total cost; and, to obtain ΣqT, we have to multiply together the amount of cost and the number of units, a pair at a time and add the resulting amounts. Hence equation **4** may be read as 'the sum of the observations of total cost is equal to (the fixed cost times the number of observations) plus (the variable cost times the sum of all the output levels)' and equation **5** as 'the sum of the product of output and total cost for each observation equals (fixed cost times the sum of output levels) plus (the variable cost times the sum of the squares of output levels)'.

The use of expressions **4** and **5** to derive a cost model from the observations given in Table 7 is described in Table 8.

Table 8 A statistical cost model for Selenedth

Output (q)	Total cost (T) (£000)	q^2 (£000)	qT (£000)	T^2 (£000 000)
500	115	250	57 500	13 225
1 000	151	1 000	151 000	22 801
2 000	205	4 000	410 000	42 025
3 000	212	9 000	636 000	44 944
5 000	328	25 000	1 640 000	107 584

$\Sigma q = 11\,500$ $\quad \Sigma T = 1011$ $\quad \Sigma q^2 = 39\,250$ $\quad \Sigma qT = 2\,894\,500$ $\quad \Sigma T^2 = 230\,579$

We substitute these numbers in equations **4** and **5**

$\Sigma T = na + b\,\Sigma q$ gives $\quad 1\,011\,000 = 5a + 11\,500b$;
$\Sigma qT = a\,\Sigma q + b\,\Sigma q^2$ gives $\quad 2\,894\,500\,000 = 11\,500a + 39\,250\,000b$

thus $\quad a = 99\,922 \quad$ and $\quad b = 44{\cdot}469$

The cost equation derived is $T = 99\,922 + 44{\cdot}5q$.

ΣT^2 is given for use in expression **6** below.

The reader will remember that we derived the observations given in Table 7 by altering slightly earlier numbers, in which a perfect linear cost–volume relationship was assumed, described by the equation $T = 100\,000 + 45q$. It will be noted that our model for the revised situation, $T = 99\,922 + 44{\cdot}5q$, is similar to the original equation. It is not identical, because our alterations to the original data were not perfectly symmetrical.

Goodness of fit

Statisticians have developed a measure to indicate how well a model derived from least-squares analysis fits the basic data, in our case the original cost–volume observations of Table 7, and hence how much confidence we may have in such a model. We note, first, that we may use two statistical measures to summarize the characteristics of the basic cost data, the arithmetic average and the variance. The average is well known as the sum of the cost observations divided by the number of observations. The variance is a measure of the range of the numbers in the basic data; it is found by calculating the difference between each item (each cost number in our case) and the average, squaring the results and calculating the average of these squares. It follows that the wider the range of numbers in the data, the larger will be the variance (we shall meet this measure again in chapter 13 where we shall use it as a measure of the risk involved in accepting a project). If we consider the average and the variance of a set of numbers, we get a summary of the range of values represented in the set.

In Table 9, we give again the cost–volume information available for Selene Ltd and calculate the average cost level and its variance. In Table 10, we tabulate the cost *predictions* for the same output levels using the model derived from least-squares analysis, $T = 99\ 922 + 44 \cdot 5q$, and calculate the average and variance for these predictions. In both tables, we also give the square root of the variance (known as the standard deviation); by 'undoing' the squaring we get a number in the same order of magnitude as the original data. The methods of least-squares analysis ensure that the average of the actual data is equal to the average of the predictions of the model – as can be verified by studying Tables 9 and 10. If our model is a good one the range of predicted cost values will be similar to the range of actual cost values – indeed if the model is perfect the two sets of numbers will be identical and have identical variances. A good measure of the success of our model in predicting the range of cost values may be obtained by comparing the variance of the original data and the variance of the predictions – and this is the measure commonly used in statistics. The ratio of the variance of predictions to the variance of actual cost levels in our example is 5 062 355/5 230 960, i.e.

Table 9 Average and variance of actual cost levels

Output level (units)	Total cost (£000)	Average cost (£000)	Difference between actual and average (£000)	Square of difference (£000)
	a	b	$c = a - b$	$d = c^2$
500	115	202·2	−87·2	7 603 840
1000	151	202·2	−51·2	2 621 440
2000	205	202·2	+2·8	7 840
3000	212	202·2	+9·8	96 040
5000	328	202·2	+125·8	15 825 640
	1011			26 154 800

Average = 202·2
Variance (average) = 5 230 960
Standard deviation = $\sqrt{}$(variance) = 72·30

96·8 per cent. We may express this result by saying that our model explains some 97 per cent of the variance observed in cost levels; the remaining 3 per cent cannot be explained by our model which deals in terms of output levels and must be attributed to random factors or to systematic influences other

Table 10 Average and variance of predicted cost levels

Output level (units)	Fixed cost (£)	Variable cost (£)	Total cost (£)	Average cost (£)	Difference between prediction and average (£)	Square of difference (£000)
q	a	$b = 44.469q$	$c = a + b$	d	$e = c - d$	c^2
500	99 922	22 234	122 156	202 200	−80 044	6 407 042
1000	99 922	44 469	144 391	202 200	−57 809	3 341 880
2000	99 922	88 938	188 860	202 200	−13 340	177 956
3000	99 922	133 406	233 328	202 200	+31 128	968 952
5000	99 922	222 344	322 266	202 200	+120 066	14 415 844
			1 011 001			25 311 674

Average = 202 200
Variance (average) = 5 062 335
Standard deviation = $\sqrt{}$(variance) = 71·15

than output (or possibly to the fact that the linear form of model we have used is not appropriate). The ratio of the variances is usually designated R^2 in statistical analysis and it is given by the formula (using the notation of Table 8)

$$R^2 = \frac{\{n \sum Tq - (\sum q)(\sum T)\}^2}{\{n \sum q^2 - (\sum q)^2\}\{n \sum T^2 - (\sum T)^2\}}. \qquad 6$$

The square root of R^2 is generally known as the coefficient of correlation. The method of calculation ensures that the value of the coefficient of correlation will vary between $+1$ (indicating a perfect positive linear relationship – costs increasing in proportion with output) and -1 (indicating a perfect negative linear relationship – which would here indicate the odd result that costs decreased in proportion with increases in output). If the coefficient of correlation had the value zero, we should conclude that there was virtually no simple relationship between output and costs. Correspondingly, R^2 may vary between $+1$, indicating that the model gives perfect predictions and 0, indicating that it has no value for predictions whatsoever.[2]

2. The reader may like to have the following account of the derivation of the formula for R^2. We denote the predicted cost levels, T^*. Then, using the notation explained in the text, we have:

$$R^2 = \frac{\text{variance } T^*}{\text{variance } T} = \frac{(1/n) \sum \{T^* - (1/n) \sum T^*\}^2}{(1/n) \sum \{T - (1/n) \sum T\}^2}$$

$$= \frac{(1/n) \sum \{(a + bq) - (1/n) \sum (a + bq)\}^2}{(1/n) \sum \{T - (1/n) \sum T\}^2}$$

$$= \frac{b^2 \sum \{q - (1/n) \sum q\}^2}{\sum \{T - (1/n) \sum T\}^2} = \frac{b^2 \{n \sum q^2 - (\sum q)^2\}}{n \sum T^2 - (\sum T)^2}.$$

Now, we know (see footnote on page 88) that $\sum T = na + b \sum q$ and $\sum qT = a \sum q + b \sum q^2$. It follows, multiplying the first expression by $\sum q$ and the second by n that

$$\sum T \sum q = na \sum q + b(\sum q)^2$$
and $$\quad n \sum qT = na \sum q + bn \sum q^2.$$

By subtraction and rearrangement

$$b = \frac{n \sum qT - \sum T \sum q}{n \sum q^2 - (\sum q)^2}$$

and substituting in our expression for R^2, we have

$$R^2 = \frac{\{n \sum Tq - (\sum q)(\sum T)\}^2}{\{n \sum q^2 - (\sum q)^2\}\{n \sum T^2 - (\sum T)^2\}}.$$

Multiple-regression analysis

Techniques have been developed for the estimation of cost relationships when more than one variable may be assumed to influence total cost. The analysis used is known as 'multiple regression' analysis. For example, it may be reasonable to suppose that total costs are influenced by the number of separate orders processed during the accounting period as well as by the volume of output. Multiple regression analysis could be applied to yield a cost model of the form:

$$T = a + b_1 q + b_2 s, \qquad\qquad 7$$

where T is total cost, a is fixed cost, b_1 is variable cost per product unit, b_2 is variable cost per order, q is the number of product units, and s is the number of orders.

Multiple regression analysis might also be applied in the analysis of the cost–volume relationship in a multi-product firm. In this case, if each product is assumed to have a constant variable cost, the total cost for a given number of units of production will depend on the product mix; the cost model will normally yield good predictions only if the output of each product is treated as an independent variable. The cost model might then have the form

$$T = a + b_1 q_1 + b_2 q_2 + b_3 q_3 + \ldots + b_n q_n \qquad\qquad 8$$

where q_1 and b_1 are the output and variable cost of product 1 and so on for n products.

An alternative approach for a multi-product firm would be to make some preliminary analysis of costs by product type, and then apply the simple regression analysis, described in the previous section, to the data for each product independently. If this approach were adopted, it is likely that the preliminary cost analysis would introduce some imprecision into the process so that the model derived would yield less good predictions than one obtained by multiple regression techniques. The degree of the imprecision would depend on the ease with which costs could be identified with different products. If the identification is simple, e.g. because products are manufactured in different departments and general overhead costs are small – a preliminary cost analysis may be a good procedure. In other cases a multiple regression analysis may be preferable; it may, however, be impracticable when a very large number of products is involved.

The method of multiple regression analysis is similar in principle to the least squares analysis described above; its detailed description is beyond the scope of this book. The interested reader is referred to one of the references listed at the end of the book for this chapter.

Some problems in the use of statistical analysis

The statistical techniques described above represent powerful means of cost estimation – perhaps the best available at the present time. Their use is, however, not without attendant difficulties and their mechanical application, ignoring such difficulties, may lead to nonsensical results. We therefore conclude our discussion of statistical cost analysis with a short review of some of the points of difficulty.

Accounting valuation conventions

We should note, firstly, that the cost models derived by statistical analysis will be no better than the basic accounting data used in the analysis. Accounting conventions commonly involve assuming that the cost of using resources (acquired by a firm at some earlier time) is equal to the original purchase price of those resources – or equal to some proportion of the purchase price, if the resources are not fully used up. But we saw, in chapter 5, that the relevant cost of using resources already owned may be their replacement cost or resale value. Original cost is not directly relevant and its use may lead to material error unless it represents a good approximation of the values that are relevant.

The cost of using a long-lived asset (depreciation) in any year is commonly calculated as the cost of the asset less any estimated scrap value divided by the estimated life of the asset. Not only does this calculation ignore replacement cost – it also ignores the sacrifice of interest involved in an effective purchase of productive services in advance. A better estimate of the cost of using a long-lived asset might be the rental which a hire company would have to charge to earn a minimum satisfactory rate of return (see chapter 17). Conventional accounting estimates may therefore require revision before they represent information which is appropriate for use in forming a cost model for decision purposes. The nature of accounting conventions will be considered in more detail in chapters 16 and 17.

Matching costs and revenues

Care should also be taken, in using conventional accounting records for cost analysis, to make sure that costs have been matched with the corresponding output. This may be particularly important if the analysis is related to a short period. The problem is that a business does not incur its expenditures in cash exactly at the time the output arises. Wages are commonly paid weekly in arrear and other expenses are often paid subject to a delay of three months or more. Normal accounting practice calls for an assessment of expenses incurred but not paid at any time, so that recorded costs represent costs incurred rather than costs paid. However, the degree of precision achieved in this process may satisfy the requirements of normal accounting and yet be insufficient for the purposes of cost analysis. Indeed, it is a deliberate policy of accounting to err on the safe side in cases of any doubt by overstating costs. It is important that data should be revised in any way necessary so that it represents the best possible assessment of the cost of the output of a period before it is used in regression analysis.

The stability of the cost–volume relationship

The use of past results for several periods in estimating a cost model rests on the assumption that the cost–volume relationship has remained stable over the periods in question and will continue to apply to a future period. In particular, it is necessary that price levels should have remained constant (or that the observations should be adjusted so that they are expressed in terms of constant prices) and that methods of operation should be constant both as regards the technology and administrative practices used and the efficiency with which they are applied. The type of error which can result when these conditions do not apply may be illustrated by simple examples.

Suppose that the cost relationship in the most recent period was the one first assumed for the case of Selene Ltd,

$$T = 100\,000 + 45q. \qquad \textbf{9}$$

If output in that period was 5000 units, total cost would have been £325 000. Suppose further that all prices had increased by 5 per cent since the previous period, whilst efficiency of operation remained constant. The cost equation for the previous period would have been:

$$T = 100\,000 \times \frac{100}{105} + \frac{45 \times 100}{105}q$$
$$= 95\,238 + 42 \cdot 9q. \qquad \textbf{10}$$

If output in that period was 4000 units, total cost would have been £266 838.

If we attempted to derive a cost model from these two observations, i.e. output 5000, cost £325 000 and output 4000, cost £266 838, we should obtain the following result. We should solve the two equations (cf. p. 84 above):

$$325\,000 = a + 5000b,$$
$$\text{and } 266\,838 = a + 4000b,$$

thus $a = 34\,190$ and $b = 58 \cdot 2$. The cost model would be assumed to be

$$T = 34\,190 + 58 \cdot 2q. \qquad \textbf{11}$$

Expression **11** has little relation to either of the actual cost relationships which prevailed during the period. Our analysis has assumed, in effect, that the whole of the increase in total cost is associated with the increase in output and ignored the effect of the price level changes. The position is illustrated in Figure 8. The lower solid line represents the cost–volume relationship for the earlier period whilst the upper solid line

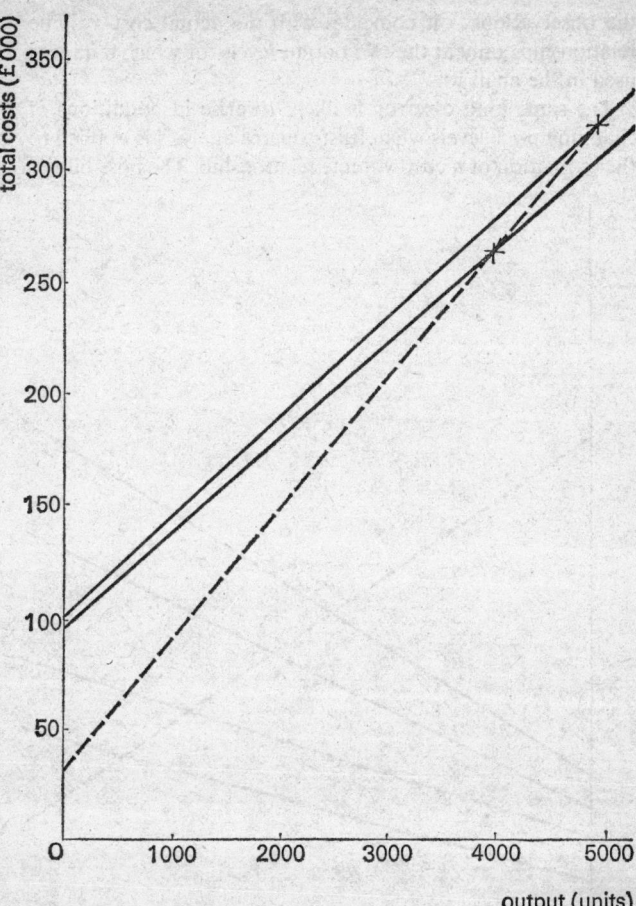

Figure 8 Cost–volume relationships with changing price levels

represents the relationship for the later period. The upper line has a higher intercept with the total-cost axis, representing the higher fixed-cost element, and a steeper slope, representing the higher variable cost. The dashed line is the line derived from the observations – it coincides with the actual cost–volume relationships only at the two output levels for which data was used in the analysis.

The same kind of error is likely to arise in conditions of changing price levels when least-squares analysis is applied to the estimation of a cost–volume relationship. The possibilities

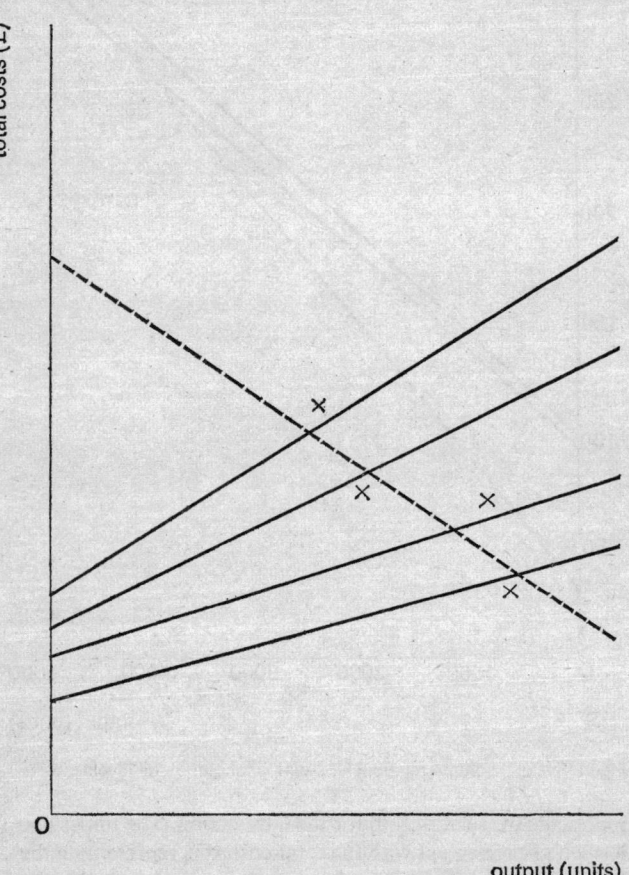

Figure 9 Cost–volume relationships with changing price levels

are illustrated in Figure 9. The solid lines represent the assumed actual cost–volume relationships at different times; and the crosses represent actual cost–volume observations, distributed about the solid lines because of chance variations. The dashed line represents the estimated cost–volume relationship, derived from a 'least squares' analysis of all the data. As Figure 9 illustrates, it is possible that the estimated relationship will be represented by a downward sloping line, implying a negative variable cost, if, for example, a trend of rising prices is combined with a trend of decreasing output.

Changes in production methods and other changes in efficiency would also cause the cost–volume line to shift position and so may give rise to precisely the same difficulty as price changes in estimating a cost model. However, whereas it may be a fairly simple matter to adjust the data to represent costs which would prevail at current price levels, it is normally impossible to adjust for changes in efficiency without assuming the answer that one is trying to establish.

The difficulties associated with changing prices and changing levels of efficiency, suggest that statistical cost analysis should be applied to observations covering a short overall time interval so that such changes are likely to be at a minimum. Since several different cost–volume observations are required to obtain reliable estimates of the relationship, the analysis should deal with data for individually short periods.

The relevant range of the analysis

Another limitation in using statistical and similar methods to learn about the behaviour of a firm's costs is that the evidence available may relate to only a small range out of the possible actions for which the predicted results are required. It is likely, for example, that actual output levels during a short period of time will lie within a small range in relation to the output levels that could have been adopted.

Figure 10 illustrates the difficulty. The crosses are actual cost–volume results as observed, covering a range of output between 1000 units and 1200 units. The solid line represents the cost model estimated by least-squares regression analysis;

it may well succeed in explaining a large proportion of observed variations in total cost. It would not be advisable, however, to use this model mechanically to predict the total cost which would be incurred for output of (say) 500 units or

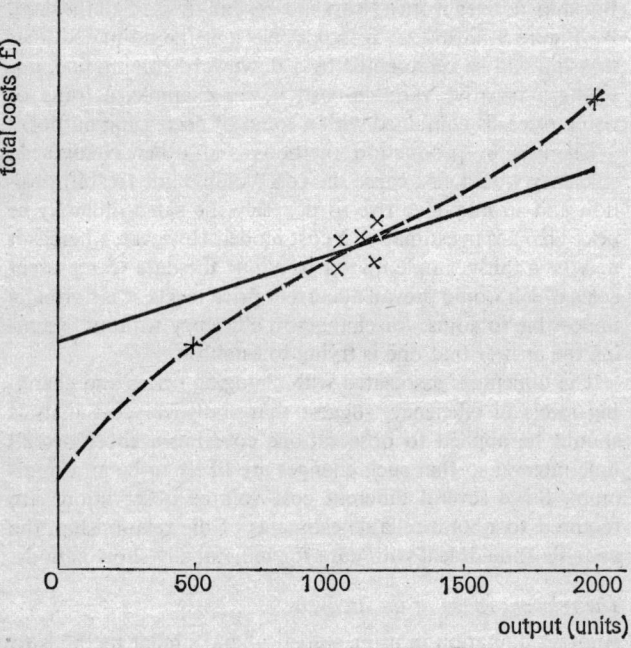

Figure 10 The relevant range in statistical cost analysis

2000 units. Such output levels lie well outside our range of previous experience and we should have little confidence in the accuracy of the predictions. Even if a calculation of R^2 yields a high value, suggesting that we have obtained a good approximation to the actual cost relationship by fitting a straight line, this indication would hold only for the range of observations available. The actual cost relationship might have the form indicated by the broken line and the positions indicated by crosses on that line might be better estimates of the cost levels at 500 units and 2000 units than those obtained from the least squares line. The further proposed output levels lie beyond the range of available observations, the less may be our confidence in predictions of corresponding costs based on regression analysis.

Multi-colinearity

Difficulties in obtaining an adequate range of observed data may be even more pervasive in a multiple regression analysis. Suppose a firm manufactures two products, a and b, and their output is always in the ratio 2:1. Observations for three periods are set out in Table 11.

Table 11

Period	Total cost (T) (£)	Units of a (q_a)	Units of b (q_b)
1	55 000	1000	500
2	75 000	1500	750
3	95 000	2000	1000

If we assume that a linear cost relationship prevails, and denote the fixed cost by f, and the variable cost of a and b by v_a and v_b, we can express this information as a set of equations:

$$f + 1000v_a + 500v_b = 55\,000$$

$$f + 1500v_a + 750v_b = 75\,000$$

$$f + 2000v_a + 1000v_b = 95\,000$$

If we attempt to solve these equations to obtain numerical values for f, v_a and v_b we shall fail – they are indeterminate. Because changes in output of a are always accompanied by proportional changes in output of b, we have no basis for the estimation of the independent contribution of each product to total cost. The best we could do is define a 'standard bundle' of goods, m, e.g. two units of a plus one unit of b, and estimate the cost of this bundle. If we assume a linear cost relationship, we should have the equations:

$$f + 500v_m = 55\,000,$$
$$f + 750v_m = 75\,000,$$
$$f + 1000v_m = 95\,000.$$

Solving these equations simultaneously, we find

$$v_m = 80 \quad \text{and} \quad f = 15\,000.$$

This example has illustrated, in an extreme form, the condition known as multi-colinearity, that is the failure of identification of the independent effects of different variables. In practice, we are unlikely to find that outputs of different products vary precisely in proportion unless there is some necessary technological relationship. In a statistical analysis of data subject to chance fluctuation we may, therefore, not fail completely to obtain estimates of the effect of changes in output of various products on total cost. However, if the ratios of outputs of different products are approximately constant, random effects on total cost may be very large relative to the effects of independent variations in the output levels of different products, and we can have little confidence in the predictions of the costs of different products from a model derived in the normal way. We may still obtain good estimates of the cost of a 'standard bundle' and this information may be valuable – but it is restricted in relation to the range of decisions that might be considered by the firm. It does not help assessments of the desirability of altering the product mix; for such a decision, it may be necessary to fall back on work study methods.

The type of cost–volume relationship

The reader will have noticed that the various forms of analysis described all require that the analyst makes some preliminary assumption about the type of equation which best describes the cost relationship. In statistical methods of analysis, we have assumed a linear relationship; the analysis has then provided estimates of the numerical coefficients – fixed and variable costs – which give the best model, judged by the least-squares criterion, but it did not indicate what relationship should be assumed in the first place. The only indication of the appropriateness of our choice has been provided by our calculation of R^2 – low values of R^2 indicate that a model has relatively poor predictive properties, but this may be due either to the existence of a large random element in the observations or to the choice of an inappropriate type of equation. In a simple regression analysis, it would be a sensible precaution to plot the available cost–volume observations on a graph to check visually whether a linear relationship appears to apply. There are some other statistical techniques for judging what type of equation best fits a particular set of observations and techniques for fitting relationships of a non-linear type to the data. Their discussion is, however, beyond the scope of this book.

Autocorrelation

There are other difficulties in statistical cost analysis of a more technical nature. We shall confine ourselves here to a short mention of one of them designed to round off a short user's guide to statistical cost estimation; for a full discussion the reader is referred to a standard text.

The condition, one which is particularly likely to cause difficulty in the estimation of cost relationships, is that of autocorrelation. This condition implies that the total cost observed for one period depends not only on the value of the variables (output and so on) during that period, but also on the cost level which prevailed during the previous period. It may arise because of 'stickiness' in costs, particularly because of difficulty in reducing costs when the rate of output is decreased. Total cost may well differ, for example, for a given output of 5000 units according to whether output in the previous period was 4000 units, 5000 units or 6000 units. When autocorrelation exists the difficulty arises that efficient cost predictions may require a specification of recent past output levels as well as the current output level. This might be eased by regarding the previous period's output as an additional variable in a multiple regression analysis. There are also some difficulties of a more technical nature associated with the estimation of the goodness of predictions of the model.

8 Price–Volume Relationships

We have now discussed the main methods of estimating models for predicting the costs of various activities, paying particular attention to the effect of different levels of output on production costs. We next consider the other main aspect of business decisions, the model expressing the relationship between receipts and level of output. We consider the relationship in terms of the main decision variable, the different pricing policies that might be adopted by the firm.

Strictly, a full analysis of pricing problems would take into account various related decisions on such things as the level of promotional and other selling costs, the level of distribution costs and policies as to discounts allowed to customers. In an attempt to identify the main features of the pricing decision, however, we shall begin by abstracting from these complications. We shall assume a firm which charges a given price for all its sales of a particular product, which offers no discounts, incurs no promotional or other selling costs and has negligible distribution costs.

General assumptions of a price–volume relationship

The essence of the pricing decision is the need to estimate the effect of changes in the price of a product on the quantity that can be sold. There is a general presumption that, other things being equal, an increase in price will cause a decrease in the quantity which can be sold and vice versa, although this is not invariably true. More precisely, we have to ask how responsive is volume of sales to changes in price and what will be the effect of such changes in terms of total receipts; or, to put it another way, by how much must price be reduced for a firm to be able to sell a given increase in output of a product. If we can answer such a question, we can compare the effect of an increase in volume on total receipts with its effect on total payments to form a view of its worthwhileness.

The pricing decision is, perhaps, one of the most difficult in business because of the lack of reliable evidence about the sales price–volume relationship. Nevertheless decisions may be improved by an understanding of the nature of the forces that influence the relationship and by developing a conceptual framework for thinking about the problem.

A good deal of the literature of economics has been devoted to the analysis of the nature of market situations in which goods and services are sold and the implications of such situations for the price–volume relationships for firms operating within the markets. Although intended originally as a means of studying various questions of macroeconomics, the analysis of market situations provides a helpful framework for considering the pricing decision from the viewpoint of the firm.

The literature has seen the development of a number of models of market situations; they may be regarded as forming a spectrum of possibilities as defined in relation to the nature and intensity of competition between firms.

Perfect competition

One extreme market situation is characterized as perfect competition. In this situation, it is supposed that a firm can sell whatever quantity of goods it wishes at a constant price, the prevailing market price. Nothing whatsoever could be sold at a higher price and there is no incentive to accept a lower price since any desired quantity can be sold at the market price. This price–volume relationship is illustrated in Figure 11.

The main assumptions underlying the model for perfect competition are as follows. The market is supposed to comprise sales by a large number of small firms, so that a change in the level of output by any one of them has no material effect on the volume of activity in the market as a whole. It is also assumed that consumers (buyers) have costless information about the prices charged by all firms, and that distribution costs are zero; furthermore there are no actual or imagined

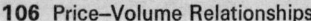

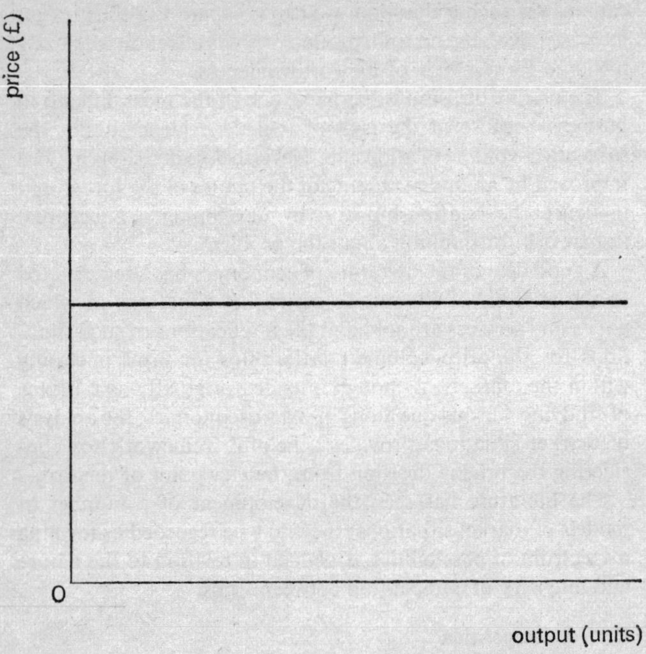

Figure 11 The sales price–volume relationship under perfect competition

differences in the quality of a product from firm to firm. It follows that no buyer would pay a specified price for the product if any firm in the market were offering the product at a lower price and hence that there would be a going price which all sellers must accept as a maximum.

It is reasonably certain that no real situation corresponds exactly to the characteristics of perfect competition. The model is useful analytically, however, as a limiting case which helps to fix ideas about more usual situations. Moreover, real markets may represent approximations to the perfect market; for example farmers and other suppliers of 'basic commodities' may have to accept the prevailing market price and be unable to influence its level themselves – although they may not discover what that price is until they actually offer their goods for sale.

Monopoly

A model of a market at the opposite extreme from perfect competition is that of monopoly, i.e. a market in which only one firm is selling a particular product. That firm has complete economic flexibility in setting the price at which it will offer its output for sale – though it will have to accept that its decision will determine the volume it is able to sell. Consumers may decide to do without the product if the price is too high, even though they are unable to buy it from another firm. We should note, however, that there is legislation in Britain which may be used to restrict the pricing power of monopolists – if it seems likely to act against the public interest – either by direct control of price or by using some device to establish competition.

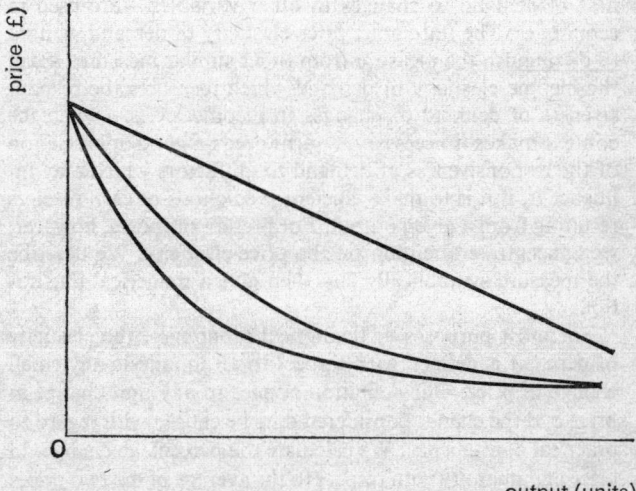

Figure 12 Possible sales price–volume relationships under monopoly

In estimating the sales price–volume relationship facing a monopolist, we might start simply with the assumption that the higher the price, the smaller the quantity that could be sold. This condition is satisfied by the models illustrated on the graph in Figure 12 and by many others. To narrow the relationship down in a more useful way, we have to describe its shape, that is we have to form a view of the responsiveness of the quantity demanded by buyers to changes in prices at various levels of price.

Price elasticity of demand

Economists have developed a measure of this responsiveness which is helpful in estimating and studying price–volume relationships. It is known as the price-elasticity of demand and may be defined as:

$$\frac{\text{percentage increase (or decrease) in quantity sold}}{\text{corresponding percentage fall (or rise) in price}}.$$

Other measures of elasticity of demand – i.e. of the responsiveness of demand to changes in other variables – are used in economics. The full name, price-elasticity of demand, is used to distinguish the measure from other similar measures – e.g. the income-elasticity of demand which measures the responsiveness of demand to changes in income levels – when the context makes it necessary. A firm needs a good appreciation of the responsiveness of demand to all factors which may influence it, if it is to make efficient predictions of cash receipts resulting from a given output. For present purposes, however, we concentrate attention on the price-elasticity. We describe the measure symbolically and then give a numerical illustration.

For most purposes of theoretical economics, the elasticity of demand is defined with respect to an infinitesimally small change in price. Our definition applies to any unit change in price and the change considered may be chosen with regard to practical convenience. We calculate the percentage changes in price and quantity with respect to the average of the two prices or quantities considered; the resulting elasticity is usually known as the arc-elasticity of demand.

Suppose that, at prices £P_1 and £P_2 a firm can sell Q_1 and Q_2 units of a product. A price increase from £P_1 to £P_2, i.e. of £P_2-P_1, equal to a percentage increase of $P_2-P_1/\frac{1}{2}(P_1+P_2)$ yields a percentage change in potential sales of $Q_1-Q_2/\frac{1}{2}(Q_1+Q_2)$. Elasticity of demand over the price interval in question would then be:

$$\frac{(Q_1-Q_2)}{\frac{1}{2}(Q_1+Q_2)} \times \frac{\frac{1}{2}(P_1+P_2)}{(P_2-P_1)} = \frac{(Q_1-Q_2)(P_1+P_2)}{(Q_1+Q_2)(P_2-P_1)}. \qquad \mathbf{1}$$

Suppose, for example, that the information in Table 12 describes parts of the estimated price–volume relationship for a particular product. The elasticity of demand over the two lowest prices would be estimated as 2000 (51)/198 000 (1) = 0·52. The measure reflects the information that a decrease of just over 2 per cent in quantity sold is associated with a price increase of just under 4 per cent, i.e. that the percentage change in demand is about one half of the percentage change in price.

Table 12 An illustrative sales price–volume relationship

Price (£)	Quantity which can be sold
25	100 000
26	98 000
50	55 000
51	54 000

We may observe also that the elasticity of demand over the two higher prices in Table 12 is 1000 (101)/109 000 (1) = 0·93. This brings out the point that there is no reason to expect elasticity of demand for a product to be the same at different levels of volume. As we shall see in chapter 9, elasticity at the optimal output level will normally be a good deal higher than either of these numbers.

Determinants of elasticity

The quantity of a product that consumers will purchase at a particular price under monopoly conditions may be supposed to depend, *inter alia*, on the satisfaction obtained from using the product and on the availability and price of other products, which may be used as substitutes. If a good is regarded as essential to the basic maintenance of life, people will try to maintain their purchases of it, or of substitutes, regardless of changes in price. In general therefore, the elasticity of 'necessities' for which there are few substitutes may be expected to be lower than that for luxuries or goods with close substitutes.

The more someone has of a good, the smaller his satisfaction from having extra units is likely to be. If the price of a good decreases from some high level, he may at first increase his purchases of it; the extra satisfaction from the extra supply may outweigh the extra cost at the lower price and he may substitute the good in question for other goods which have become relatively more expensive. Eventually, however, if price decreases still further, the increase in the quantity purchased will become very small because the possibility of further substitution will be reduced and extra satisfaction from further consumption of the item will become negligible. People would prefer to use money saved from the price reduction to increase their purchases of other goods. Hence it may be reasonable to suppose that elasticity of demand falls as price falls and consumption rises towards satiation point.

Some standard price–volume models

Table 13 gives the characteristics of some standard forms of algebraic expression which may be used as models of price–volume relationships. The four models chosen (linear, quadratic, hyperbolic and constant elasticity) are merely illustrative – there are many other possibilities.

We will consider the contents of Table 13 using one column – that giving the hyperbolic model – as an illustration; all the columns have similar contents. The first row gives the general expression of the class of model: $q = a/(p+b)-c$; we can give any value to the parameters a, b and c and the result will be a member of the same class of model. The second row gives an expression for calculating the elasticity of demand for a member of the class of model in terms of price, quantity and the parameters a, b, c (and k); the strict definition of elasticity in terms of an infinitesimal change in price has been used to derive the expression in the second row with calculation by differential calculus – elasticity is given by $(dq/dp) \times (p/q)$.

The remaining rows give numerical illustrations of the model. For the hyperbolic model, we put $a = 300\,000$, $b = 10$ and $c = 1000$. Using the model, we predict sales volume if price is set at £20, £21, £40 and £41 (i.e. we evaluate q having substituted the appropriate values for p in the model). Finally we calculate the exact elasticities of demand for prices of £20.5 and £40.5, using the expressions given in row two and, in order to evaluate their worth as approximations, the corresponding arc-elasticities of demand using expression 1. In all cases, the answers coincide to within one per cent.

All the models in Table 13 have the property that quantity demanded falls as price rises. The first three have the property discussed above that elasticity of demand falls as price falls and quantity demanded increases. The linear model is, perhaps, implausible in assuming that a given change in price produces a fixed change in demand at all levels of price; but it may represent a good approximation of the price–volume relationship over small changes in price. The fourth model is a limiting case in which elasticity of demand is constant at all price levels.

As we shall see in chapter 9, an estimate of the whole sales price–volume relationship may be derived conveniently from an estimate of the type of model applicable, the elasticity of demand and one or a few observations of price and corresponding volume.

Long-run effects

Amongst the several complications neglected in our discussion so far are possible inter-connections between price–volume relationships for a particular product at different times. If price is reduced in a current period, consumers may stockpile items in the expectation that the price will rise again subsequently – hence more may be sold at a particular price in the

Table 13 Some standard forms of sales price–volume models with elasticities

Type of model	Linear	Quadratic	Hyperbolic	Constant elasticity
general form of model	$q = a - bp$	$q = a - bp - cp^2$	$q = \dfrac{a}{p+b} - c$	$q = ap^k$
elasticity	$\dfrac{bp}{q}$	$\dfrac{bp + 2cp^2}{q}$	$\dfrac{ap}{q(p+b)^2}$	k
example of model	$q = 5000 - 50p$	$q = 5800 - 50p - 2p^2$	$q = \dfrac{300\,000}{p+10} - 1000$	$q = 2\,000\,000p^{-2}$
predicted sales volume if price = 20	4000	4000	9000	5000
21	3950	3868	8677	4535
40	3000	600	5000	1250
41	2950	388	4882	1190
elasticity $p = 20\cdot5$	0·26	0·69	0·75	2·00
$40\cdot5$	0·68	17·38	0·96	2·00
approximate elasticity price 20/21	$\dfrac{50}{7950} \times \dfrac{41}{1} = 0\cdot26$	$\dfrac{132}{7868} \times \dfrac{41}{1} = 0\cdot69$	$\dfrac{323}{17\,677} \times \dfrac{41}{1} = 0\cdot75$	$\dfrac{465}{9535} \times \dfrac{41}{1} = 2\cdot00$
if 40/41	$\dfrac{50}{5950} \times \dfrac{81}{1} = 0\cdot68$	$\dfrac{212}{988} \times \dfrac{81}{1} = 17\cdot38$	$\dfrac{118}{9882} \times \dfrac{81}{1} = 0\cdot97$	$\dfrac{60}{2440} \times \dfrac{81}{1} = 1\cdot99$

q represents potential sales quantity, p is price and a, b, c, k are numerical constants.

current period than would be sold at the same price in a subsequent period – all other things being equal. On the other hand, a current price increase may provoke consumers to search for substitutes, the effect of which, in reducing demand, may not be felt fully until some subsequent period. The difficulties in estimating such effects are considerable and we must restrict ourselves to the observation that the effects should be kept in mind in building models for decisions.

Imperfect competition

The main usefulness of the analysis of monopolistic conditions is as an extreme case which helps to fix principles – as was the case with perfect competition. It is very unusual for full-blooded monopoly conditions to be found in practice although approximations to such conditions exist.

The most realistic descriptions of actual market situations normally fall between the extremes of monopoly and perfect competition. The analysis of various such situations has received extensive attention in the economic literature; they have been described variously as monopolistic competition, oligopoly and so on. It is beyond the scope of this book to study a variety of possible market situations in detail. It is relevant, however, to consider the essence of the considerations that arise.

In the two extreme market situations considered, we were justified in assuming that the sales price–volume relationship for one firm would not be influenced by the behaviour of competing firms. In the case of monopoly, indeed, it was assumed that there were no such firms; in the case of perfect competition it was assumed that no single firm was large enough to influence the activities of another firm – so that the activities of other firms, considered individually, were irrelevant to one firm's decisions. In the intermediate situation we have a few firms selling a product which is basically similar though, perhaps, not strictly identical: it may be distinguished by factors such as the reputation of the firm for quality and service or its geographical location; because of difference in perceived quality or lack of information, one firm may be able to obtain a higher price for its product than that charged by a competitor, without losing all its sales.

Assumptions about competitors' reactions

The quantity of a product that a firm can sell at a particular price under imperfect competition must be assumed to depend not only on the strength of consumers' desires for the product and the availability of substitute products but also on the price at which other firms are offering the same or similar products. Moreover it cannot be assumed that each firm fixes its prices independently. A change in price by one firm may provoke a change by its competitors and this would influence the effect of the original price change on sales volume.

In estimating a model of the sales price–volume relationship for a firm in an imperfectly competitive situation, it may be best to include competitors' prices as independent variables. The model would be difficult to estimate but any pricing decision must imply some assumption about competitors' reaction. The relationship might, for example, be expressed:

$$q = a - bp_1 - c(p_1 - p_2) - d(p_1 - p_3), \qquad\qquad 2$$

where p_1 is the price set for the firm in question, p_2, p_3 are prices set by competitors, and a, b, c, d are constants.

If a firm has several competitors it might be preferable for the model to reflect the prices of some or all of them by means of an average rather than individually. The explicit inclusion of the prices of competitors in a model is most appropriate if a firm believes that it has information which would enable it to make predictions of competitors' pricing policy but this information cannot be handled conveniently as a mathematical expression.

If a firm can express algebraically its views on the likely relationship between the prices of its competitors and its own prices, the model can be expressed in terms of its own price alone, competitors' prices being reflected implicitly. Let us continue the example of three competing firms and suppose that firm 2 always charges £2 more than firm 1 and firm 3 charges £1 less: we have

$$p_2 = p_1 + 2$$
and $\quad p_3 = p_1 - 1,$

thus (by substitution in expression 2)

$$q = a - bp_1 - c(p_1 - p_1 - 2) - d(p_1 - p_1 + 1)$$
$$= (a + 2c - d) - bp_1.$$

It may also be appropriate to leave a competitor's price to be reflected implicitly in a model where a firm has little information about his likely reaction, and so has to fall back on some general assumption.

The literature has developed a number of general models of ways in which competing firms respond to changes in each others' prices and these may be helpful in developing a model of sales price–volume relationships in a particular situation. Let us consider some of the possibilities briefly.

Market leadership

One firm amongst a group of competitors may be a market leader. Thus one firm, particularly if it is large and prestigious, may so dominate a market that other firms tend to follow its pricing practices either exactly or with some identifiable differential. Such a firm may ignore the pricing policies of other firms *as independent variables* in setting its own policies; it will behave similarly to a monopolist. The other firms are, however, particularly dependent on predicting the policies of the market leader – for these will directly affect their own prices. Indeed they are in a position similar in some respects to that of the firm in a perfectly competitive market – they virtually take the price as given, even though they cannot sell an indefinitely large quantity at that price. The rationale of this situation is that the non-leaders cannot afford to attempt to undercut the leader and cannot get away with charging a materially higher price.

Collusion

Another possibility is that there is collusion explicitly or tacitly between competing firms. This again is tantamount to saying that prices of various firms are not independent variables. Collusion is seen as a means of achieving, by using the power of the monopolist, an aggregate cash surplus for all firms which is so large that it may be divided in a way that leaves each firm better off than it would be without collusion. Firms participating in collusion run the risk that some participators will opt out and secure an especially high part of the cash surplus for themselves. They also run the risk that the Government will use its statutory powers to restrict their activities. Tacit collusion exists when it is normal practice for firms to follow price changes of their competitors – although the changes may not be initiated by a market leader. It may also exist where firms tend to use a standard formula for pricing based on costs (see chapter 18), or relate their prices to some independent variable which provides equal information to them all, e.g. the index of retail prices.

The 'kinked' demand curve

Another model of the relationship between pricing policies of competing firms is one in which the elements of competition are more evident. The assumption is made that if a firm reduces its price, competitors will do likewise (because they believe that they cannot afford not to do so) so that the increased demand will be shared amongst them; by contrast, it is assumed that price increases will not be followed, competitors preferring to get the benefit of increased sales from customers who switch. These assumptions lead to the expectation that changes in demand are more sensitive to price increases than to price decreases – hence that the curve representing the price–volume relationship has a 'kink' at the current price as illustrated in Figure 13.

The asymmetry implied by these assumptions makes them seem rather implausible. Furthermore, empirical analysis suggests that they are not broadly representative of actual behaviour.

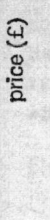

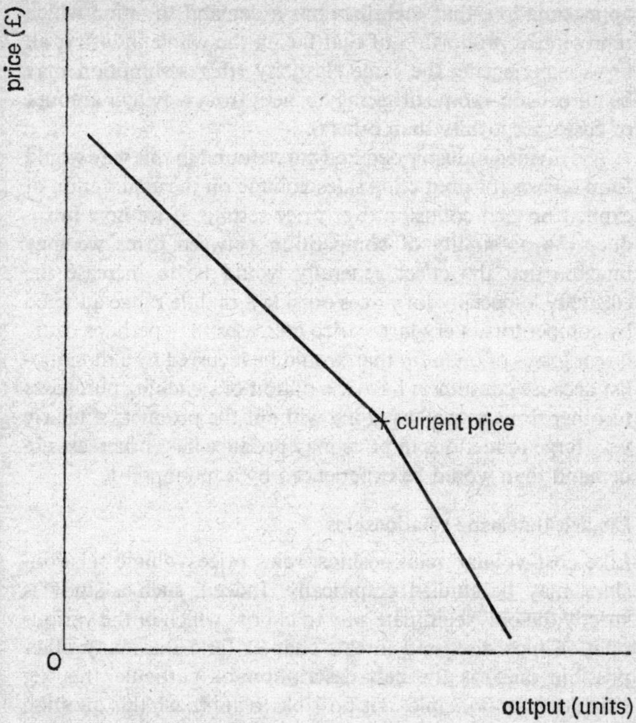

Figure 13 A firm with a 'kinked' demand curve

Elasticity of demand under imperfect competition

The idea of elasticity of demand is useful in developing models of sales price–volume relationships in imperfectly competitive markets in the same way as it is in studying monopoly. One might approach the estimation of elasticity of demand by firstly imagining that all firms in the industry were joined together to form a monopoly, and estimating the elasticity of demand for a product judged in accordance with its role in consumers' budgets, its degree of necessity, the availability of substitutes and so on. It might then be assumed, as a first approximation, that each firm has a demand situation which represents a proportion of that facing the whole industry, all firms experiencing the same elasticity (this assumption may be unrealistic – some firms may benefit from a greater amount of customer loyalty than others).

The divided industry demand curve found in this way would form a basis for predicting sales volume on the assumption of explicit or tacit collusion over price setting. If we now introduce the possibility of competition between firms we may imagine that the effect generally would be to increase the elasticity, especially for prices outside a middle range adopted by competitors. Very large price increases may perhaps cause larger losses of quantity than would be incurred by a monopolist because consumers have the option of switching purchases to other firms as well as going without the product; similarly very large reductions in price may produce larger increases in demand than would be experienced by a monopolist.

Empirical demand relationships

Like cost–volume relationships, sales price–volume relationships may be studied empirically. Indeed, such a study is strictly the only legitimate way to choose which of the various relationships discussed in this chapter (and the many other possible ones) is the best description of particular market situations. In principle, it is possible to approach this question by assuming a standard form of model for price–volume relationships (such as one given in Table 13), collecting observations of actual prices and corresponding volumes in recent experience, and finding what values for the parameters give a model which best fits the data by the statistical means described in relation to costs in chapter 7.

The empirical study of a sales price–volume relationship is inevitably beset by particular difficulties, however. Changes in taste, income levels, the availability of substitute products and so on may alter the price–volume relationship facing a particular firm for a particular product from period to period. If we study a number of observed pairs of prices and sales volumes over some past interval of time, we may in effect be studying one result from each of a number of different relationships. In order to obtain a good estimate of a model for a particular decision period we need a record of prices and corresponding volumes of sales over a time during which the factors which influence demand may be assumed to be similar to those prevailing during the decision period. Failure of availability of such information leads to the same difficulty as we met in discussing cost–volume relationships when prices and efficiency were changing, i.e. the difficulty that the information available may be insufficient to identify the relationship. The identification of the sales model may present greater difficulty than the identification of the cost model, however, because it may be harder to judge independently whether there have been material changes in taste and so on than to judge whether there have been changes in efficiency. Moreover, a good estimate of the model would require observations of sales volume corresponding to a wide range of different prices. Typically, the information available will relate to only a narrow range of prices and the effects of price movements may be obscured by random fluctuations.

Standard patterns of demand curves

It may be, in practice, that the empirical estimation of the price–volume relationship, using actual data, is too complex for the attempt to be worthwhile. Actual statistical studies might yield conclusions which were highly unreliable and, at best, valid only for small variations in price from the level currently adopted. Nevertheless it is relevant for a businessman to consider how quantities demanded of his products will respond to price changes. The actual price–volume relationship may materially affect results from different decisions and therefore deserves explicit attention. One means of expressing the relationship involves using the general ideas described in this chapter, without attempting to measure empirically the price–volume relationship for each product. Managers might adopt a number of 'standard' models for use, choosing them to reflect different assumptions about elasticity, and then select one of them to describe the relationship for each product. The selection might be guided by general indications of elasticity of demand at the price in question, as suggested by the qualitative factors considered above – degree of necessity, availability of substitutes, intensity of competition and so on. Sales managers and their assistants collect a great deal of information in the course of their business activities which is indicative of the responsiveness of demand to changes in price; indeed the feasibility of using explicit estimates of sales price–volume relationships for business decision purposes is supported by the author's observation that businessmen are willing to give some estimate of the effect of a price change, if pressed to do so. Moreover, this type of information may be supplemented by special market surveys in some situations.

Any business pricing decision must imply some view of the sales price–volume relationship. Although the procedure suggested here is less than ideal, it does at least provide a framework within which managers can make their assumptions numerically explicit and analyse their consequences. They can also repeat the analysis using different assumptions to study the sensitivity of the optimal decision to different assumptions. Furthermore, the framework may be one in which, by comparing predictions of standard models and actual results, managers may learn about the elasticity of demand for their products. We shall study the application of such an analysis further in the next chapter.

Other bases for pricing policies

It is as well that we should conclude this chapter by noting that some managers respond to the difficulty of estimating the elasticity of demand for their products by avoiding an explicit consideration of price–volume relationships and basing the pricing decision on other factors, often average costs. These methods will be considered more fully in chapter 18. However, one should not avoid making a relevant estimate because it is difficult. It is probably better to use a relevant measure with a chance of error than to use an irrelevant measure – one which avoids explicit attention to the dependence of sales volume on price.

9 Optimal Price–Volume Decisions

In the past three chapters we have examined relationships between the level of output and total cost, and relationships between sales volume and selling price. These topics pave the way for the estimation of the optimal output level. If we assume that sales and output are precisely equal, i.e., that there is no increase or decrease in stocks, we have merely to put the two relationships together to estimate what plan will yield the maximum short-run cash flow – and hence satisfy the objective that we have assumed for the firm.

Marginal revenue and cost

First, however, it is convenient to consider two related concepts which will be useful in the analysis; the concepts of marginal revenue and marginal cost. Marginal revenue may be defined as the amount by which total receipts from sales increase as a result of selling one extra unit of a product. Marginal revenue would be equal to selling price in the case of a product sold in a perfectly competitive market; in such a case, it would not be necessary to decrease price in order to increase the quantity sold.

In more usual situations, however, it is assumed that price has to be reduced to make it possible to dispose of an increased volume; hence marginal revenue is less than selling price. Suppose a firm has to reduce its price from p to $p-s$ (where s is some small positive sum) in order to increase its sales volume by one unit from q to $q+1$. Total sales revenue at the lower quantity is £pq and at the higher quantity £$(p-s)(q+1)$. Hence marginal revenue is

$$£(p-s)(q+1)-pq = (p-s)-sq,$$

i.e. marginal revenue is equal to the new price £$(p-s)$ less the reduction in revenue resulting from the need to accept a price reduction of £s per unit on the q units which could have been sold at the higher price.[1]

Marginal cost may be defined similarly as the increase in total cost resulting from an increase in output of one unit.

Conditions for optimal output level

Let us now consider the identification of the optimal level of sales for a product. The normal rule is that to maximize net receipts a firm should evaluate successive small increases in sales volume and accept each one, provided that the amount expected to be added to receipts exceeds the expected addition to costs, i.e. provided that marginal revenue exceeds marginal cost by some amount, however small; marginal cost and marginal revenue will be approximately equal for the last output unit added. Any further increase would reduce the net surplus provided marginal revenue is below marginal cost for all higher output levels.

This rule holds good given the assumption that, as sales volume is increased, marginal revenue steadily decreases and marginal cost remains constant or steadily increases. If this assumption is not valid the simple rule *may* break down. We shall examine this possibility in more detail below.

It is necessary, having identified the output level at which marginal cost equals marginal revenue, to undertake a further check to make sure that total revenue is likely to exceed total costs, including any fixed costs at that point and thereby establish that some output is worthwhile. Let us consider the application of the normal rule in a simple example.

An illustration of the selection of output level

Capricornus Ltd manufactures a single product. We assume that its managers have a clear idea of the cost–volume and

1. Marginal revenue may be defined more precisely using the calculus. If $p = f(q)$, total revenue $R = pq = q\,f(q)$ and marginal revenue is $\frac{dR}{dq} = f(q) + q\,f'(q)$, i.e. the rate of change of total revenue with respect to quantity.

sales price–volume relationships for the business. They believe that total costs are predicted well by the simple model $T = 65\,000 + 50q$ where q is the number of units produced; i.e. costs comprise a fixed element of £65 000 and an element of £50 per unit which is variable linearly with output.

Managers have decided to adopt a simple linear model for predicting the relationship between selling price and quantity of sales; $q = 5100 - 30p$, where p is selling price.

A decision on the optimal level of output might be reached by preparing a series of estimates of the cash flow generated at various levels of output, or, what is much the same, at various prices (see Table 14). These calculations indicate that the best policy is to set the price at about £110 and plan to produce 1800 units (it can be shown by mathematical methods that £110 is the strictly optimal price).[2] It is worth noting that there is a range of prices over which net cash inflows do not vary greatly. Variations in selling price between £100 and £120 seem likely to affect net cash earnings only by some $7\frac{1}{2}$ per cent at most. This is probably a fairly common consequence of reasonable assumptions about price–volume relationships; it is comforting in view of the speculative nature of some of the estimates used.

Total (gross) receipts are commonly maximized at a level of output in excess of the optimal level because marginal revenues

2. $T = 65\,000 + 50q$,

thus marginal cost $= \dfrac{dT}{dq} = 50$.

$q = 5100 - 30p$; thus $p = 170 - \dfrac{q}{30}$.

Total revenue $= 170q - \dfrac{q^2}{30}$.

Marginal revenue $= \dfrac{d(pq)}{dq} = 170 - \dfrac{q}{15}$.

At optimum, marginal cost = marginal revenue,

i.e. $50 = 170 - \dfrac{q}{15}$,

$q = 1800$.

Substituting in sales price–volume relationship,

$p = 170 - \dfrac{1800}{30} = 110$.

Table 14 Capricornus Ltd – net cash inflow related to output (£)

Price p	Quantity sold q = 5100−30p (units)	Total receipts (1)×(2)	Fixed costs	Variable costs 50q	Total cash outflow (4)+(5)	Net cash inflow (3)−(6)
(1)	(2)	(3)	(4)	(5)	(6)	(7)
70	3000	210 000	65 000	150 000	215 000	(5 000)
80	2700	216 000	65 000	135 000	200 000	16 000
90	2400	216 000	65 000	120 000	185 000	31 000
100	2100	210 000	65 000	105 000	170 000	40 000
105	1950	204 750	65 000	97 500	162 500	42 250
110	1800	198 000	65 000	90 000	155 000	43 000
115	1650	189 750	65 000	82 500	147 500	42 250
120	1500	180 000	65 000	75 000	140 000	40 000
130	1200	156 000	65 000	60 000	125 000	31 000

are usually positive for some higher output levels even though they are less than marginal costs. (In the case of Capricornus, maximum receipts arise at a price in the range £80–£90 and at a quantity in the range 2400–2700 units.) Marginal revenue at the optimal output level may be estimated as follows:

Since $q = 5100 - 30p$,

it follows that $p = \dfrac{5100 - q}{30}$.

Hence the price required to dispose of 1801 units is:

$$p = \frac{5100 - 1801}{30} = \frac{3299}{30}.$$

Total revenue is then $£\dfrac{3299}{30} \times 1801 = £198\ 049\ 97$

Total revenue from sales of 1800 units $= £198\ 000 \cdot 00$

Marginal revenue $= £ \qquad 49.97$

Hence marginal revenue is approximately equal to marginal cost (£50) in accordance with the rule described above.

Marginal revenue and demand elasticity

It may sometimes be helpful to incorporate an estimate of the elasticity of demand directly into the analysis of optimal sales-volume; this requires that marginal revenue be expressed in terms of elasticity of demand. Let us consider how marginal revenue is related to elasticity of demand. We shall derive the relationship in a way that is somewhat contrived in order to avoid the use of calculus in the main text.[3] Recall that elasticity of demand may be expressed as:

$$e = \frac{(Q_2-Q_1)(P_1+P_2)}{(Q_2+Q_1)(P_1-P_2)};$$ 2

(expression **1** in chapter 8, revised to relate to a price decrease). Now suppose that we are considering an increase in sales volume from q units to $q+1$ (i.e. $Q_2-Q_1 = 1$) and that this calls for a price reduction from £p to £$(p-s)$, where s is some small amount. Using expression **2**, we have:

$$e = \frac{1(2p-s)}{(2q+1)s},$$

thus $\quad 2sq+s = \dfrac{2p-s}{e}$

and $\quad 2sq = \dfrac{2p-s}{e}-s$, which may be rewritten as:

$$\frac{2p-2s}{e}+\frac{s(1-e)}{e}.$$

Thus $\quad sq = \dfrac{p-s}{e}+\dfrac{s(1-e)}{2e}.$

Since s is relatively small, the second fraction on the right-hand side is also relatively small and may be ignored. We thus have:

$$sq = \frac{p-s}{e}.$$ 3

3. A more precise derivation would run:

$$p = f(q); \quad R = pq = qf(q),$$

and $\quad R' = \dfrac{d(pq)}{dq} = p+q\dfrac{dp}{dq} = p\{1+(q/p)(dp/dq)\},$

$$e = (-p/q)(dq/dp).$$

Hence $\quad R' = p\left\{1-\dfrac{1}{e}\right\}.$

We found above that marginal revenue $R' = (p-s) - sq$ (expression **1**).

Hence $R' = (p-s) - \dfrac{p-s}{e}$ (substituting expression **3**)

$$= (p-s)\left(1 - \frac{1}{e}\right), \qquad\qquad 4$$

i.e. the marginal revenue associated with a small reduction in price and the consequent increase in volume is approximately equal to the new price times the difference between one and the reciprocal of elasticity of demand.

We can draw some useful results from a study of equation **4**. Marginal revenue is less than price provided that elasticity is positive, i.e. provided quantity demanded increases as price decreases and vice versa. We argued, in chapter 8, that it is normally reasonable to assume that the elasticity of demand for a product decreases steadily as the quantity sold increases. It follows from equation **4** that marginal revenue then decreases as the quantity sold increases (i.e. as price decreases). If elasticity of demand is close to or equal to one, marginal revenue is close to or equal to zero. If elasticity is less than one but greater than zero, marginal revenue is negative – increases in sales volume reduce total receipts from sales; a firm will wish to expand sales of a product to this extent only in exceptional circumstances.

The relationship between marginal revenue and elasticity of demand may be illustrated by a further reference to the example of Capricornus Ltd. Optimal output for Capricornus was found to be 1800 units with a selling price of £110 and 1801 units could be sold at £3299/30 per unit. Elasticity of demand at the optimal output level may be seen – by substitution in expression **1** in chapter 8 – to be approximately

$$e = \frac{1801-1800}{1801+1800} \times \frac{110+(3299/30)}{110-(3299/30)} = 1{\cdot}833.$$

Expression **4** gives marginal revenue as $(p-s)(1-1/e)$; we shall now write $p = p-s$, assuming s to be indefinitely small (i.e. using the expression derived strictly in the footnote), and express marginal revenue as $p(1-1/e)$; this should be equal to marginal cost at the optimal output level. We may now verify that our solution to the problem satisfies this condition:

$$p(1-1/e) = 110(1-1/1{\cdot}833) = 110 \times 0{\cdot}4545 = 49{\cdot}99$$

approximately £50, the marginal cost, as required.

The use of the concept of demand elasticity

It is probably rare for the concept of elasticity of demand to be used explicitly in the analysis of decisions in actual business practice. The responsiveness of sales volume to changes in price is, however, doubtless considered informally by managers – in a qualitative rather than a quantitative manner. The lack of explicit use of the concept is perhaps due to the difficulties of assigning numerical values in actual problems. It may be argued, however, that it is desirable to consider explicitly some measure of the responsiveness of sales volume to price changes. It is a relevant consideration in decision-taking and it may not receive adequate attention if it remains implicit. Indeed the justification for making an explicit estimate of elasticity is much the same as that for any estimate of an uncertain event made for decision purposes. It focuses the attention of the decision-taker on the relevant variables and helps him to explore their inter-relation in the structure of the problem. It therefore seems worthwhile to consider an illustration of how elasticity of demand might be incorporated explicitly in a firm's decisions.

The analysis might proceed in the following way. Some selling price and corresponding sales volume would be selected as a base point for the estimation of elasticity of demand – the actual price and volume for a recent period in the case of established products, some target price and estimated volume for new products. The estimate of elasticity might be based on a consideration of the nature of the product, e.g. whether it is a luxury or a necessity, the nature of similar products offered by competitors and their prices, the availability and prices of substitute products and so on. A numerical estimate might be made directly by estimating the percentage change in sales volume which would result from a given small percentage change in price. Alternatively, the estimate might be expressed qualitatively in the first place, e.g. 'moderate' or 'small' and converted to a numerical estimate subsequently, according to some standard conversion table. Such a table is given in Table 15 for purposes of illustration. The values adopted may not be appropriate to particular cases – careful study would be needed of actual situations to estimate the most suitable range of values.

Table 15 A standard scale of elasticities of demand

Qualitative description	Elasticity of demand (numerical value assigned)	Implied percentage decrease in volume for 5 per cent increase in price
very small	1·5	7·5
small	2·0	10·0
moderate	2·5	12·5
large	3·0	15·0
very large	3·5	17·5

The next step might be to compute the elasticity of demand which would be implied if the present price and marginal cost relationship for a product were optimal. We know that, at the optimal output, marginal cost c is equal to marginal revenue, i.e.

$$c = p(1 - 1/e) \text{ (using expression 4),}$$

hence
$$\frac{c}{p} = 1 - \frac{1}{e},$$

$$\frac{1}{e} = \frac{p-c}{p},$$

and
$$e = \frac{p}{p-c}. \qquad 5$$

At the optimum, elasticity of demand equals price divided by the difference between price and marginal cost.

We may use this calculation of implied elasticity in various ways. We might simply compare the estimated elasticity with that implied by the present price, deduce whether the present price seems too high, too low or about right and if the present price does not seem optimal, make some adjustment that seems in the right direction. It would be prudent to restrict the adjustment to a small percentage (e.g. 5 per cent or 10 per cent at any time) in view of the speculative nature of the estimates. If, for example, too large a price increase were made, the firm might incur a substantial loss and it might take some time to recover the previous position. If price changes are restricted, it would be possible to study the consequences of the changes over a reasonable period and ascertain whether they accorded with the estimates before considering further changes.

Alternatively, we might use the estimates of demand elasticity, in conjunction with some assumption about the shape of the demand curve, to estimate the actual price–volume relationship for the product and deduce the optimal price. Again, it might be prudent to limit any change in selling price suggested by the analysis to some percentage of the current price of existing products.

It should be noted that strictly the optimal price cannot be calculated from the relationship $e = p/(p-c)$ without making some assumptions about the way in which elasticity changes as price is changed – for elasticity is not normally constant at all relevant price levels. Suppose, for example, that some product is currently priced at £20 and has a marginal cost of £8 whereas elasticity is estimated at 2·0. The present price would be optimal if elasticity of demand were $20/(20-8) =$ 1·67. We might estimate the optimal price by substituting estimated elasticity and marginal cost in our equation and solving for p; we should have $2·0 = p/(p-8)$ whence $p = $ £16. However elasticity of demand would probably not equal $p/(p-c)$ at a price of £16 either. More would be sold at a price of £16 than at a price of £20 and elasticity might well be lower at the new level (according to the assumption discussed above, that elasticity falls as volume increases). The optimal price would be a little higher than £16. However, the element of approximation caused by neglecting this factor may be unimportant if price changes are limited to small percentages at one time.

A process for learning about actual elasticity

The first time a firm uses a procedure such as that described above, the results will be particularly uncertain. However the usefulness of the procedure, hopefully, may increase with time because it encourages a programmed learning process. If the procedure leads to a price alteration for a product, it will be possible to compare the actual result with the result expected. If there is a difference, there may be several possible explanations, for example:

The elasticity was wrongly estimated;
The elasticity was rightly estimated at the time but
   conditions subsequently changed; or
The assumed type of price–volume relationship was wrong.

In the event of unexpected consequences a study should be undertaken of the reason for the difference and the decision will have to be revised in the light of the new evidence. A study of various cases in which elasticity has apparently been wrongly estimated is likely to improve the ability of estimators in identifying the factors which contribute to elasticity and hence help them to make better estimates.

It may be objected that this type of analysis implies the possibility of frequent adjustments to selling prices whereas, in practice, frequent changes are undesirable because they are costly, and they harm the company's reputation and create a feeling of uncertainty on the part of its customers. The quantity of a product that can be sold may depend not only on the current price but also on the frequency of price changes. However, this consideration does not strike at the principles of the proposals but rather argues for the setting of a reasonably long interval between successive uses of the proposals for the review of prices. The general upward trend of prices, found when there is a rapid level of inflation, may give a firm extra flexibility in implementing any proposals for adjustments in prices; if some prices seem too high and others too low in one period, the position may be remedied by small or large increases relative to the rate of inflation in the following period.

An illustration using the concept of demand elasticity

Let us now turn to a particular numerical example. Sagittarius Ltd is currently selling five products. Details of current prices, sales volumes, marginal costs and estimated elasticities are given in Table 16. Prices have previously been fixed by some

Table 16 Product data for Sagittarius

Product	Current price (£)	Quantity sold in current period (units)	Marginal cost per unit (£)	Implied elasticity $e = \dfrac{p}{p-c}$	Estimated elasticity
1	25	4000	15	2·5	3·5
2	40	3000	20	2·0	1·5
3	32	5000	24	4·0	3·0
4	54	2000	36	3·0	1·5
5	10	7000	4	1·7	2·0

rule of thumb technique. Elasticities of demand represent estimates of (say) the percentage increase in volume of sales which would result from a decrease in price of 1 per cent.

It is assumed that costs are linearly variable; total costs may be predicted by the model:

$$T = 125\,000 + 15q_1 + 20q_2 + 24q_3 + 36q_4 + 4q_5,$$

where $q_1, \ldots, q_5$ represent the quantities produced of products $1, \ldots, 5$, and £125 000 is a fixed cost.

Table 16 also gives calculations of implied elasticities, that is the elasticity which would have to exist if present prices were optimal; an optimal pricing structure would involve equality between implied elasticity and estimated elasticity. We may make use of the assumption that actual elasticity normally falls as price falls and quantity sold increases. Consider product 1. Estimated elasticity currently exceeds implied elasticity. Price should be altered in a way which reduces estimated elasticity and increases implied elasticity until they become equal. If price is reduced, the value of implied elasticity – the value of

$p/(p-c)$ – will increase; correspondingly, at the associated higher volume, estimated elasticity is likely to be lower. Hence it seems that the optimal price for product 1 is lower than the present price. Similarly it seems that the price of product 5 should be reduced and that prices of products 2, 3 and 4 should be increased.

Given this evidence, it might simply be decided that prices of products 1 and 5 would be reduced and prices of the other products increased by (say) 5 per cent or 10 per cent. A more precise formulation might be sought, however, and this would require the estimation of the full sales price–volume relationship.

Suppose, to take the simplest possibility, that managers assume the sales price–volume relationship to be linear, i.e. of the form $q = a - bp$. We noted in chapter 8 (Table 13) that the elasticity of such a relationship is given by the expression $e = bp/q$, thus $b = eq/p$. We may use this relationship in conjunction with the data in Table 16 to deduce b in the sales model for each product, e.g. for product 1,

$$b = (3 \cdot 5 \times 4000)/25 = 560.$$

Given an estimate of b, we may infer a value for a, e.g. for product 1, $q = a - bp$: but when $q = 4000$, $p = 25$, hence $4000 = a - 560 \times 25$, whence $a = 18\,000$.

Next we evaluate marginal revenue. If the sales price–volume relationship is

$$q = a - bp$$
it follows that $\qquad p = (a-q)/b,$
and total revenue $\qquad pq = (aq-q^2)/b.$ **6**

Consider a very small increase, h, in quantity sold. Total revenue now becomes – by substituting $(q+h)$ for q in **6**

$$\frac{a(q+h)-(q+h)^2}{b},$$ **7**

an increase of $\qquad \dfrac{ah-2qh-h^2}{b}$ **8**

– expression **7** less **6**,

and marginal revenue, the rate of increase per unit,

$$R' = \frac{ah - 2qh - h^2}{bh} = \frac{a - 2q - h}{b},$$

dividing **8** by h. Since h is very small, we may ignore the last term and regard marginal revenue as:

$$R' = \frac{a - 2q}{b}. \qquad \qquad 9$$

At the optimal price, marginal cost equals marginal revenue, i.e.

$$\frac{a - 2q}{b} = c,$$

thus $a - 2(a - bp) = bc$ (substituting $q = a - bp$),

and $2bp = bc + a;$

$$p = \frac{c}{2} + \frac{a}{2b}. \qquad \qquad 10$$

Table 17 gives the optimal prices calculated from expression **10** and also recommended prices on the assumption that any price changes are restricted to 10 per cent of the original prices

Table 17 Optimal prices for Sagittarius (£)

Product	Estimated linear sales price–volume relationship $q = a - bp$	Optimal price $p = \frac{c}{2} + \frac{a}{2b}$	Original price	Revised price restricted by percentage	Predicted volume (units)
1	$q = 18\,000 - 560p$	23·5	25	24	4560
2	$q = 7500 - 112·5p$	43·3	40	43	2662
3	$q = 20\,000 - 469p$	33·3	32	33	4523
4	$q = 5000 - 55·5p$	63·0	54	59	1725
5	$q = 21\,000 - 1400p$	9·5	10	10	7000

given in Table 16 and rounded to the nearest whole number. In Table 18, we set out estimates of the net cash inflows given the original prices and the revised prices; the revised prices are expected to yield an extra surplus of £6648.

Table 18 Net cash flows for Sagittarius Ltd

Product	Original prices per unit				New prices per unit				
	Price (£)	Cost (£)	Net (£)	Quantity (units)	Total cash flow (£)	Price (£)	Cost (£)	Net (£)	Quantity (units)	Total cash flow (£)
1	25	15	10	4000	40 000	24	15	9	4560	41 040
2	40	20	20	3000	60 000	43	20	23	2662	61 226
3	32	24	8	5000	40 000	33	24	9	4523	40 707
4	54	36	18	2000	36 000	59	36	23	1725	39 675
5	10	4	6	7000	42 000	10	4	6	7000	42 000
total					218 000					224 648
less fixed costs					125 000					125 000
net cash surplus					93 000					99 648

Let us now consider how these decisions might be revised in the event that some errors of estimation become apparent. Suppose it turns out that sales of product 1 are 4800 units and those of product 4 are 1850 units, and suppose that the errors are attributed to incorrect estimates of elasticity. In the case of product 1 we have a larger than expected change in quantity for a given price change; elasticity of demand was presumably larger than we estimated. Hence it seems likely that price should have been reduced by a larger sum to reduce estimated elasticity further and bring estimated and implied elasticity into equality; a further reduction should be made for the next period.

In the case of product 4, however, quantity has changed less than expected for a given price change. Elasticity of demand, it seems, was less than we estimated. Since implied elasticity was originally above estimated elasticity, we needed to increase the price; since actual elasticity appears to have been even lower than estimated, we should now increase the price still further.

An illustration involving a non-linear cost model

In the first two examples in this chapter, we assumed a simple linear cost–volume relationship for the product under review. We also assumed that marginal revenue was greater than marginal cost at all levels of output below the optimum and that marginal revenue was less than marginal cost at all higher levels. Another possibility is that marginal cost is high initially, and falls, as output increases, up to some limit after which it rises again. The decline may be explained by the possibility that a more efficient production process may be applied with larger volumes of output and the increase may be explained by the eventual need to press into service some relatively inefficient resources. In such a case marginal cost and marginal revenue may be equal at two or more output levels, and the simple rule that the optimal output level may be found by equating marginal cost and marginal revenue is insufficient. It is necessary to examine all the output quantities for which marginal cost equals marginal revenue to discover if any is worthwhile and which is best.

Suppose that the marginal cost of unit q of a certain product produced by Scorpius Ltd is predicted by the model:

$$c = 15 - \frac{q}{200} + \frac{q^2}{1m}$$

(m denotes million). Thus the first unit costs about £15, the one thousandth £11 and the five thousandth £15. Suppose, further, that Scorpius sells in conditions approximating to perfect competition; it can sell any likely quantity at a price of £12 per unit (but nothing at a higher price). Marginal revenue is therefore also £12 and marginal cost equals marginal revenue when:

$$12 = 15 - \frac{q}{200} + \frac{q^2}{1m}$$

i.e. $q^2 - 5000q + 3m = 0$,

and $q = \dfrac{5000 \pm \sqrt{(25m - 12m)}}{2} = 697$ or 4303.

It can be shown that where

$$c = 15 - \frac{q}{200} + \frac{q^2}{1m},$$

total cost $T = 15q - \dfrac{q^2}{400} + \dfrac{q^3}{3m}$ (assuming that there are no fixed costs).[4]

The two output levels for which marginal cost and marginal revenue are equal, approximately 700 units and 4300 units are

Table 19 Cash flow for Scorpius Ltd

Quantity (units)	Total cost (£) $15q - (q^2/400) - (q^3/3m)$	Total revenue (£) $12q$	Net surplus (£)
700	$10\,500 - 1225 + 114 = 9389$	8400	-989
4300	$64\,500 - 46\,225 + 26\,502 = 44\,777$	51 600	$+6823$

evaluated in Table 19. It can be seen that a loss would be incurred on production of 700 units but a surplus of £6823 would be earned on the output of 4300 units. The latter is the

4. $T = \int c\, dq$, using integral calculus; alternatively, if total cost is $T = 15q - (q^2/400) + (q^3/3m)$, marginal cost may be found as the first derivative (the technique used in obtaining expression 9).

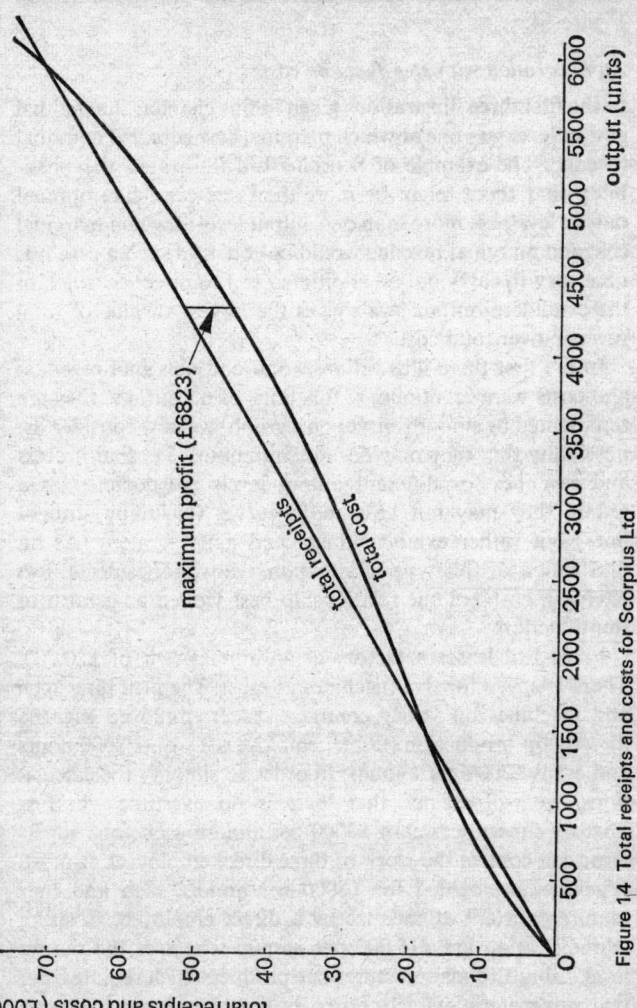

Figure 1.4 Total receipts and costs for Scorpius Ltd

best possible output level. These results are illustrated in Figure 14.

An illustration with step-function costs

In the first three illustrations given in this chapter, the optimal output level was one at which marginal cost equalled marginal revenue. The example of Scorpius Ltd illustrated the possibility that there might be more than one candidate optimal output level, i.e. more than one output level at which marginal cost and marginal revenue would be equal. In such a case it is necessary to carry out an additional test to discover which of the candidate output levels gives the largest surplus of total revenue over total cost.

In the first three illustrations, total and marginal revenues and costs were 'continuous' functions of output, i.e. they are represented by smooth curves on a graph; we now consider the possibility that they may be 'discontinuous', i.e. that if costs and revenues for different output levels are depicted as a graph, they may not be smooth curves (including straight lines) but rather exhibit 'kinks' and gaps or steps. As an illustration of this type of situation, we will consider a firm having a cost–volume relationship best viewed as a form of step-function.

Libra Ltd leases a factory at an annual rent of £20 000. There is space for five machines at most. The firm hires men and machines on yearly contracts. Each employee engaged directly on production ('direct employees') works 2000 hours and earns £2000 per annum; in order to simplify the calculations, we will assume that there is no overtime working. Factory supervisors earn £3000 per annum each; one supervisor can control the work of three direct employees at most. Machines are rented for £5000 per annum each and they require constant attendance by a direct employee. Costs of administration are £15 000 per annum whatever the output level. Libra Ltd manufactures one product which requires, per unit, raw materials which cost £6, two machine hours (with two hours of a direct employee's time in operating the machine), and three other direct labour hours, a total of five labour hours.

It is estimated that the sales price–volume relationship has the linear form:

$$q = 9600 - 160p,$$

thus

$$p = 60 - \frac{q}{160},$$

and total revenue

$$pq = 60q - \frac{q^2}{160}.$$

We may now estimate total revenue and costs for various output levels. We will consider each level at which there is a step in the cost function. Each product unit requires five labour hours – hence one man can make 400 product units in his working year of 2000 hours. A product unit also requires two machine hours; one machine can undertake the work involved in the production of 1000 units in its working year of 2000 hours. Hence steps in the cost function take place at intervals of 400 units and 1000 units. Steps associated with supervisory labour take place every 1200 units, once for every three direct employees. Maximum output is 5000 units, set by the limit of factory capacity to five machines.

Cost data for the output levels at which there are steps in total costs are given in Table 20 and total costs and revenues are summarized in Table 21 and in Figure 15.

Inspection of Table 21 indicates that the best output level of those considered is 3600 units: net cash surplus is then £31 400. We cannot be sure that this is the overall optimum, however, until we have considered costs and revenue associated with other output levels. Let us approach this question by examining the relationship between marginal cost and marginal revenue.

Marginal cost, the increase in total costs for a unit increase in output, is generally £6 per unit – the cost of materials. It is constant for all output levels except those at which step-like increases take place in total costs; the concept of marginal cost lacks its usual significance at such points because the increase in total costs then reflects the acquisition of resources which contribute not just to one extra unit of output but to a range

Table 20 Total costs for Libra Ltd

Number of product units	Direct labour (employees)	(£)	Machines (number)	(£)	Supervisors (employees)	(£)	Materials (£)	Fixed cost (£)	Total cost (£)
1	1	2 000	1	5 000	1	3 000	6	35 000	45 006
400	1	2 000	1	5 000	1	3 000	2 400	35 000	47 400
401	2	4 000	1	5 000	1	3 000	2 406	35 000	49 406
800	2	4 000	1	5 000	1	3 000	4 800	35 000	51 800
801	3	6 000	1	5 000	1	3 000	4 806	35 000	53 806
1000	3	6 000	1	5 000	1	3 000	6 000	35 000	55 000
1001	3	6 000	2	10 000	1	3 000	6 006	35 000	60 006
1200	3	6 000	2	10 000	1	3 000	7 200	35 000	61 200
1201	4	8 000	2	10 000	2	6 000	7 206	35 000	66 206
1600	4	8 000	2	10 000	2	6 000	9 600	35 000	68 600
1601	5	10 000	2	10 000	2	6 000	9 606	35 000	70 606
2000	5	10 000	2	10 000	2	6 000	12 000	35 000	73 000
2001	6	12 000	3	15 000	2	6 000	12 006	35 000	80 006
2400	6	12 000	3	15 000	2	6 000	14 400	35 000	82 400
2401	7	14 000	3	15 000	2	6 000	14 406	35 000	87 406
2800	7	14 000	3	15 000	2	6 000	16 800	35 000	89 800
2801	8	16 000	3	15 000	3	9 000	16 806	35 000	91 806
3000	8	16 000	3	15 000	3	9 000	18 000	35 000	93 000
3001	8	16 000	4	20 000	3	9 000	18 006	35 000	98 006
3200	8	16 000	4	20 000	3	9 000	19 200	35 000	99 200
3201	9	18 000	4	20 000	3	9 000	19 206	35 000	101 206
3600	9	18 000	4	20 000	3	9 000	21 600	35 000	103 600
3601	10	20 000	4	20 000	4	12 000	21 606	35 000	108 606
4000	10	20 000	4	20 000	4	12 000	24 000	35 000	111 000
4001	11	22 000	5	25 000	4	12 000	24 006	35 000	118 006
4400	11	22 000	5	25 000	4	12 000	26 400	35 000	120 400
4401	12	24 000	5	25 000	4	12 000	26 406	35 000	122 406
4800	12	24 000	5	25 000	4	12 000	28 800	35 000	124 800
4801	13	26 000	5	25 000	5	15 000	28 806	35 000	129 806
5000	13	26 000	5	25 000	5	15 000	30 000	35 000	131 000

Table 21 Total receipts and costs for Libra Ltd

Number of product units	Price (£) $p = 60 - \dfrac{q}{160}$	Total receipts (£)	Total costs (£)	Net cash surplus/deficit (£)
1	60.	60	45 006	−44 946
400	57.50	23 000	47 400	−24 400
401	57.50	23 058	49 406	−26 348
800	55	44 000	51 800	−7 800
801	55	44 055	53 806	−9 751
1000	53.75	53 750	55 000	−1 250
1001	53.75	53 804	60 006	−6 202
1200	52.50	63 000	61 200	+1 800
1201	52.50	63 053	66 206	−3 153
1600	50	80 000	68 600	+11 400
1601	50	80 050	70 606	+9 444
2000	47.50	95 000	73 000	+22 000
2001	47.50	95 048	80 006	+15 042
2400	45	108 000	82 400	+25 600
2401	45	108 045	87 406	+20 639
2800	42.50	119 000	89 800	+29 200
2801	42.50	119 043	91 806	+27 237
3000	41.25	123 750	93 000	+30 750
3001	41.25	123 791	98 006	+25 785
3200	40	128 000	99 200	+28 800
3201	40	128 040	101 206	+26 834
3600	37.50	135 000	103 600	+31 400
3601	37.50	135 038	108 606	+26 432
4000	35	140 000	111 000	+29 000
4001	35	140 035	118 006	+22 029
4400	32.50	143 000	120 400	+22 600
4401	32.50	143 033	122 406	+20 627
4800	30.	144 000	124 800	+19 200
4801	30	144 030	129 806	+14 224
5000	28.75	143 750	131 000	+12 750

of output levels. We noted above that if a firm's sales price–volume relationship has the form

$$q = a - bp,$$

marginal revenue is equal to $\dfrac{a - 2q}{b}$ (expression **9**).

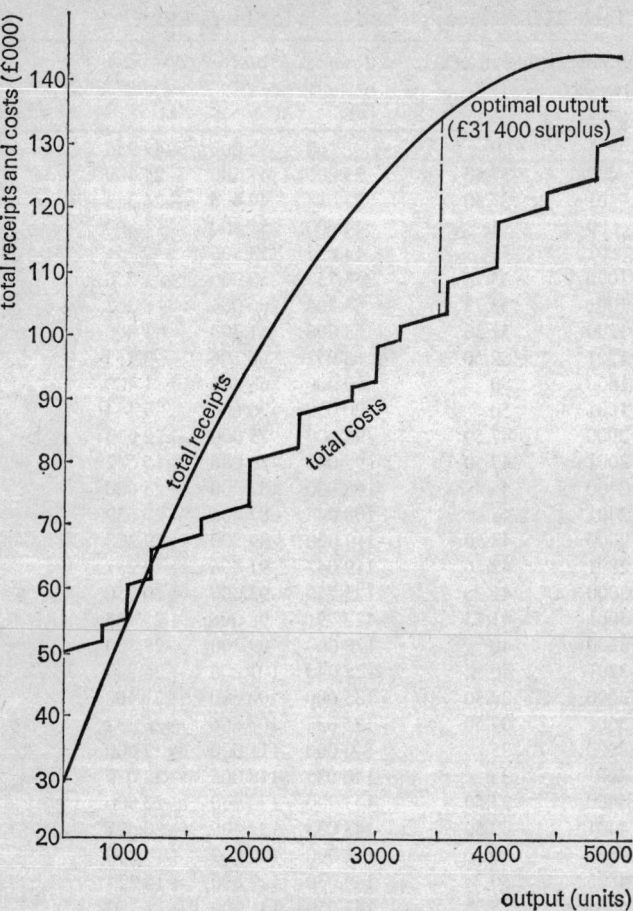

Figure 15 Total receipts and costs for Libra Ltd

In the case of Libra Ltd, $a = 9600$ and $b = 160$ – hence marginal revenue is

$$\frac{9600 - 2q}{160}.$$

11

Marginal cost and marginal revenue are equal when:

$$\frac{9600-2q}{160} = 6,$$

i.e. when $q = 4320$.

At this output level:

total revenue $= 60q - \frac{q^2}{160} =$ £142 560

and total cost $=$ cost of 4001 units
                 $+319$ at £6
           $=$ £118 006$+(319 \times$ £6$) =$ £119 920

Net surplus: £22 640

It can be seen by inspection of expression **11** that marginal revenue (as usual) decreases as output increases. Hence at output levels below 4320 marginal revenue always exceeds marginal cost. Increases in output levels between steps in total costs and below 4320 always increase the cash surplus because the increase in revenue exceeds the increase in costs. Increases in output between steps and beyond 4320 result in a decrease in the cash surplus, however, as marginal revenue is then less than marginal cost. Although the cash surplus fluctuates up and down as output is increased over steps there are 'local optima' (the best of a range of nearby output levels) just before a step in the cost function, up to the point where marginal cost and revenue are equal.

The above argument indicates that optimal output can be estimated by considering total costs and total revenues at output levels where there are steps in total costs and at the level(s) where marginal cost and marginal revenue are equal.

In our illustration, the optimal output level can now be seen to be 3600 units – the surplus earned at this point is greater than that for the output of 4320 units. Marginal revenue at this point (substituting $q = 3600$ in expression **11**) is £15 and this is not equal either to the marginal cost (£6) or the increase in cost in adding one unit to the output of 3600 (£5006).

The inclusion of the cost of machines in this example serves to remind us that such costs are relevant to short-term decisions even though they are usually incurred by the purchase of a machine having a long life and hence the subject of an investment decision. Such costs should include an element for interest as noted in chapter 2 and hence may be appropriately calculated as the annual rental which would enable a leasing company to break even on the hire of machines, after meeting interest, over their working lives.

The preparation of estimates of total cost and total revenue for the output level(s) at which marginal cost and marginal revenue are equal and for each level at which there is a step in the cost function may be a formidable computational task in practice – even though it may be possible to exclude many output levels which are clearly uneconomic. The problem may be reduced to manageable proportions, however, by programming an electronic computer with the cost and revenue models and using it for the detailed computations.

The reader may feel that it is unrealistic to suppose that steps in total costs take place at hard and fast points in the output schedule – that some increase in output may be squeezed from a given collection of resources. Whilst this possibility may be granted, the point of the illustration is that the potential for such extra output is limited and there will be a level of output at which resources must be increased; at that level, costs increase sharply rather than by a small amount. In practice, step-like cost increases associated with increases in the labour force may not be significant and labour costs may be treated as strictly variable; but it is otherwise with the costs of expensive machines, factory space and large plants.

Finally we should note that the optimal level of sales price and volume, calculated by the methods described in this chapter, may not be attainable in practice if there is some form of governmental control of prices. In such a case a firm may have to operate at a lower level of price and a higher volume than optimal and hence accept a lower level of net cash earnings.

10 Optimal Output: Promotion and Distribution

In this chapter, we conclude our discussion of the basic features of the model-building approach to the identification of optimal output and pricing policy with a note on two important factors which we have ignored so far, the effect of sales promotional costs and distribution costs. We cannot, in the space available, attempt more than an outline of the main principles at issue.

Sales promotion

Let us consider the setting of the optimal level of advertising as an example of the general category of sales promotional costs. The object of advertising may be considered to be the achievement of a favourable shift in the sales price–volume relationship. Given any output-volume which a firm may wish to sell, it would expect to receive a higher price with advertising than without it.

The position is complicated in practice because the impact of advertising may be delayed and it may be cumulative. Advertising during the current period may bring some benefit in the current period, but it may also bring some benefit (possibly greater) in the following period and indeed in several subsequent periods. Furthermore its impact on results in the next period may depend partly on the level of advertising expenditure in that period and so on.

However it will help our development of a conceptual framework for the study of advertising if we abstract from these complications and assume that whatever benefit is derived from advertising is derived solely in the period in which the expenditure is incurred. The extension of the model involves little extra difficulty of principle.

Let us pursue the idea that advertising expenditure makes it possible to sell a given quantity of a product at an increased price. The optimal level of advertising at any level of sales is found by increasing the expenditure on advertising up to the point at which the marginal increase in sales revenue is just equal to the marginal advertising cost. This is another application of the rule that optimality calls for the equation of marginal cost and marginal revenue and again rests on the assumption that the relationship is 'well-behaved' – that each extra pound spent on advertising produces successively smaller increases in total revenue.

The optimal level of advertising could also be studied by taking the view that advertising makes it possible to sell a larger quantity of a product at a given price. An increase in advertising expenditure would improve the cash flow by the difference between the extra sales proceeds from the increased quantity and the cost of producing it – and advertising expenditure should be increased as long as increases lead to improvement in net cash receipts. This approach would necessarily lead to the same conclusion as the former.

A model of the effect of advertising

Let us examine a model which describes the results of advertising when advertising is assumed to affect sales potential only in the period during which it is incurred.

Virgo Ltd sells a single product. We consider firstly models which describe total revenues and costs if there is no advertising.

Suppose that $\qquad q = 18\,000 - 200p,$

thus $\qquad p = 90 - \dfrac{q}{200}.$ **1**

Total revenue $\quad pq = 90q - \dfrac{q^2}{200}$

and marginal revenue is $\quad 90 - \dfrac{q}{100}$ (calculated in accordance with expression **9** in chapter 9). Total cost is the simple linear relation

$$T = 15q + 150\,000 \quad \text{i.e. marginal cost is £15.} \qquad \mathbf{2}$$

The optimal output level, obtained by equating marginal cost and revenue is q in

$$90 - \frac{q}{100} = 15,$$

thus $\quad q = 7500$.

Suppose that the possibility of advertising is now introduced. Successful advertising makes it possible to obtain a higher price for a given sales quantity. We require a model which describes the relationship between the expenditure on advertising and the increase in price made possible. Let us denote by p' the new price which can be obtained with advertising and by A the expenditure on advertising. We will assume that an investigation has indicated that the effect of advertising may be estimated by the model:

$$p' = p + \frac{A}{100} - \frac{A^2}{1m} \qquad \mathbf{3}$$

$$= 90 - \frac{q}{200} + \frac{A}{100} - \frac{A^2}{1m} \qquad \mathbf{4}$$

(substituting expression **1** in expression **3**).

Total revenue is

$$p'q = 90q - \frac{q^2}{200} + \frac{Aq}{100} - \frac{A^2q}{1m}. \qquad \mathbf{5}$$

Total cost, including advertising, is given by the expression

$$T = A + 15q + 150\,000. \qquad \mathbf{6}$$

We might use expressions **5** and **6** to explore the effect on total costs and revenues of different output levels and different expenditures on advertising. Suppose, for example, that £5000 is spent on advertising. Substitution in expression **3** indicates that the new price

$$p' = p + \frac{5000}{100} - \frac{25m}{1m} = p + 25. \qquad \mathbf{7}$$

Table 22 summarizes the calculations of the total costs and revenues for different output levels when either nothing or £5000 is spent on advertising, and price is set at the estimated levels which make it possible to dispose of the entire output (as estimated by expressions **1** and **7**). A study of Table 22 indicates that it is better to spend £5000 on advertising than nothing and that the best output level associated with advertising expenditure of £5000 is 10 000 units with a price of £65 – yielding an estimated surplus of £345 000. It would be possible to use a computer to explore the effect on net cash earnings of adopting a large number of different output levels and advertising expenditure levels (instead of the few representative levels illustrated in our example). Given the simple models that we have assumed in the example of Virgo, it is also possible to find the strict optimum by direct calculation; it involves an output level slightly below 10 000 units and advertising expenditure of about £4950 – and is close to the best possibility shown in the Table.[1]

1. Total net revenue,

$$R = 75q - \frac{q^2}{200} + \frac{Aq}{100} - \frac{A^2 q}{1m} - A - 150\,000,$$

(expression **5** less equation **6**).

We find the optimum by taking partial derivatives and setting them equal to zero:

$$\frac{\partial R}{\partial q} = 75 - \frac{q}{100} + \frac{A}{100} - \frac{A^2}{1m} = 0, \qquad 8$$

and $\quad \dfrac{\partial R}{\partial A} = \dfrac{q}{100} - \dfrac{2Aq}{1m} - 1 = 0 \qquad 9$

Rearrangement of **9** gives $\quad A = 5000 - \dfrac{500\,000}{q}, \qquad 10$

and substitution in **8** gives

$$75 - \frac{q}{100} + \frac{1}{100}\left(5000 - \frac{500\,000}{q}\right) - \frac{1}{1m}\left(5000 - \frac{500\,000}{q}\right)^2 = 0,$$

i.e. $\quad 100 - \dfrac{q}{100} - \dfrac{250\,000}{q^2} = 0,$

$$q^3 - 10\,000q^2 + 25m = 0 \qquad 11$$

The value for q at the optimal output level can be seen by inspection of expression **11** to be slightly under 10 000 units (i.e. this value satisfies the equation). Substitution in **10** indicates that the optimal advertising expenditure is approximately £4950.

It is not a simple matter to formulate the models appropriate to deal with promotional expenditures in an actual problem. Potential sales in any particular period are likely to depend on a formidable number of variables: the current selling prices of the firm and of its competitors, the current advertising expenditure of the firm and its competitors – for competition may be waged through advertising policy as well as pricing policy – and so on. Statistical methods of investigation of the models are likely to be of limited value because the models would exhibit in extreme form the difficulties discussed in chapters 7 and 8. However the attempt at formulation directs attention to relevant questions for a firm's decisions and provides a framework within which managers can learn about the critical relationships (by comparing forecast and actual results). Uncertainty about the choice of model can be met in part by analysing a range of different but promising models and studying the sensitivity of the optimal results to the differing assumptions reflected in each one. It is also possible, within the analytic framework described, to focus attention on relevant questions such as: 'If the price is £p and we spend £A on advertising, how many extra units must we sell to earn a larger surplus overall (than with no advertising or some alternative level) and what are the chances of doing so successfully?' We may edge towards the optimal plan by considering the effect of small changes in advertising in a manner similar to that suggested for the use of elasticity in chapter 9.

The results given in Table 22 are depicted in Figure 16 which shows total costs excluding advertising, total revenue without advertising and total revenue less the cost of advertising when advertising expenditure is at the optimal level.

The example of Virgo Ltd shows that the optimal plan is not necessarily to be found by estimating what the optimal output level (or price) would be without advertising and then estimating the optimal amount of advertising expenditure given this base. The best output level with advertising – 10 000 units – is different from the best output level if there is no advertising – 7500 units – and the optimal prices differ by £12.50.

Decisions on desired levels of selling costs are more complex

Table 22 Total costs and receipts for Virgo Ltd

Output level (q units)	Without advertising				With advertising			
	Price (£) $p = 90 - \dfrac{q}{200}$	Total revenue (£000) pq	Total cost (£000) $c = 15q + 150\,000$	Net revenue (£000) $pq - c$	Price (£) $p' = p + 25$	Total revenue less advertising cost (£000) $p'q - a$	Total cost (£000) $c + a$	Net revenue (£000) $p'q - (c+a)$
6 000	60	360	240	120	85	505	240	265
7 000	55	385	255	130	80	555	255	300
7 500	52.50	393.75	262.50	131.25	77.50	576.25	262.50	313.75
8 000	50	400	270	130	75	595	270	325
9 000	45	405	285	120	70	625	285	340
10 000	40	400	300	100	65	645	300	345
11 000	35	385	315	70	60	655	315	340
12 000	30	360	330	30	55	655	330	325

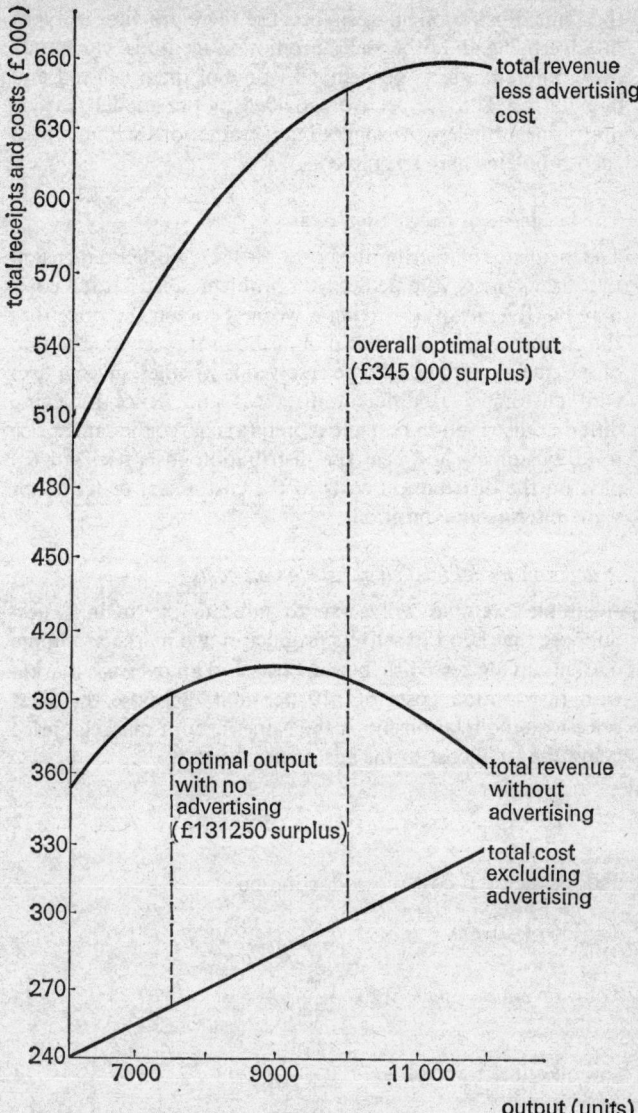

Figure 16 Total receipts and costs for Virgo Ltd

than our illustration suggests because there are various types of advertising and other sales promotion methods which may have different effects on demand, some of them delayed and cumulative. The perspective provided by our model may be useful, nevertheless, in suggesting a framework within which such problems may be studied.

The incidence of distribution costs

The incidence of distribution costs adds yet another dimension to a firm's price–volume decision problem. Distribution costs may be thought of as driving a wedge between the price that the customer pays and the amount the firm receives. The nub of the question that has to be resolved is whether, given a firm with customers at different distances and hence involving different distribution costs, it should (a) charge the same price to all customers and bear the distribution costs itself, or (b) pass on the distribution costs to the customers, or (c) adopt some intermediate position.

A decision model involving distribution costs

A simple example will serve to indicate the main issues. Suppose that Leo Ltd sells its product in two markets, a home market having zero distribution costs and an overseas market with distribution costs of £10 per unit. Suppose the sales price–volume relationship is the same in both markets, price being the total cost to the customer:

$$p = 120 - \frac{q}{300}, \qquad\qquad 12$$

and let the total cost of production be

$$T = 36q + 40\,000.$$

$$\text{Total revenue} = pq = 120q - \frac{q^2}{300}, \qquad\qquad 13$$

and marginal revenue is $120 - \dfrac{q}{150}$. $\qquad\qquad 14$

Marginal cost in the home market is £36 and in the overseas market £36+£10 = £46 (including distribution). It follows, equating marginal revenue and marginal cost, that in the home market sales quantity should be q in

$$120 - \frac{q}{150} = 36,$$

i.e. $q = 12\ 600,$

and in the overseas market it should be q in

$$120 - \frac{q}{150} = 46,$$

i.e. $q = 11\ 100.$

Price in the home market would be $p_h = 120 - \frac{12\ 600}{300} = £78$ (substituting in **12**), and delivered price to the customers in the overseas market

$$p_o = 120 - \frac{11\ 100}{300} = £83.$$

This is a simplified example. In practice it is possible that the price–volume relationships would differ from market to market because of competitive considerations or for other reasons. In the example, however, the best plan is for the firm in effect to pass on some of the distribution costs but not the whole amount (£5 out of £10); i.e. the differential price including distribution should be less than the distribution costs. Similar results are likely to hold generally, provided the sales price–volume models are the same in the various markets. It follows from this analysis that in a firm's optimal plan the average percentage surplus (after deducting distribution costs) earned on a product may well be lower in a market in which distribution costs are high, than in a market in which they are low. This result is relevant to the question of the best price for a product sold both in domestic and export markets.

It should be noted that the separate calculation of optimal output for each market was appropriate only because marginal cost was a constant, independent of output level. In other cases it would be necessary to formulate a model of overall cash surplus and estimate the overall optimum in one set of calculations. If q_1 units are sold in market 1 and q_2 units in market 2, the model would have the form:

Overall surplus = (total revenue from selling q_1 units in market 1)

$plus$ (total revenue from selling q_2 units in market 2)

$less$ (total cost of producing $q_1 + q_2$ units)

$less$ (distribution costs, $d_1 q_1 + d_2 q_2$).

11 Optimal Use of Scarce Resources (1)

In chapter 9, we assumed that the gain from the manufacture of one product was independent of whatever other products were manufactured and hence that the optimal output level for each product could be estimated independently. The optimal mix of products did not require special attention – it would be whatever was implied by the independent decisions.

We discussed the existence of resource constraints briefly in chapter 5 and we now consider in more detail the difficulties posed by their existence. Suppose we use the procedures described in chapter 9 to estimate the optimal output level for each of a firm's products. We may find that the resources required to implement the plan are more than the firm can obtain. In such cases, the resource constraints will cause us to modify our plans; we must decide which parts of the production originally planned should be given priority. It is necessary to ration the use of the resources. Production possibilities must be measured against each other to find which is best – it is no longer satisfactory to consider them independently.

Before we consider the methods of analysis adapted to this type of problem, we should perhaps consider shortly the practical significance of resource constraints.

The supply of all resources is subject to some upper limit; most resources are scarce in relation to their conceivable uses. In capitalist economies, it is assumed that the price mechanism will normally operate to ration resources between competing uses. If the worthwhile uses of a resource, at a particular price, cause a demand for the resource in excess of the available supply, competition would be expected to drive up the price. The increase in price would continue until some of the uses were no longer worthwhile and supply and demand were in balance. Decisions in the firm would then be (relatively) straightforward. Sufficient resources would be available to undertake all activities judged to be worthwhile on independent appraisal.

The allocation of scarce resources presents a special problem only if there are material imperfections in the market pricing mechanism which prevent the elimination of a firm's excess demand for a resource. This consideration has led some writers to ignore the problem, asserting that in the long run, at least, it may be assumed to be immaterial.

Practical existence of resource constraints

There are two reasons why we do not dismiss the problem so shortly. First, in the short period, with which we are concerned, it seems likely that significant constraints exist. They may be particularly likely to arise if one firm dominates the use of a resource so that competition (which might drive up the price) for the resource is at a minimum. They may arise anyway because of normal delays in market adjustment to competitive pressures (even if it does adjust eventually). They may be especially common in the case of resources which require complex and costly plant for their production; the delay in adjustment of the level of output of the resource to the demand is then especially likely to be lengthy and meanwhile, prices may not rise sufficiently to eliminate the excess demand, partly as a result of deliberate policy on the part of the supplier.

Secondly, a situation analagous to resource scarcity may arise as a result of a firm's operating policy even if it does not arise because of market conditions. The existing managers of a firm may have the capacity to manage only a limited size of undertaking; they may prefer to limit the size of the management team (and retain the existing 'social structure' in the firm) rather than increase the size of the firm. Similarly they may set a limited size of operation because their objectives attach great value to leisure. In either case they may decide that the best plan is to set some appropriate limit on the volume of resources that they are willing to manage – particularly labour and factory space which make notable demands on managers' time.

Assumptions of analysis

We shall begin our analysis of methods for taking decisions where there are resource constraints, as usual, with particular simplifying assumptions designed to highlight main principles. We shall assume, for each product considered, that there is a simple linear relationship between the quantity made and sold on the one hand and each of (a) the total quantity of resources required, (b) the total cost of the resources and (c) total sales receipts on the other. The quantity of resources used and the cost of such resources will be assumed to comprise a fixed element plus a variable element which is a constant amount per product unit. Selling price is assumed to be set at some predetermined level because of strategic considerations. In such a model, consistency requires that potential sales volume should be assumed to be unlimited (an appropriate assumption if selling conditions approximate to perfect competition), or subject to some upper limit (presumably the more usual situation).

Furthermore, we assume perfect divisibility of resources (apart from the element corresponding to fixed cost) and products; i.e. the firm can make and sell any quantity of a product including fractions (subject to some upper limit only) and the quantity and cost of resources used will vary in direct proportion to output and sales. These simplifying assumptions will be relaxed in chapter 12.

Decisions with one resource constraint

Let us begin our analysis of resource constraints by considering a situation in which only one resource comprises an effective limit on output. We will develop the argument with the help of an example.

The products which can be manufactured by Andromeda Ltd during the coming period are described in Table 23. Andromeda Ltd uses one grade of labour, the supply of which

Table 23 Products available to Andromeda Ltd

Maximum sales volume	Product	Selling price (£) p	Variable cost excluding labour (£) v	Gross contribution (£) $G = p - v$	Labour hours L	Labour cost (£) $W = 0.75L$	Net contribution (£) $G - W$
3000	A	79	24	55	16	12	43
2000	B	77	35	42	20	15	27
3500	C	41	17	24	10	7.50	16.50
2500	D	58	21	37	12	9	28
4500	E	44	28	16	8	6	10

is limited to 120 000 hours per annum, at a wage rate of £0.75 per hour.

We wish to maximize:

$$(79-24)x_a+(77-35)x_b+(41-17)x_c+(58-21)x_d$$
$$+(44-28)x_e-0.75L-185\ 000,$$

subject to the constraints:

$$16x_a+20x_b+10x_c+12x_d+8x_e-L \leqslant 0,$$
$$L \leqslant 120\ 000,$$
$$x_a \leqslant 3000,$$
$$x_b \leqslant 2000,$$
$$x_c \leqslant 3500,$$
$$x_d \leqslant 2500,$$
$$x_e \leqslant 4500,$$

where $x_a,\ldots,x_e$ represent the quantities manufactured and sold of products $A,\ldots,E$ (quantities which cannot be negative) and L represents the number of labour hours hired.

The expression to be maximized (the objective function) represents net cash receipts. If we assign values to $x_a,\ldots,x_e$, corresponding to some production plan, the terms concerned give total sales receipts less variable costs from which we deduct $0.75L$, the cost of labour used and £185 000, the amount of fixed costs. In the first constraint $16x_a+\ldots+8x_e$ represents the number of labour hours required for a production plan and these must not exceed L, the labour hours hired; or, equivalently, in the form in which the constraint is expressed, the labour hours required, minus the labour hours hired must not exceed zero. The remaining constraints give the limits to the number of labour hours that can be hired and the product quantities which can be sold.

The contribution per unit of the limiting resource

In this type of problem, the optimal plan may be estimated by a simple procedure. It is necessary, firstly, to calculate for each product the contribution to cash earnings per unit of the resource which limits output. The best plan can then be built up by ranking products in the order of the size of their contribution per unit of the resource, and selecting for manufacture firstly as much as can be sold of the product with the highest ranking; other products are then added in the order of their ranking until the supply of the resource is exhausted.

Table 24 Contributions per labour hour for Andromeda Ltd (£)

Product	Selling price per unit	Variable costs per unit excluding labour	Contributions per unit	Labour hours per unit	Contributions per labour hour	Ranking
A	79	24	55	16	3.4	1
B	77	35	42	20	2.1	4
C	41	17	24	10	2.4	3
D	58	21	37	12	3.1	2
E	44	28	16	8	2.0	5

For the case of Andromeda Ltd, calculations of contributions are given in Table 24 and the optimal plan is described in Table 25. The contributions were calculated in Table 24 without any deduction for labour costs; it would be necessary to discard any products which earn a contribution per labour hour which is less than 75p, the cost of labour per hour – for

Table 25 The optimal plan of Andromeda Ltd

Product	Amounts per unit		Quantity	Totals	
	Contribution (£)	Labour hours		Contribution (£)	Labour hours
A	55	16	3000	165 000	48 000
D	37	12	2500	92 500	30 000
C	24	10	3500	84 000	35 000
B	42	20	350	14 700	7 000
maximum supply of labour					120 000
total				356 200	
less labour cost 120 000 hours at £0.75	£90 000				
less fixed costs	£185 000			275 000	
Net cash surplus				£81 200	

such products would yield a deficit after allowing for labour costs. Identical results would have been obtained had labour been included with variable costs and had zero contribution been used as the signal for discarding products. The contribution per labour hour for each product would then have been reduced by £0.75 and the ranking of products unaffected.

It will be noted that fixed costs have no effect on the selection of the best products; fixed costs are kept in the calculations so that we can check that they are likely to be covered by the aggregate contributions earned – a necessary condition if the continuation of the firm in business is to be justified. The objective of the firm is essentially to earn as large a pool of contributions from its products as possible, at least enough to cover fixed costs.

The substitution test of optimality

We may show formally that our ranking method has led to an optimal plan by the following argument. The objective is to maximize the cash surplus earned. The chosen plan may be seen to be optimal if we investigate the effect of altering it in all possible ways and find that none leads to an increase in cash surplus. All possible alterations may be viewed as substitutions – increases in output of some products offset by decreases in others. In our example, all possible substitutions may be described in terms of changes in the use of labour, e.g. taking one labour hour provisionally assigned to one product and applying it to the manufacture of another. The use of labour may be regarded as a 'pivotal' consideration; we must find a plan of production which requires no more than 120 000 hours of labour: moreover, given the abundant availability of worthwhile products, the firm will clearly not want to use less.

One possible substitution in the plan suggested for Andromeda would involve withdrawing one labour hour provisionally assigned to product C and applying it in the manufacture of product B instead. This would involve giving up manufacture of one-tenth units of C and adding one-twentieth units of B (C and B require ten and twenty labour hours per unit) – readers will remember that we are assuming for convenience of exposition that fractions of products may be counted as valued in proportion to whole units. The effect of this substitution would be to lose contributions of £24 × 1/10 on C and gain £42 × 1/20 on B, a net loss of £3/10. Such a substitution is not worthwhile. Apart from the 'marginal' product B, C earns least per labour hour of the products included in the plan and all the products wholly excluded earn less per labour hour than B. Hence it can be seen that any other substitution would involve a loss. The plan chosen is therefore optimal.

A generalization of the above argument indicates that a ranking of products by contribution per unit of a resource which limits output will always lead to an optimal plan if there is one and only one such resource. Many, no doubt, would acknowledge the usefulness of calculating the contribution per unit of the 'scarce' resource in this situation without requiring rigorous justification in terms of substitutions; a similar analysis is often given in accounting texts with some title such as 'key factor analysis'. The concept of substitution was introduced at this point in order to pave the way for a demonstration of its usefulness in more complex analysis.

The link with opportunity cost

As further preparation for subsequent analysis, it will be useful to study the applicability of opportunity cost concepts to the situation in which there is one resource constraint. The opportunity cost of a resource is defined in relation to some provisional plan of activities under consideration; it is the gross amount (before deducting the cost of the resource) that can be earned from a resource in the best alternative use, apart from activities included in the provisional plan. It follows that opportunity cost is also the amount by which the value of the provisional plan could be increased if one extra unit of a resource could be used – again without deduction for the cost of the resource. We noted in chapter 5 that the opportunity cost of a resource would exceed external cost (purchase price or realizable value) if the supply of the resource was subject to an effective constraint. It can now be seen that opportunity cost may be used as a ranking (or at least a 'cut-off') device in conditions of resource constraints. Products manufactured must earn more than available alternatives which set the opportunity costs; if the provisional plan is optimal all activities must show a surplus when resources required are valued at their external cost, or opportunity cost if higher.

In our illustration, only labour has an opportunity cost in excess of external cost; increased usage of other resources would not make it possible to improve the value of the plan whilst labour remained in fixed supply. If one extra labour hour were to become available, it could be applied in manufacturing more of product B – the next best use available. One hour would yield a gross contribution of £2.10 and this is the opportunity cost of labour; we may regard it as being made up of the external cost of labour of £0.75 per hour and a surplus earned from the use of labour of £1.35 per hour.

We may now demonstrate the significance of opportunity cost. Contributions on products available to Andromeda are restated in Table 26 with resources costed at opportunity cost

Table 26 Revised costings for Andromeda Ltd., including opportunity costs

| Product | Selling price (£) | Labour | | Other variable costs (£) | Total costs (£) | Surplus or deficit (£) |
		Hours	Cost at £2.10			
A	79	16	33.6	24	57.6	+21.4
B	77	20	42	35	77	0
C	41	10	21	17	38	+3
D	58	12	25.2	21	46.2	+11.8
E	44	8	16.8	28	44.8	−0.8

or external cost, whichever is higher. It is the general rule, consistent with Table 26, that when we value all resources on this basis:

1 Those products of which we wish to make as much as we can sell have surpluses (in our example A, C, D).

2 Those products which we do not wish to make have deficits (in our example E).

3 There is normally one or a few marginal products which have neither surplus nor deficit – we wish to make some units but fewer than we could sell (in our example *B*).

We shall discuss the practical usefulness of opportunity costs later.

Decisions with many resource constraints

Let us now consider the position when a firm has more than one resource constraint. There is no simple computational rule for selecting the optimal plan in this case. Contributions per unit of a resource which constrains output may well give different rankings of products or other activities according to which resource is used as a base; and we need, at least, some means for choosing between them.

We can solve problems of product selection with several resource constraints provided we retain our simplifying assumptions of constant variable costs, fixed selling prices and divisibility of resource and product units. We need to use the technique of computation known as linear programming. It is beyond the scope of this book to explain the technique in detail or to justify the method by rigorous mathematics. We shall simply consider the main principles involved in the method, study an example of its application and discuss the interpretation of solutions obtained.

The method of linear programming

The method of considering substitutions – used above to demonstrate the optimality of the plan chosen for Andromeda – underlies the basic method of linear programming. The method involves adopting a provisional plan, one that is feasible having regard to the availability of resources; several possible changes (including substitutions) are then evaluated and one is selected for adoption from amongst those that yield increased surpluses. This gives a new provisional plan. The procedure is repeated with successive plans until one is found for which no improvement is possible. That last provisional plan is the optimal plan.

Linear programming techniques, such as the simplex method, enable the process described to be carried out with reasonable efficiency; for example, they ensure that the number of provisional plans that has to be examined is small relative to the total number of possible plans. It can be shown by rigorous mathematical arguments that the procedure does lead to an optimal plan; for example that a better plan will not be found by accepting a substitution that reduces the surplus and then seeking a larger improvement.

An illustration of linear programming methods

Let us see how these ideas work out in a numerical example. Cygnus Ltd uses three resources that are subject to constraints, labour of three grades, skilled, unskilled and semi-skilled, with wage costs of £1, £0.50 and £0.75 per hour. Maximum available supplies for the coming year are estimated at 16 000 hours each of skilled and unskilled labour and 12 000 hours of semi-skilled labour. No transfers are possible between the different grades of labour. Fixed costs are £29 000 per annum. Details of the products being considered for manufacture are given in Table 27. The problem is described by the following mathematical model.

We wish to maximize:

$$26{\cdot}5x_a + 10{\cdot}5x_b + 15x_c + 19x_d + 28{\cdot}5x_e + 8x_f,$$

subject to the constraints:

$$10x_a + 8x_b + 4x_c + 8x_d + 2x_e + 4x_f \leqslant 16\ 000,$$
$$4x_a + 8x_b + 10x_c + 4x_d + 4x_e + 2x_f \leqslant 16\ 000,$$
$$2x_a + 2x_b + 8x_c + 4x_d + 10x_e + 4x_f \leqslant 12\ 000,$$
$$x_a \leqslant 800,$$
$$x_b \leqslant 400,$$
$$x_c \leqslant 1000,$$
$$x_d \leqslant 600,$$
$$x_e \leqslant 500,$$
$$x_f \leqslant 1000,$$
$$x_a, x_b, x_c, x_d, x_e, x_f \geqslant 0.$$

The expression to be maximized simply represents the cash surplus that will be earned, before meeting fixed costs if

Table 27 Products available to Cygnus Ltd

Maximum quantity that can be sold	Product	Labour requirements						Other variable costs (£)	Total costs (£)	Selling price (£)	Net contribution (£)
		Skilled		Unskilled		Semi-skilled					
		Hours	Cost (£)	Hours	Cost (£)	Hours	Cost (£)				
800	A	10	10	4	2	2	1.5	27	40.5	67	26.5
400	B	8	8	8	4	2	1.5	9	22.5	33	10.5
1000	C	4	4	10	5	8	6	18	33	48	15
600	D	8	8	4	2	4	3	19	32	51	19
500	E	2	2	4	2	10	7.5	12	23.5	52	28.5
1000	F	4	4	2	1	4	3	19	27	35	8

$x_a, \ldots, x_f$ units of products $A, \ldots, F$ are manufactured and sold.

The first three constraints (restrictions to be observed in maximizing the objective function) deal with the limited supply of the three grades of labour; the left-hand side represents the number of hours required to manufacture $x_a, \ldots, x_f$ units of products $A-F$ and the whole expression stipulates that the hours used must not exceed the supply available. For simplicity, the use of labour is not included as a separate variable as it was in the case of Andromeda, but such a formulation would have led to the same result. The next six constraints require that output should not exceed the number of units which the firm expects to be able to sell at the prices set. The final set of constraints $x_a \geq 0$ and so on formalize the requirement that negative production is impossible.

Table 28 gives a summary of the solution to the problem obtained by applying the simplex method – though technical refinements are omitted. The last three columns keep a running tally of the use made of the limited resources. The other columns will be referred to in the description of the calculations.

We begin the calculations by selecting a provisional plan which is feasible, i.e. which can be carried out within the restrictions set by the supply of resources and other constraints. A safe starting point, with this type of formulation, is a plan to manufacture nothing (provisional plan 1). The first section of Table 28 records this decision and notes that the available resources remain at 16 000, 16 000 and 12 000 hours. Now we seek a change of plan which will improve the earnings – not a difficult task at this stage. We consider introducing product A. The order in which we consider the introduction of products is rule of thumb – in this case we choose the product with the greatest surplus of selling price over variable costs other than labour. Whatever order we select, we shall get to the optimal plan eventually – only the speed of getting there is at issue.

In the section of the Table describing the transition from plan 1 to plan 2, the numbers in brackets $(10, 4, 2)$, referring to

Table 28 Calculations of optimal plan for Cygnus Ltd

	Limits imposed by:				Units of resources (labour)		
	Skilled labour	Unskilled labour	Semi-skilled labour	Demand	Skilled	Unskilled	Semi-skilled
initial supply of resources					16 000	16 000	12 000
provisional plan 1: produce $A, B, C, D, E, F, = 0$ resources used					0	0	0
resources still available					16 000	16 000	12 000
change in plan: increase output of product A (10, 4, 2)	1600	4000	6000	800			
provisional plan 2: produce $A = 800$, $B = C = D = E = F = 0$ extra resources used 800 (10, 4, 2)					8 000	3 200	1 600
resources still available					8 000	12 800	10 400
change in plan: increase output of product E (2, 4, 10)	4000	3200	1040	500			

provisional plan 3:
produce E = 500, A = 800,
B = C = D = F = 0
extra resources used

500 (2, 4, 10)	875	2700	1350	600	1000	2000	5000
resources still available					7000	10800	5400

change in plan: increase output of product D (8, 4, 4)

provisional plan 4:
produce D = 600, A = 800,
E = 500, B = C = F = 0
extra resources used

600 (8, 4, 4)	550	840	375	1000	4800	2400	2400
resources still available					2200	8400	3000

change in plan: increase output of product C (4, 10, 8)

provisional plan 5:
produce C = 375, A = 800,
D = 600, E = 500,
B = F = 0
extra resources used

375 (4, 10, 8)			375		1500	3750	3000

Continued overleaf

Table 28 – continued

	Limits imposed by:				Units of resources (labour)		
	Skilled labour	Unskilled labour	Semi-skilled labour	Demand	Skilled	Unskilled	Semi-skilled
resources still available					700	4 650	0
change in plan: increase output of product B by one unit and reduce output of product C by ¼ unit (7, 5.5, 0) can carry out 375×4 =1500 times before C reduced to zero	100	845.5	∞	400			
provisional plan 6: produce B = 100 units C = 375 − (100 × ¼) = 350 units A = 800, D = 600, E = 500, F = 0 extra resources 100 (7, 5.5, 0)					700	550	0
resources still available					0	4 100	0

product A, are the numbers of units of each resource required to manufacture one unit of the product. The numbers represent skilled labour, unskilled labour and semi-skilled labour in that order. We use these numbers to calculate how many units of product A can be made. If skilled labour represented the only restriction, we could manufacture $16\,000/10 = 1600$ units, i.e. the number of hours available divided by the number required per unit; this number is recorded in column 1. Similarly, we record in columns 2 and 3, the restrictions imposed by the other two resource limitations, $16\,000/4 = 4000$ units and $12\,000/2 = 6000$ units. The fourth column records the limitation imposed by demand considerations, the maximum number that can be sold. Production is effectively limited by the most restrictive of the four factors – in the case of product A, demand. Hence we decide to manufacture 800 units of product A and this gives us our second provisional plan.

We then move to provisional plans 3, 4 and 5 introducing products E, D and C, in a precisely similar manner. Demand sets the limit of output in the case of the first two products and the supply of semi-skilled labour sets the limit in the case of product C.

Provisional plan 5 involves using the entire supply of semi-skilled labour; any further changes in the plan must therefore involve reducing output of some product previously included in order to set some semi-skilled labour free. In seeking an improvement to plan 5, we consider introducing product B, the next in order according to our rule of thumb for introducing products (in the order of the size of contribution without deduction for labour costs). The various ways in which we could do this are described in Table 29. They involve reducing output of A, C, D or E. Consider a reduction in output of product E, for example. Product B requires two hours of semi-skilled labour per unit and product E requires ten hours. Hence enough semi-skilled labour for the manufacture of one unit of B can be set free by giving up $1/5$ units of E. If we manufacture one unit of B we require 1 (8, 8, 2) units of resources and we can earn an extra contribution of £10.5;

Table 29 Substitutions for introducing one unit of product B to provisional plan

	Skilled labour			Unskilled labour			Semi-skilled labour			Contribution (£)		
	+	−	Net	+	−	Net	+	−	Net	+	−	Net
reduce A by 1 unit (10, 4, 2, £26.5)	8	10	−2	8	4	+4	2	2	0	10.5	26.5	−16
reduce C by ¼ units (4, 10, 8, £15)	8	1	+7	8	2·5	+5·5	2	2	0	10.5	3.75	+6.75
reduce D by ½ units (8, 4, 4, £19)	8	4	+4	8	2	+6	2	2	0	10.5	9.5	+1
reduce E by ⅕ units (2, 4, 10, £28.5)	8	0·4	+7·6	8	0·8	+7·2	2	2	0	10.5	5.7	+4.8

against this, if we give up 1/5 units of E, we save 1/5 (2, 4, 10) = (0·4, 0·8, 2) units of resources and we lose £1/5 × 28·5 = £5.7 in contribution.

A study of Table 29 indicates that the most worthwhile substitution (per unit) involves increasing B and reducing C – the net cost in resources being (7, 5·5, 0) each time we carry it out. We still have available (see Table 28) 700 units of skilled labour and 4650 units of unskilled labour – these limit the number of times we carry out the substitution to 700/7 = 100 and 4650/5·5 = 845·5; another limitation is that we cannot sell more than 400 units of B. Each time we make the substitution, we give up $\frac{1}{4}$ units of C; since plan 5 included only 375 units of C, the availability of C limits the substitutions to 375 ÷ $\frac{1}{4}$ = 1500. We can carry out the substitution one hundred times, the limit set by skilled labour, the most restrictive factor; i.e. we increase output of B by one hundred units and reduce output of C by 100 × $\frac{1}{4}$ = 25 units.

This substitution leads to provisional plan 6 – the plan which is found to be optimal. It is summarized in Table 30 which also shows that cash earnings cover fixed costs. In order to demonstrate the optimality of this plan, we could again consider all possible changes in terms of substitutions; we should find that all would lead to decreases in the contributions earned. The calculations have not been given as they are rather tedious in the context of our informal description of linear programming – they are carried out automatically as part of the solution process of the simplex method.

The reader will note that the optimal plan does not involve using the entire supply of all resources in strictly limited supply. The limitation to the supply of unskilled labour is not effective. Such a result is not uncommon when there are several resource limitations. Indeed we should have noted other unused resources had we included constraints relating to the supply of other resources – e.g. materials – which are presumably subject to some limit even though it may be large. In formulating a linear programme, one cannot always be sure which constraints will be critical. The formulation would normally include constraints for any resources for which the

Table 30 Summary of optimal plan for Cygnus Ltd

Product	Amounts per unit			Output		Totals			
	Skilled labour	Unskilled labour	Semi-skilled labour	Output	Contribution (£)	Skilled labour	Unskilled labour	Semi-skilled labour	Contribution (£)
A	10	4	2	800	26.5	8 000	3 200	1 600	21 200
B	8	8	2	100	10.5	800	800	200	1 050
C	4	10	8	350	15	1 400	3 500	2 800	5 250
D	8	4	4	600	19	4 800	2 400	2 400	11 400
E	2	4	10	500	28.5	1 000	2 000	5 000	14 250
F	4	2	4	0	8	0	0	0	0
Gross cash earnings									53 150
Resources used						16 000	11 900	12 000	
Resources unused						0	4 100	0	
Resources available						16 000	16 000	12 000	
Fixed costs									29 000
Net cash earnings									24 150

limitation seemed significant in relation to production possibilities; but it is necessary to check subsequently that enough is available of *all* resources required for the optimal plan and to revise the formulation if this condition is not met.

Opportunity costs in linear programming

The optimality of our solution to the problem of Cygnus may be demonstrated without explicitly examining all possible substitutions, and in a way that leads on to a discussion of one important interpretation of the results of linear programming calculations. It involves the identification of the opportunity costs of the scarce resources.

Let us calculate opportunity costs from the fundamental definition given above (page 69), the definition which regards the opportunity cost of a resource as the amount by which the value of the optimal plan can be increased if the supply of the resource is increased by one unit, without deduction for the cost of the resource, all other things being unchanged. First suppose that we had one extra hour of skilled labour available. Refer again to Table 28. With one extra hour of skilled labour, we could have carried out the last change (substituting B for C) $701/7 = 100\frac{1}{7}$ times, i.e. $\frac{1}{7}$ times more than previously. Since each substitution earns £6.75 (see Table 29), we could have increased contributions by £6.75/7 = £0.96; we add the wage rate of £1, since this has been deducted in calculating contributions, and find the total opportunity cost of skilled labour to be £1.96 per hour.

Secondly, consider semi-skilled labour; suppose we had 12 001 hours available. In introducing product C, moving from plan 4 to plan 5, we should have been able to produce $3001/8 = 375\frac{1}{8}$ units of C, $\frac{1}{8}$ units more than before, increasing contributions by £$\frac{1}{8} \times 15$ = £1.88. Product C requires four hours of skilled labour, however, and so we should have had $\frac{1}{8} \times 4 = \frac{1}{2}$ hours less, i.e. $699\frac{1}{2}$ hours of skilled labour available for the last substitution. We could have carried out the last substitution only $699\frac{1}{2}/7$ times, i.e. $99\frac{13}{14}$ times, $\frac{1}{14}$ less than previously, thereby losing £$\frac{1}{14} \times 6.75$ = £0.48. The net gain from one extra hour of semi-skilled labour is thus £1.88 less

£0.48 = £1.40 and, adding the wage rate of £0.75, we find the total opportunity cost to be £2.15. It is noteworthy that the opportunity cost of semi-skilled labour exceeds that of skilled labour. Cygnus would earn a larger surplus if some of the skilled employees could be persuaded to do the work of the semi-skilled, even without a cut in their wage rate. We assume this to be impracticable however. It might lead to demands by the semi-skilled to be paid the same wage as the skilled and the granting of such demands for the whole workforce would more than eliminate any gain from the arrangement.

The opportunity cost of unskilled labour does not exceed the wage cost. The optimal solution derived in Table 28 does not use all the unskilled labour available; and an increase in the supply would therefore not enable an increase in earnings.

In Table 31 we review the product data for the problem, valuing resources at their opportunity cost or external costs, whichever is higher. The rule noted above still holds – those products of which we wish to make as much as we can sell have a surplus, other products included in the plan just break even and products excluded have deficits. The fact that the rule holds for the production plan derived in Table 28, demonstrates the optimality of that plan. The opportunity cost values for resources may actually be obtained as a by-product of the simplex calculations. In linear programming terminology they are known as dual prices – or shadow prices. We must be careful, in interpreting dual price data, to deal consistently with the external cost of the resource. A dual price is the increase in the value of the objective function of a linear programme made possible by a unit relaxation in one of the constraints. The cost of the resource will be deducted in the objective function either explicitly, as in the formulation used for Andromeda, or by deduction in calculating the contribution for each product, as in the formulation for Cygnus. In both cases, we must add the cost of the resource to the dual price to obtain the full opportunity cost as defined here.

Table 31 Opportunity cost data for Cygnus Ltd

Product	Labour requirements						Other variable costs (£)	Total costs (£)	Selling price (£)	Surplus/deficit (£)
	Skilled		Unskilled		Semi-skilled					
	Hours	Cost (£) at £1.96	Hours	Cost (£) at £0.50	Hours	Cost (£) at £2.14				
A	10	19.60	4	2.00	2	4.28	27	52.88	67	+14.1
B	8	15.68	8	4.00	2	4.28	9	32.96	33	0
C	4	7.84	10	5.00	8	17.12	18	47.96	48	0
D	8	15.68	4	2.00	4	8.56	19	45.24	51	+5.8
E	2	3.92	4	2.00	10	21.40	12	39.32	52	+12.7
F	4	7.84	2	1.00	4	8.56	19	36.40	35	-1.4

The usefulness of dual prices

Let us now consider the practical usefulness of opportunity cost, or dual price, data. It may at least be said that opportunity cost analysis gives us additional insight into decision problems. If we have effectively 'scarce' resources, we should husband their use by attributing a high price to them in costing any activity in which they would be used.

The practical use of opportunity cost is not immediately clear however. If we could estimate it, in some simple way, we could use the information to obtain an approximate indication of the best plan by evaluating each product, costing resources at opportunity costs, in an analysis such as that given in Table 31. However we cannot know opportunity costs unless we firstly calculate the optimal plan (or at least we calculate the opportunity costs and the optimal plan concurrently) and once we know the optimal plan it might seem that opportunity costs are redundant.

Dual prices and sensitivity analysis

However, this would be too hasty a conclusion. One use of dual prices is in sensitivity analysis, a study of the effect on the optimal plan of changes in assumptions in the specification of the problem, designed to evaluate the implications of uncertainty in those assumptions. The conditions assumed in formulating a linear programming problem are rarely entirely fixed and beyond the control of the firm. The quantities of products which can be sold at various prices are subject to uncertainty; moreover, it may be possible, by special effort, to increase the supply of some resources beyond the assumed limit.

Dual prices represent estimates of the effect of small changes in conditions assumed in the formulation of a problem. We have already seen, for example, that dual prices indicate by how much the net cash surplus earned by a firm may be increased if the supply of a resource is increased by one unit. The firm would therefore be well advised to put a good deal of effort into increasing the supply of resources which have the highest dual prices. The dual prices plus the assumed external cost, indeed indicate the maximum price a firm could afford to pay to increase the supply of a resource. In the case of Cygnus, for example, it would be worthwhile to have semi-skilled workers work overtime at any wage rate up to £2.14 per hour – up to this level there would be some net gain – provided the skilled workers did not object!

Dual prices also provide a basis for estimating how much the cash surplus of a firm could be increased if the sales potential of a product could be increased. The cash gain is measured by the surplus attributed to a product after costing resources at opportunity costs, e.g. the figures given by the final column of Table 31. This amount is equal to a dual price associated with the constraints specifying the limit to the potential sales of each product. Cygnus Ltd could earn an extra £14.1 if one more unit of product A could be sold, but the supply of resources remained constant. This represents the gain from the sale of A less the contribution lost by reducing output of other products in order to keep within the resource constraints. A firm might decide to put particular effort into selling products which have large surpluses calculated with respect to dual price data.

A given set of dual prices may hold valid only for small changes from the optimal plan. Consider again the example of Cygnus Ltd. If one extra hour of skilled labour were available, we could have used it to manufacture more of product B (giving up some of product C to get the mix of resource usage right) and contributions would have increased by £0.96, the dual price of skilled labour less the extra £1 of wage cost. If supply increased by 2100 hours, however, and it was applied in the manufacture of B as optimality dictates, the firm would be making as much of B as it could sell. The last substitution in Table 28 could have been carried out 2100/7 more times, involving increasing output of B by 300 units and bringing output up to 400 units, the maximum that can be sold. Any further increase in supply would have to be applied to the manufacture of other products and the increase per hour in net cash earnings would be different. There is no general rule for estimating the range of validity of a dual price – it depends on the conditions of each case.

It is likely, given the restricted validity of dual prices, that a firm will not wish to rely entirely on the approach described for sensitivity analysis. It may wish to formulate its decision problem on the basis of various assumptions concerning the production opportunities and resource supplies available, and study the implications of the variations for the optimal plan by making fresh calculations from scratch. It may wish, particularly, to estimate the effects of various pricing policies in the context of various formulations of a problem. It may thereby discover that some features of the optimal production plan have a high degree of certainty, i.e. are constant over a wide range of different assumptions – and in what respects the uncertainties are critical. We shall discuss decisions under uncertainty further in chapter 13.

Estimated dual prices

In studying linear programming methods of product selection, we have assumed that a firm will be able to make adequate estimates of the products or other activities available, during the period for which plans are being made. In some situations this may be unrealistic. New products may become available at frequent intervals with sparse advance information concerning their characteristics. A firm in this position would like to develop a sort of league table, ranking products by 'profitability' so that it can seek to replace products near the foot of the table with others which are more worthwhile when they become available.

In such a case, it may be helpful to select activities by costing resources at estimated dual prices using the technique of calculation illustrated in Table 31. Dual prices may be estimated from data for the previous period or from a solution to a linear programme using fictitious data, representing managers' estimates of the main characteristics of activities available. Each activity would be appraised when sufficient details become known. At any time, resources would be devoted to the best available activities, as indicated by dual price data, and new activities would replace old ones if they seemed likely to yield a higher surplus. A running comparison would be kept of actual activities appraised and the activities on which dual price estimates were based to ensure consistency. Dual price estimates would be revised when the comparison of actual and assumed data showed material differences.

Dual prices have various other uses – notably in setting transfer prices in a system of divisional control. A discussion of such uses, however, is beyond the scope of this book.

12 Optimal Use of Scarce Resources (2)

We began our discussion of linear programming methods by considering the solution to a product selection problem, arising in a situation which was reduced by a number of simplifying assumptions. Particularly significant were the assumptions (a) that product units and resource units were perfectly divisible and (b) that the relationship between sales volume, sales revenue and total costs had a linear form. These assumptions helped us to identify the main characteristics of linear programming, but they are not universally valid in actual business situations. We now consider how the technique must be modified to obtain useful results when the assumptions are inapplicable. We consider the assumptions in turn.

The assumption of divisibility

The optimal solution to a linear programme gives, implicitly or explicitly, instructions concerning what resources a firm should acquire and what activities it should carry out. One of the ways in which we may judge the usefulness of a linear programming model is by asking whether all instructions which might emerge from the solution could be implemented precisely. There are two reasons why a model founded on the assumption of divisibility may fail to satisfy this criterion.

First, it may be impossible to purchase the quantity of a resource required by the optimal solution on the terms assumed. In the case of Cygnus Ltd, considered in chapter 11, the solution called for the use of 11 900 hours of unskilled labour on the assumption that it would cost 119/120 times the cost of 12 000 hours. Suppose the firm has a standard working year of 2000 hours and suppose that policy is to offer employment on contracts for a whole year (or that people will only accept employment on this basis); the practice of 'hiring and firing' is ruled out. The purchase of 11 900 hours of unskilled labour at the price assumed would then be ruled out. It would be necessary to purchase, say, 10 000 hours or 12 000 hours. An intermediate number of hours could be used but the cost would not vary in proportion to usage; the cost of using 11 900 hours would be the same as the cost of using 12 000 hours.

However it may sometimes be possible to hire labour by the hour – the chances of hourly hiring are better with labour than some other resources. For example, it is rarely possible to hire machine services for short periods, at least without incurring a relatively high rate of cost. The normal position is that whole machines may be purchased or leased for a minimum standard period at a given rate and used for whatever length of time is dictated by the firm's working year and other factors. It is not possible to buy half a machine for half the cost and hence some unused machine capacity is a normal part of business situations. If a machine is not fully used there may be some cost saving because its life is prolonged and it may be possible to buy machines with different capacities or to hire a machine by the hour. In all these cases, however, the average cost per hour would vary; it would not be constant as assumed in the simplest form of linear programming model.

Secondly, the solution to a linear programme may call for the completion of a fraction of an activity. The fact that Cygnus Ltd was advised to manufacture whole numbers of units of each product arose from the design of the problem – such a result would not be guaranteed generally. We should not worry unduly if a programme called for the manufacture of a fraction of a unit of a product of small value; we might neglect the fraction as immaterial or we might regard it as planned work in progress, to be completed during the following period. It would be otherwise if a major contract was involved. It would not be valid to assume that half a contract could be fulfilled at half the cost of the whole contract and to yield half the revenue. Nor should we assume that the best plan for the following period would necessarily involve completion of the contract even if this were feasible.

Suppose a contract would yield receipts of £1200 and involve costs of £1100, and a linear programme gives the result that it would be optimal to accept one-half of the contract in the current period; but completion of the project would involve displacing a contract yielding a net £300 in the following period. If the contract is half completed in the first period, it would be best to complete it in the following period because if this were not done the total receipts of £1200 would be lost (presumably and ignoring any penalties for non-completion) and the costs saved would be only £550; completion would add £650 to net income against the alternative of £300. However, a better decision would have been to reject the first contract and accept the second, earning £300 overall rather than £100. If the contract in the second period had a surplus of £30 instead of £300, however, acceptance of the first contract would have been optimal. This suggests that the significance of losses associated with the false assumption of divisibility may be reduced by extending the planning horizon. Nevertheless, in view of the difficulty in looking far ahead and since there might be several projects marked for fractional acceptance, involving significant values, a firm may prefer instead to restrict itself to the best 'whole number' solution.

Integer programming

The difficulty of indivisibilities is not solved in a satisfactory manner by calculating the optimal plan involving fractions and rounding to the nearest whole numbers. There may be much greater difference than provided in rounding off between the ingredients of an optimal plan with fractions and those of an optimal plan restricted to whole numbers. Consider a simple analogy. Suppose we are given a wooden crate and a large number of blocks of different materials and of various shapes and sizes. We are told to pack blocks into the crate so as to pack the maximum possible weight, but we must be able to close the rigid lid at the end. If we are able to cut the blocks without restriction, we shall start with the heaviest block (per unit of volume) and add blocks in the order of heaviness, dividing them where necessary, until we run out of space. However, if we are unable to divide the blocks (accept fractional activities) any combination of blocks may fail to take up the space (use the resources) available exactly. We may then achieve our objective most effectively by discarding some of the heaviest blocks (most profitable projects) in favour of others that fit in better. The larger the blocks and the more eccentric their shapes, the more likely it is that there will be substantial differences in ingredients between the optimal solutions with and without divisibility.

A method is available for dealing with problems of indivisibility in linear programming. It is known as integer programming. In order to use integer programming, it is necessary to formulate the problem in a model which includes the purchase of resources as explicit variables, expressed in units in which acquisitions may actually take place and which allows the quantity of resources used to differ from the quantity purchased (so that spare capacity may be part of the optimal plan).

Suppose, for example, that a firm has five contracts available for acceptance during a period, with expected cash surpluses of £7000, £6500, £6000, £5500 and £5000, before deducting the cost of labour or machine time. Each contract must be completed during the period or rejected. The requirements of labour, for each contract in hours, are 2500, 2200, 1800, 1600 and 1500 and the requirements of machine time in hours, are 2200, 2400, 2700, 2800 and 3100. Each man and each machine can work up to 2000 hours during the period. Each man earns a salary of £1800 during the period and each machine is hired at a cost of £1500 per period; and both men and machines must be hired for the whole period or not at all. There are only four men and five machines available for hiring.

A formulation of the problem, for solution by integer programming methods, might run as follows:

We wish to maximize
$$7000x_1 + 6500x_2 + 6000x_3 + 5500x_4 + 5000x_5 - 1800L - 1500M,$$
subject to the constraints:

$$2500x_1 + 2200x_2 + 1800x_3 + 1600x_4 + 1500x_5 - 2000L \leqslant 0$$
$$2200x_1 + 2400x_2 + 2700x_3 + 2800x_4 + 3100x_5 - 2000M \leqslant 0$$
$$x_1 \leqslant 1$$
$$x_2 \leqslant 1$$
$$x_3 \leqslant 1$$
$$x_4 \leqslant 1$$
$$x_5 \leqslant 1$$
$$L \leqslant 4$$
$$M \leqslant 5.$$
$$x_1, x_2, x_3, x_4, x_5, L, M \geqslant 0 \text{ and an integer}$$

where $x_1, \ldots, x_5$ represent the acceptance or rejection of contracts $1, \ldots, 5$, L represents the number of men employed, and M represents the number of machines hired.

The constraints require that $x_1, \ldots, x_5$ should be (a) greater than or equal to zero, (b) equal to or less than one and (c) integer; hence each can have only the value one, representing acceptance of the contract, or zero, representing rejection. When the values zero or one are given to the variables $x_1, \ldots, x_5$, the objective function represents the surplus earned on contracts accepted less the cost of men employed ($1800L$) and machines hired ($1500M$). The first two constraints require that labour hours used should not exceed labour hours available from the men employed ($2000L$) and that machine hours used should not exceed machine hours available from machines hired. Other constraints require the number of men employed to be a whole number in the range 1 to 4 inclusive or zero, and the number of machines hired to be a whole number in the range 1–5 inclusive or zero.

The optimal solution will be the set of whole number values for the variables which satisfies the constraints and gives the largest value to the objective function.

Integer programming methods are quite complex and their detailed description is beyond the scope of this book. The integer restriction is achieved by introducing extra constraints which rule out the feasibility of fractional solutions. Since every constraint which is operative has an associated dual price, integer programming methods give dual prices to the integer constraints as well as to the more usual constraints. Moreover, the giving of dual prices to the integer constraints alters the values of the other dual prices, and consequently the dual prices of integer programming are not readily interpretable as opportunity costs as are the dual prices of linear programming. The methods of integer programming are well developed theoretically and can be guaranteed to lead to a determinate solution. However they are not economical of computing time and they are much more likely to be too expensive for use on practical problems than are ordinary linear programming methods. In such cases, it may be necessary to fall back on linear programming as providing the best feasible appropriate solution.

Non-linear relationships

The other main simplifying assumption with which we prefaced our discussion of linear programming was that all relevant relationships between variables could be represented aptly in linear terms, i.e. we required a linear relationship between the output levels of each activity on the one hand and each of total receipts, total usage of resources and total costs on the other. As its name implies, linear programming is designed to yield solutions only for problems in this form.

No general methods are yet available for obtaining strictly optimal plans when relationships in the decision model may take any mathematical form. However, special methods of analysis are available for some particular types of problem. Perhaps the simplest of these deals with the model in which the relationship between total sales receipts and output volume is non-linear and output is subject to one resource constraint of linear form. Ability to solve problems in this form may have significant value because it enables selling price to be included in the model as a variable.

An example with one resource constraint

We will illustrate the main principles of the method with an example. Coggia Ltd manufactures and sells two products, S and T. For some short period, the sales price–volume relationships are estimated as $q_s = 260 - 20p_s$ (thus $p_s = 13 - q_s/20$) and $q_t = 190 - 10p_t$ (thus $p_t = 19 - q_t/10$). Total costs are estimated from the model $T = 50 + 10q_s + 15q_t$, i.e. product S has a constant marginal cost of £10 per unit and product T a constant marginal cost of £15 per unit. Products S and T require two and four hours of labour per product unit (the cost of which is included in marginal cost estimates) and Coggia can hire only 104 labour hours during the period, at most.

We found in chapter 9 (expression **9**) that where the sales price–volume relationship has the form $q = a - bp$, marginal revenue is equal to $(a - 2q)/b$.

We may use this expression to find the unconstrained optimal output for Coggia, substituting appropriate values for a and b and equating marginal cost and marginal revenue; optimal output levels are q_s and q_t in expressions **1** and **2**:

$$\frac{60 - 2q_s}{20} = 10 \quad \text{thus} \quad q_s = 30; \tag{1}$$

and $$\frac{190 - 2q_t}{10} = 15 \quad \text{thus} \quad q_t = 20. \tag{2}$$

However, the manufacture of thirty units of S and twenty units of T would require 140 hours of labour – $(30 \times 2) + (20 \times 4)$ – and is not feasible.

The decision problem of Coggia may be expressed in the model:

Maximize: total revenue less total costs

$= p_s q_s + p_t q_t - T$

$= 13q_s - \dfrac{q_s^2}{20} + 19q_t - \dfrac{q_t^2}{10} - 50 - 10q_s - 15q_t,$

subject to the constraints:

$2q_s + 4q_t \leqslant 104,$
and $q_s, q_t \leqslant 0.$

We derived, in chapter 11, the optimal decision rule for the situation in which there was one resource constraint and each product earned a constant contribution to cash earnings, independent of the output level (i.e. selling price and marginal cost were assumed to be fixed). The optimal decision involved accepting products in the order of the ranking given by the contribution per unit of the resource in limited supply. We established the optimality of this rule by showing that having used it to allocate the limited resource we could not find any substitution which would improve cash earnings. The problem of Coggia calls for a similar method. Again we have one resource in limited supply on which we want to maximize cash earnings; and again, by the same process of logic, it can be seen that optimality requires allocation of the resource to products in the order of the magnitude of their contribution per unit of the resource. The special feature of the case of Coggia is that we assume the need to reduce price to sell increased quantities of each product and so the contribution to cash earnings per unit of labour – the limited resource – is not a fixed quantity for each product.

The calculations of contributions for determining the optimal decision are set out in Table 32. The calculations may be explained with reference to the second row under the heading product S. This deals with the manufacture of the second unit of S. The price at which two units can be sold is £12.90 (column 2) giving total revenue of £25.80 ($2 \times$ £12.90, column 3). The marginal (variable) cost for two units of S is £20, hence there is a contribution of £5.80 from the sale of two units (£25.80 − £20, column 4). The second unit increases total contributions by £2.85 (£5.80 for two units less £2.95 for one unit, column 5) and since each product unit requires two labour hours, the second unit yields £2.85/2 = £1.425 per labour hour (column 6). Table 32 gives calculations only for selected output levels which are useful for purposes of illustration.

Now consider the process of allocation of the limited supply of labour. We allocate each successive labour hour to its most profitable use. The first hour may be allocated to product S or T: it would earn £1.475 on S against £0.975 on T in use

Table 32 Contributions per labour hour for Coggia Ltd

Product S

Quantity q	Price (£) $p = 13 - \frac{q}{20}$	Total revenue (£) pq	Total contributions (£) pq − 10q	Contribution (£) from qth unit	Marginal contribution per labour hour (£)
1	12.95	12.95	2.95	2.95	1.475
2	12.90	25.80	5.80	2.85	1.425
.					
.					
10	12.50	125.00	25.00	2.05	1.025
11	12.45	136.95	26.95	1.95	0.975
12	12.40	148.80	28.80	1.85	0.925
.					
.					
20	12.00	240.00	40.00	1.05	0.525
21	11.95	250.95	40.95	0.95	0.475
22	11.90	261.80	41.80	0.85	0.425
23	11.85	272.55	42.55	0.75	0.375
24	11.80	283.20	43.20	0.65	0.325
25	11.75	293.75	43.75	0.55	0.275

Product T

Quantity q	Price (£) $p = 19 - \frac{q}{10}$	Total revenue (£) pq	Total contributions (£) pq − 15q	Contribution (£) from qth unit	Marginal contribution per labour hour (£)
1	18.90	18.90	3.90	3.90	0.975
2	18.80	37.60	7.60	3.70	0.925
.					
.					
10	18.00	180.00	30.00	2.10	0.525
11	17.90	196.90	31.90	1.90	0.475
12	17.80	213.60	33.60	1.70	0.425
13	17.70	230.10	35.10	1.50	0.375
14	17.60	246.40	36.40	1.30	0.325
15	17.50	262.50	37.50	1.10	0.275

on the first unit of each product; we therefore allocate it to S, the more profitable use. The second labour hour follows the first since two hours are required for the first product unit. Indeed we allocate enough labour hours to S for the manufacture of ten units before the contribution per hour falls to the level of that on the first unit of T. We then allocate labour hours to each product in turn (two hours to S and four to T); the eleventh unit of S yields the same as the first unit of T; the twelfth unit of S yields the same as the second of T; and so on. This process is continued until we run out of labour, i.e. until we have decided to manufacture twenty-four units of S and fourteen units of T (use of labour $24 \times 2 + 14 \times 4 = 104$ hours). At this point, the marginal contribution per labour hour is equal for each product at £0.325 per hour. The optimal plan for Coggia would yield a net cash flow of £29.60 (total contributions from S and T, £43.20 + £36.40 less fixed costs £50). The optimality of the plan can be shown formally by the substitution test. If we were to shift one labour hour from the use proposed to use on the other product, cash earnings would fall (by £0.327 less £0.275, assuming divisibility).

It can be shown, by differential calculus, that the rule which emerged from the analysis of Coggia's decision holds valid generally. The optimal allocation of one limited resource implies equality between the marginal contributions per unit of the resource arising on every use (every product or whatever). Hence a firm may test the optimality of its resource allocation by estimating the marginal contribution per resource unit for each product. If (say) product Q has a higher marginal contribution per unit of resource than product R, net cash earnings would be increased by making more of Q and less of R.

The methods used to discover the optimal solution for Coggia cannot be generalized to obtain an optimal solution for a decision problem in which there is more than one resource constraint – nor are modified versions of linear programming able to deal with all mathematical forms which may arise. This is a severe restriction on the practical usefulness of programming. There may be many practical situations in which non-linear cost–volume relationships are met (in conjunction with resource rationing) and many more in which it is desired to consider various prices for different products and hence to consider non-linear receipts–volume relationships.

Such difficulties are not altogether intractable, however. Some progress may be made by approximating non-linear relationships by linear ones and then applying standard linear programming techniques. This method will now be illustrated.

Linear approximations of non-linear relationships

Donati Ltd estimates the price–volume relationship for one of its products – A – to be

$$p_a = 120 - \frac{q_a}{240}, \qquad\qquad 3$$

thus total receipts $R_a = p_a q_a = 120 q_a - \frac{q_a^2}{240}. \qquad\qquad 4$

This relationship is represented by the curve shown in the graph of Figure 17. A linear relationship always appears as a straight line on a graph; the receipts–volume relationship for Donati's product is non-linear. However, we may derive linear expressions which approximate the non-linear one. The three straight lines given in Figure 17 represent linear expressions; and if we estimate total receipts for any volume of output, from the straight lines, we derive an approximation to the estimate of receipts given by the curve. The approximation may be improved by increasing the number of straight lines used in the process. Such an increase would also increase the burden of calculations, however, and we shall restrict ourselves to three for purposes of illustration.

Let us consider the derivation of an approximate linear expression for the original receipts–volume relationship. The first step is to establish the range of output values in which we are interested. Suppose the marginal cost of the product is a constant – £40. Marginal revenue is $120 - 2q/240$ (using expression **9** in chapter 9): optimal output, if the supply of resources

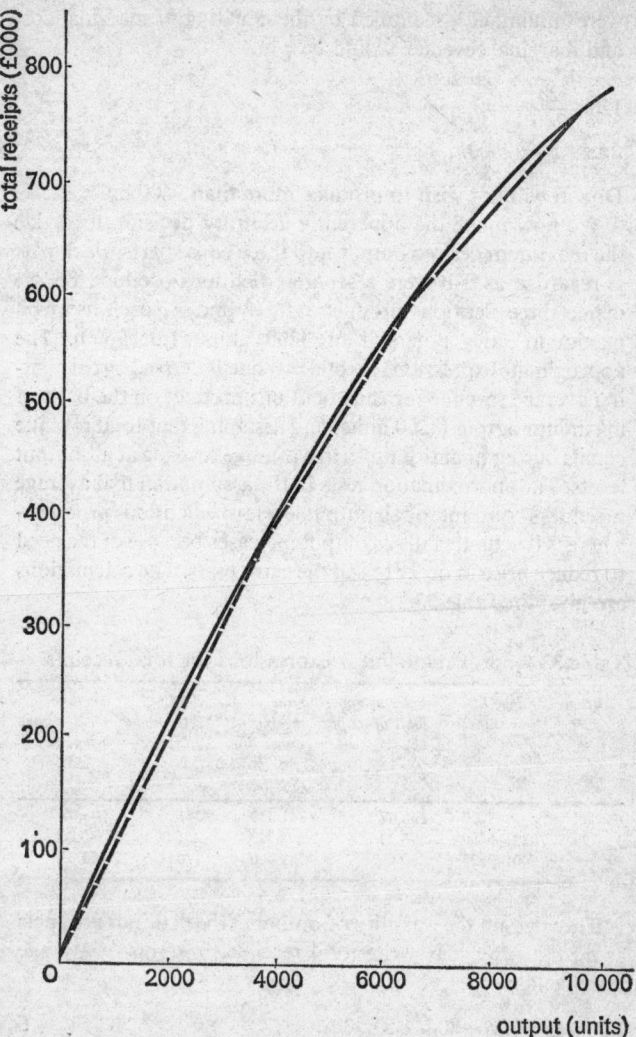

Figure 17 Linear approximation to non-linear curve

were 'unlimited', identified by the equating of marginal cost and marginal revenue, would be q in

$$120 - \frac{2q}{240} = 40,$$

thus $q = 9600$.

Donati will not wish to produce more than 9600 units.

We now make the apparently arbitrary decision to divide the maximum desired output into three equal parts. Each part is regarded as if it were a separate fictitious product, i.e. we define three fictitious products, A_1, A_2 and A_3, each having a maximum sales potential of 3200 units ($1/3 \times 9600$). The approximate expression for total revenue is derived by calculating average revenue for each fictitious product on the basis of maximum output (3200 units) and assuming that total revenue equals output quantity times this average revenue at all output levels. The approximation rests in the assumption that average revenue is constant for all output levels of a fictitious product – whereas it actually falls as output increases because of the need to reduce price in order to sell the extra units. The calculations are given in Table 33.[1]

Table 33 Approximate linear expressions for total receipts

Fictitious product	Range of quantities	Price at upper limit of output (£) $p = 120 - \frac{q}{240}$	Total receipts at upper limit of output (£) $R = pq$	Receipts attributable to range (£) R	Average receipts for range (£) $R/3200$
1	0–3200	106.67	341 333	341 333	106.67
2	3201–6400	93.33	597 333	256 000	80.00
3	6401–9600	80	768 000	170 667	53.33

If we denote the quantity of output of the fictitious products as a_1, a_2, a_3 we may write total receipts, in terms of average revenue, as:

$$R_a = 106.67a_1 + 80a_2 + 53.33a_3. \qquad 5$$

1. For simplicity, we ignore the fractional elements in the actual linear programming computations.

We may use our linear approximations to estimate total receipts for some level of output of the actual product by expressing the output in terms of the fictitious products, e.g. for output of 4500 units we assign product A_1 output of 3200 units, the maximum in the first range (a_1), and product A_2, output of 1300 units (a_2). Our linear estimate will equal the value given by the assumed non-linear relationship at quantities corresponding to the maximum outputs of fictitious products (e.g. 6400 units) – points at which the curves and the linear segments meet in Figure 17. The divergence will be greatest halfway between these points (in our example). These assertions are illustrated in Table 34 by calculation of the value of receipts given by the non-linear expression (using expression 4) and by the linear approximation (expression 5) for output of 6400 units, the upper limit for the second fictitious product, and for output of 4800 units, the mid-point of the output range covered by that product.

Table 34 Linear approximations to non-linear receipts

Output	Receipts	
	Linear estimate (£)	Non-linear value (£)
4800	$(106.67 \times 3200) + (80 \times 1600)$	$(120 \times 4800) - \dfrac{1}{240}(4800^2)$
	$= 469\,330$	$= 480\,000$
6400	$(106.67 \times 3200) + (80 \times 3200)$	$(120 \times 6400) - \dfrac{1}{240}(6400^2)$
	$= 597\,330$	$= 597\,330$

We may now consider further the case of Donati Ltd. Suppose the firm has two other products available for manufacture, with the following price and cost data:

Product B: $p_b = 80 - \dfrac{q_b}{200}$; marginal cost £20, 6

Product C: $p_c = 90 - \dfrac{q_c}{160}$; marginal cost £30. 7

The maximum desired output for each product may be calculated as before:

Product B: $80 - \dfrac{q_b}{100} = 20$; $q_b = 6000$,

Product C: $90 - \dfrac{q_c}{80} = 30$; $q_c = 4800$.

Linear expressions approximating total receipts are calculated in Table 35 to be:

Product B: $R_b = 70b_1 + 50b_2 + 30b_3$,   **8**

Product C: $R_c = 80c_1 + 60c_2 + 40c_3$.   **9**

Table 35 Calculation of average receipts

Fictitious product	Range of quantities	Price at upper limit of output (£)	Total receipts at upper limit of output (£)	Receipts attributable to given range (£)	Average receipts for given range (£)
product B:		$p_b = 80 - \dfrac{q_b}{200}$	$R = p_b q_b$	R'_b	$R'_b/2000$
1	0–2000	70	140 000	140 000	70
2	2001–4000	60	240 000	100 000	50
	4001–6000	50	300 000	60 000	30
product C:		$p_c = 90 - \dfrac{q_c}{160}$	$R = p_c q_c$	R'_c	$R'_c/1600$
1	0–1600	80	128 000	128 000	80
2	1601–3200	70	224 000	96 000	60
3	3201–4800	60	288 000	64 000	40

Donati Ltd has two scarce resources, labour grade A (maximum supply 100 000 hours) and labour grade B (maximum supply 80 000 hours). Labour requirements of the three products, per unit (grade A; grade B) are: product A (10; 4); product B (8; 8); and product C (4; 10). The best estimate of receipts less costs for Donati is given by the following expression (excluding fixed costs):

$$
\begin{aligned}
C &= R_a - 40q_a + R_b - 20q_b + R_c - 30q_c \\
&= p_a q_a - 40q_a + p_b q_b - 20q_b + p_c q_c - 30q_c \\
&= \left(120 - \frac{q_a}{240}\right)q_a - 40q_a + \left(80 - \frac{q_b}{200}\right)q_b - 20q_b \\
&\quad + \left(90 - \frac{q_c}{160}\right)q_c - 30q_c \\
&= 80q_a - \frac{q_a^2}{240} + 60q_b - \frac{q_b^2}{200} + 60q_c - \frac{q_c^2}{160}.
\end{aligned}
$$

10

This expression is derived by substituting for p_a, p_b, p_c, expressions **3**, **6** and **7** and including costs, as estimated above, of £40 per unit, £20 per unit and £30 per unit.

The model that we shall use, incorporating the linear approximation of total receipts (expressions **5**, **8** and **9**) and setting costs for each fictitious product equal to the estimates given above runs as follows:

Maximize $\quad 106a_1 + 80a_2 + 53a_3 - 40(a_1 + a_2 + a_3) + 70b_1 + 50b_2$
$+ 30b_3 - 20(b_1 + b_2 + b_3) + 80c_1 + 60c_2 + 40c_3 - 30(c_1 + c_2 + c_3)$
$= 66a_1 + 40a_2 + 13a_3 + 50b_1 + 30b_2 + 10b_3 + 50c_1 + 30c_2 + 10c_3,$

subject to the restrictions:

$10a_1 + 10a_2 + 10a_3 + 8b_1 + 8b_2 + 8b_3 + 4c_1 + 4c_2 + 4c_3 \leqslant 100\,000$
$4a_1 + 4a_2 + 4a_3 + 8b_1 + 8b_2 + 8b_3 + 10c_1 + 10c_2 + 10c_3 \leqslant 80\,000$
$a_1 \leqslant 3200$
$a_2 \leqslant 3200$
$a_3 \leqslant 3200$
$b_1 \leqslant 2000$
$b_2 \leqslant 2000$
$b_3 \leqslant 2000$
$c_1 \leqslant 1600$
$c_2 \leqslant 1600$
$c_3 \leqslant 1600$
$a_1, a_2, a_3, b_1, b_2, b_3, c_1, c_2, c_3 \geqslant 0.$

Any results from this model will make sense only if each fictitious product is taken in order, i.e. a_1 must have the value 3200 before any positive number is assigned to a_2 and so on. However we need take no special steps to ensure that this happens. Fictitious products representing low output volumes have larger contributions than those representing high output volumes (e.g. A_1 has a higher contribution than A_2), for the same requirements of resources – they are more 'profitable' and will automatically be given priority in an optimal solution. Fictitious products representing low output volumes will not always have the largest contributions, however, e.g. unit costs may fall over some range of output. In such cases, it may be

Table 36 Calculation of optimal plan

	Limits imposed by			Units of resources – labour	
	Grade A labour	Grade B labour	Demand	Grade A	Grade B
initial supply of resources				100 000	80 000
provisional plan 1: produce $a_1 = a_2 = a_3 = b_1 = b_2 = b_3 = c_1 = c_2 = c_3 = 0$.					
resources used				0	0
resources still available				100 000	80 000
change in plan: increase output of product A_1 (10, 4)	10 000	20 000	3200		
provisional plan 2: produce $a_1 = 3200$, $a_2 = a_3 = b_1 = b_2 = b_3 = c_1 = c_2 = c_3 = 0$					
resources used; 3200 (10, 4)				32 000	12 800
resources still available				68 000	67 200
change in plan: increase output of product B_1 (8, 8)	8500	8400	2000		
provisional plan 3: produce $b_1 = 2000$, $a_1 = 3200$, $a_2 = a_3 = b_2 = b_3 = c_1 = c_2 = c_3 = 0$					
resources used; 2000 (8, 8)				16 000	16 000
resources still available				52 000	51 200
change in plan: increase output of product C_1 (4, 10)	13 000	5120	1600		
provisional plan 4: produce $c_1 = 1600$, $a_1 = 3200$, $b_1 = 2000$, $a_2 = a_3 = b_3 = b_2 = c_2 = c_3 = 0$.					

				8400	16 000
resources still available					
change in plan: increase output of product A_2 (10, 4)	4560	8800	3200	45 600	35 200
provisional plan 5: produce $a_2 = 3200$, $a_1 = 3200$, $b_1 = 2000$, $c_1 = 1600$, $a_3 = b_2 = b_3 = c_2 = c_3 = 0$					
resources used; 3200 (10, 4)				32 000	12 800
resources still available				13 600	22 400
change in plan: increase output of product B_2 (8, 8)	1700	2800	2000	13 600	22 400
provisional plan 6: produce $b_2 = 1700$, $a_1 = 3200$, $a_2 = 3200$, $b_1 = 2000$, $c_1 = 1600$, $a_3 = b_3 = c_2 = c_3 = 0$					
resources used; 1700 (8, 8)				13 600	13 600
resources still available				13 600	13 600
change in plan: increase output of product C_2 by 1 unit and reduce output of product b_2 by $\frac{1}{2}$ units (0, 6) (see Table 37) can carry out $1700 \times 2 = 3400$ times before b_2 reduced to zero	∞	$1466\tfrac{2}{3}$	1600	0	8800
provisional plan 7: produce $c_2 = 1466\tfrac{2}{3}$ units, $b_2 = 1700 - \tfrac{1}{2}(1466\tfrac{2}{3}) = 966\tfrac{2}{3}$, $a_1 = 3200$, $a_2 = 3200$, $b_1 = 2000$, $c_1 = 1600$, $a_3 = b_3 = c_3 = 0$					
resources used; $1466\tfrac{2}{3}$ (0, 6)				0	8800
resources still available				0	0

necessary to introduce special constraints to secure the desired result.

We shall not describe in detail the steps in the calculation of the optimal solution. The calculations are summarized in Tables 36 to 38 and they follow exactly the principles described in chapter 11. The optimal solution calls for the manufacture of some units of each product. This is a likely result of the type

Table 37 Substitutions for introducing one unit of product C_2 to provisional plan

	Labour grade A			Labour grade B			Contribution (£)		
	+	−	Net	+	−	Net	+	−	Net
reduce A_1 by $\frac{2}{3}$ units (10, 4, 66)	4	4	0	10	1·6	8·4	30	26.4	3.6
reduce A_2 by $\frac{2}{3}$ units (10, 4, 40)	4	4	0	10	1·6	8·4	30	16	14.0
reduce B_1 by $\frac{1}{2}$ units (8, 8, 50)	4	4	0	10	4	6	30	25	5.0
reduce B_2 by $\frac{1}{2}$ units (8, 8, 30)	4	4	0	10	4	6	30	15	15.0
reduce C_1 by 1 unit (4, 10, 50)	4	4	0	10	10	0	30	50	−20.0

of model used and seems to be a desirable result. With the type of model used in chapter 11, if a product is not sufficiently profitable, at the one assumed price, it will simply be excluded from the plan. With the formulation used in this chapter, the price–volume relationships are considered explicitly (even though approximately) in order to form a view as to whether production is worthwhile at *any* price. A product will be judged worthwhile if the opportunity cost of the resources it requires is less than estimated marginal revenue at some price.

The cash surplus predicted for a plan of production under a model of the type used in this chapter will normally be less than the best attainable because of the nature of the approximation involved. Table 38 estimates that Donati Ltd will earn a contribution of £594 333$\frac{1}{3}$ from the optimal plan derived using linear programming. Output required, in terms of actual rather than fictitious product units is 6400 units of product A, 2966$\frac{2}{3}$ units of product B and 3066$\frac{2}{3}$ units of product C. We

Table 38 Summary of optimal plan based on linear approximation for total revenue

Product	Amounts per unit		Contribution (£)	Output	Totals		Contribution (£)
	Labour grade A	Labour grade B			Labour grade A	Labour grade B	
A_1	10	4	$66\frac{2}{3}$	3200	32 000	12 800	213 333$\frac{1}{3}$
A_2	10	4	40	3200	32 000	12 800	128 000
A_3	10	4	$13\frac{1}{3}$	0	0	0	0
B_1	8	8	50	2000	16 000	16 000	100 000
B_2	8	8	30	$966\frac{2}{3}$	7 733$\frac{1}{3}$	7 733$\frac{1}{3}$	29 000
B_3	8	8	10	0	0	0	0
C_1	4	10	50	1600	6 400	16 000	80 000
C_2	4	10	30	$1466\frac{2}{3}$	5 866$\frac{2}{3}$	14 666$\frac{2}{3}$	44 000
C_3	4	10	10	0	0	0	0
Resources used and available					100 000	80 000	
Contributions earned							594 333$\frac{1}{3}$

refer to the original estimates of price–volume relationships to find the prices at which these quantities can be sold:

Product A:

$$p_a = 120 - (q_a/240) = 120 - \frac{6400}{240} = £93\tfrac{1}{3} \text{ (expression 3)}$$

Product B:

$$p_b = 80 - (q_b/200) = 80 - \frac{2966·6}{200} = £65\tfrac{1}{6} \text{ (expression 6)}$$

Product C:

$$p_c = 90 - (q_c/160) = 90 - \frac{3066·6}{160} = £70\tfrac{5}{6} \text{ (expression 7)}$$

If these prices are adopted, the contribution earned may be estimated as in Table 39.

Table 39

	A	B	C
Selling price per unit	£93$\tfrac{1}{3}$	£65$\tfrac{1}{6}$	£70$\tfrac{5}{6}$
Cost per unit	40	20	30
Average contribution per unit	£53$\tfrac{1}{3}$	£45$\tfrac{1}{6}$	£40$\tfrac{5}{6}$
Volume of output	6400	2966$\tfrac{2}{3}$	3066$\tfrac{2}{3}$
Total contribution = £341 333$\tfrac{1}{3}$ + £133 994$\tfrac{4}{9}$ + £125 222$\tfrac{2}{9}$ = £600 550			

The optimal plan for Donati Ltd, given the actual price–volume relationships for its products, may be even better than this – in view of the approximations used in our calculations of optimal output. However, the linear approximation may well make it possible to choose a better plan than any practicable alternative.

13 Risk and Uncertainty: Attitudes to Risk

Up to now, the methods advocated for the analysis of business decisions have considered only a single set of estimates of the consequences of accepting each activity; in estimating the demand for a product, for example, we have considered only one possible quantity resulting from each price. Such estimates may be viewed as values somehow distilled from many sets of estimates representing all the various outcomes that might arise – for it is impossible to be completely certain what the outcome will be. In this chapter, we consider methods of incorporating directly in the analysis, estimates of a range of possible outcomes.

The relevance of a range of values

In principle, it is important to consider all possible outcomes of an activity – a single estimate does not convey all the information which might reasonably influence a decision. Suppose, for example, that Centaurus Ltd has been offered two contracts but is able to accept only one of them. Each would yield a receipt of £1500. The costs of carrying out contract A can be predicted with considerable confidence. They would almost certainly fall in the range £1075 to £1125; £1100 might be taken as a representative estimate of cost. Contract B is subject to much more uncertainty, since it involves a new technology. It is thought that cost might fall anywhere between £700 and £1400; £1050 might be selected as a representative estimate. If we consider the single representative estimates above, contract B looks preferable; it would yield a larger surplus by £50. A consideration of the range of possible outcomes, however, might well lead Centaurus to accept contract A, taking the view that it would be better to have a fairly certain surplus of £400 than take the chance of earning only £100 (even though that chance is balanced by a chance of gaining £800 at the other extreme).

Our illustration assumes a degree of uncertainty which is by no means unknown in actual practice. It serves to demonstrate that consideration of the range of possible outcomes from an activity may add a relevant dimension to decision processes. It will be helpful to our subsequent discussion of the analysis of risk and uncertainty if we now identify some basic concepts.

Probability distributions

Estimates of the various possible outcomes of an activity can conveniently be described as a probability distribution, that is, a list of all possible outcomes and the probability that each will occur.

Probability as long-run relative frequency

The probability of an outcome is usually defined as the long-run relative frequency of its occurrence, the number of occasions on which it does arise as a proportion of the total number of occasions on which it could arise in a long sequence of trials. Suppose we examine 1000 light bulbs produced in a factory and discover that 147 are defective, 853 are good. The probability of discovering a good bulb by taking one at random is 0·853 (85·3 per cent) and the probability of a defective bulb is 0·147 (14·7 per cent).

By definition, the probabilities of all possible outcomes of a particular activity must add up to one (100 per cent). Strictly, probabilities are defined in relation to actual observation of a relevant series of events, even though, in some cases, we may feel well able to predict what would be observed. We might expect that the probability of obtaining a six from rolling a dice would be $\frac{1}{6}$; but we might be wrong if the dice were not well made, and we can check our ideas only by testing them in observations.

Probability applied to business projects

Estimates of probabilities derived from past experience are useful if we would take them into account in predicting the likelihood of various outcomes of future events. Strictly, according to the above definition of probability, we may derive a probability distribution for a future event only if that event has taken place frequently in identical – or closely similar – circumstances; if such experience is lacking, we lack a basis for observing the relative frequency of different outcomes. Such previous experience is rarely available in business. Business activities take place in the context of a changing environment so that an activity can rarely be said to be repeated in similar circumstances. Suppose for example, that we have produced a fixed quantity of a given product for a large number of periods; we might list the total costs incurred in each period and use the list to derive a probability distribution of total costs for the next period. Such a procedure would strictly be justified only if it could be assumed that all conditions affecting costs had remained unchanged over the past observations and would be unchanged in the next period. Any change in quality of materials, the skill and morale of employees, the methods of production and so on would invalidate the use of past data for deriving probabilities of future cost levels.

Nevertheless, it would be a pity to discard a potentially useful tool because of excessive strictness of definition; it may be useful to describe the outcomes of business projects as probability distributions. Probability distributions provide a vehicle which a forecaster may use for expressing his opinion on the possible values of results and putting a numerical value on the degree of likelihood of each. They are an aid to clear thinking about relevant considerations. One should, perhaps, think of probabilities in business as representing not long-run relative frequencies but rather as fair betting odds, odds which the forecaster would be prepared to offer in a small wager that the outcome of a project would have a particular value.

Expected values and most likely values

The idea of a probability distribution provides a vehicle for describing the ways in which a single value may be selected as representative of the estimated outcome of a project. One common practice is to select the most likely value, the value of the outcome assigned the largest probability of occurrence. Another is to compute what is called the 'expected' value, a weighted average value of all possible outcomes, using probabilities as weights.

Consider the following numerical illustration. Orion Ltd has been offered two contracts, each at a fixed price of £1200. Probability distributions for the costs of the contracts have been estimated as shown in Table 40. For purposes of estimat-

Table 40 Probability distribution of results

Contract A

Cost (£)	Price (£)	Surplus (£)	Probability
700	1200	500	0·1
800	1200	400	0·2
900	1200	300	0·4
1000	1200	200	0·2
1100	1200	100	0·1

Contract B

Cost (£)	Price (£)	Surplus (£)	Probability
550	1200	650	0·05
750	1200	450	0·10
900	1200	300	0·15
1050	1200	150	0·4
1250	1200	−50	0·3

ing the probability distributions, we have chosen a number of key cost levels and assumed them to be the only ones possible. It would presumably have been more realistic to consider the possibility of any cost level within a certain range and to assign some probability to each one. The probability distribution might be described by a continuous curve such as that

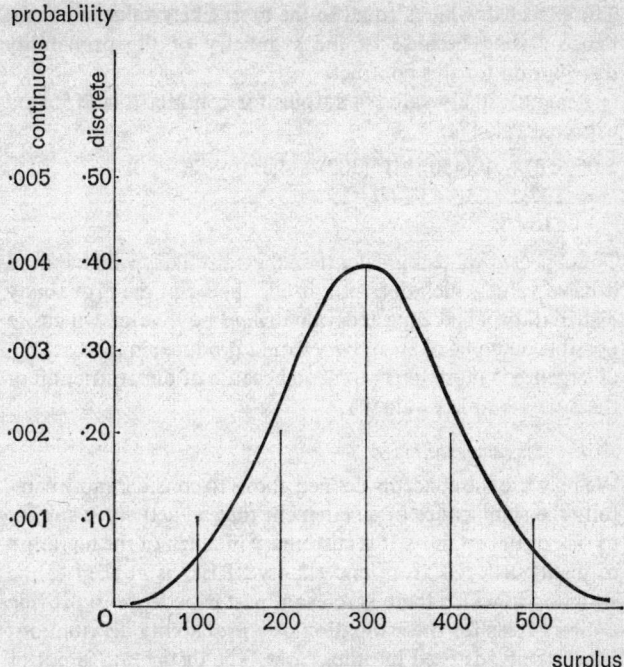

Figure 18 Continuous and discrete probability distributions

shown in Figure 18. However, the analysis of continuous probability distributions involves more complicated mathematical manipulation and we shall therefore confine ourselves to a consideration of key values (discrete probability distributions) in illustrating the principles of analysis of risk and uncertainty.

The most likely surplus of contract A is £300 and the expected surplus is:

$$£.1(500)+.2(400)+.4(300)+.2(200)+.1(100)$$
$$= £50+80+120+40+10$$
$$= £300.$$

The expected value is equal to the most likely value, a coincidence arising because of the symmetry of the probability distribution for this contract.

The most likely value of surplus for contract B is £150 and expected value is:

$$£.05(650) + .10(450) + .15(300) + .4(150) + .3(-50)$$
$$= £32.5 + 45 + 45 + 60 - 15$$
$$= £167.5.$$

The expected value is greater than the most likely value; indeed it has a value which does not, itself, appear in the probability distribution. (The expected value *could* be a value which no possible outcome of an activity would produce; in this case the divergence is more likely to arise because of our restriction of the analysis to key values.)

Risk versus uncertainty

We may use the concepts defined above to consider more carefully the significance of a statement that an activity is subject to risk or uncertainty. It is customary in much of the literature to distinguish risk from uncertainty. 'Risk' is applied to the situation in which there is relevant past experience to provide a direct basis for the estimation of a probability distribution; 'uncertainty' is used in other cases. The distinction is not of great importance for our analysis; indeed, it is hard to find practical business examples of pure risk according to this definition. We shall use the two terms interchangeably.

The measurement of risk

When we say that a project is subject to a high degree of risk, we assume, instinctively, that it is hard to estimate its outcome; we have to admit some probability that the outcome will fall anywhere in a relatively wide range of values. We may have in mind particularly that there is a material probability of incurring a loss on the project. However, it is convenient to define risk in terms of variability of outcome alone, so that the risk may be large even if all possible outcomes involve earning a surplus.

A useful measure of risk is one based on a statistical measure of variability, the variance or its square root, the standard deviation. As noted in chapter 7, the variance is calculated by finding the differences between each possible result and the average (or expected) result; squaring those differences; and computing the average of the squares (in this case weighted by the probabilities). The calculation of variance and standard deviation and their relevance are demonstrated for two pairs of projects in Table 41. Project P has the same expected value as project Q: projects S and T are also equivalent in this respect. Intuitively we would say that project Q is more risky than project P because its possible outcomes cover a wider range of values than those of project P, even though corresponding outcomes for the two projects have the same probabilities. Similarly project T seems more risky than project S; the possible outcomes are the same for each project but the extreme values have the higher probability in the case of project T. In both cases, the projects which seem more risky, intuitively, have the larger variances and standard deviations. The standard deviation is, perhaps, the better of the two measures to use because it yields values of the same order of magnitude as the basic outcomes.

The results of Table 41 may give us some confidence in the use of standard deviation as a measure of risk. However, we have been comparing projects with identical expected values. Standard deviation may not be such a good measure for comparing projects with different expected values. Consider the data for project Z, given in Table 42. Project Z has possible outcomes each of which is ten times as large as corresponding outcomes for project S and the same pattern of probabilities. It might be said, therefore, that the two projects are equally risky. However, the standard deviation of the surplus of project Z is ten times as large as that of project S. This scale effect may be removed by adopting as a measure of risk the standard deviation divided by the expected value. This would give a value of

$$\frac{28 \cdot 3}{110} = \frac{283}{1100} = 0 \cdot 25 \text{ for each project.}$$

Table 41 Standard deviation as a measure of risk

Project P

Surplus (£) s	Probability p	£ps	Difference d = s − V	d²	pd²
150	0·5	75	+20	400	200
110	0·5	55	−20	400	200
	1·0				
expected value (V)		130	variance (Var)		400
standard deviation = √(Var) = £20					

Project Q

Surplus (£) s	Probability p	£ps	Difference d = s − V	d²	pd²
170	0·5	85	+40	1600	800
90	0·5	45	−40	1600	800
	1·0				
expected value (V)		130	variance (Var)		1600
standard deviation = √(Var) = £40					

Project S

Surplus (£) s	Probability p	£ps	Difference d = s − V	d²	pd²
150	0·25	37·5	+40	1600	400
110	0·5	55	0	0	0
70	0·25	17·5	−40	1600	400
	1·0				
expected value (V)		110	variance (Var)		800
standard deviation = √(Var) = £28.3					

Project T

Surplus (£) s	Probability p	£ps	Difference d = s − V	d²	pd²
150	0·40	60	+40	1600	640
110	0·20	22	0	0	0
70	0·40	28	−40	1600	640
	1·0				
expected value (V)		110	variance (Var)		1280
standard deviation = √(Var) = £35.8					

Table 42 The relation of size and standard deviation

Project Z					
Surplus (£) s	Probability p	£ps	Difference d = s−V	d²	pd²
1500	0·25	375	+400	160 000	40 000
1100	0·5	550	0	0	0
700	0·25	175	−400	160 000	40 000
	1·0				
expected value (V)		1100	variance (Var)		80 000
standard deviation = √(Var) = £283					

The foregoing discussion suggests that we might summarize the characteristics of a business project by two measures, its expected value and its standard deviation divided by the expected value. However, there is no single measure for risk that can be said to be unambiguously the best; and as we shall see, summary measures of a project's characteristics are of limited use as guides to decision. Their role is rather in clarifying the conceptual issues at hand.

In order to assess whether a risky project is worthwhile, we have to know the attitude to risk of people whose interests are at stake. The objectives of the firm have to be modified to include an operational statement of attitude to risk.

Attitudes to risk by individuals

Let us consider what basic forces may be supposed to shape an individual's attitude to risk. Most people think of great risk as an unpleasant thing, something to be avoided if possible; and there is a good deal of evidence of the existence of people who are more reluctant to undertake uncertain projects than certain ones. This attitude may not be shared by all people but it is easy to rationalize.

The rationale of risk aversion

The basic rationalization of risk aversion is that it is more unpleasant to lose a given sum than pleasant to gain the same amount; for a loss may cause a reduction in the standard of living to which one has become accustomed – a particularly unpleasant occurrence. In an extreme case, a risky venture may be shunned because it puts basic necessities at risk. Imagine an individual, with no savings, faced with a choice for his sole activity between one which would yield £1500 per annum for certain and one which would be equally likely to yield £0 or £5000. If there were no welfare state as a guarantee against starvation (and often even if there were one), it would not be hard to believe that the former activity would be chosen even though the latter has the larger expected value.

More generally, we may assume that an individual uses available money firstly to buy the things that give him the most satisfaction. Each successive £1 added to his resources may be supposed to add a smaller amount to the total satisfaction that he derives. We might assume that the relationship between satisfaction (or utility as it is generally called in economic analysis) and money income has some such form as that depicted in Figure 19. It follows, as we shall see, that such an individual will normally prefer an activity which offers a given sum for certain to an alternative with the same expected value from uncertain outcomes.

The utility of money

Let us assume, for purposes of illustration, a model describing the relationship between utility and cash earnings for a particular individual, Mr Cepheus. If Mr Cepheus has tastes with the general characteristics discussed above, our model should have the property that each successive one pound added to earnings should increase total utility by a smaller amount; but total utility should always increase as earnings increase – one is unlikely to experience a fall in satisfaction as a result of an increase in earnings. A model which has this property is

$$U = 1000 \log_{10} Y, \qquad\qquad 1$$

where U represents total utility
and Y represents total earnings.

For example, if earnings are £1000, utility is

$1000 \log_{10} (1000)$
$= 3000$ units;

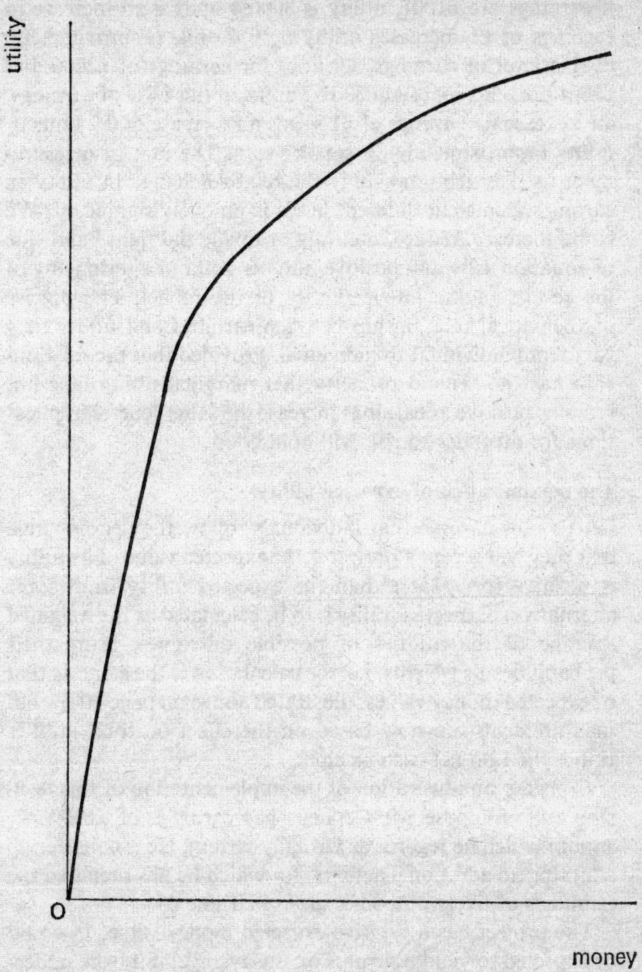

Figure 19 The relationship between utility and money

if earnings are £1001, utility is 3000·4 units – an increase in earnings of £1 increases utility by 0·4 units (approximately) at this level of earnings. Utilities for earnings of £2000 and £2001 are 3301 units and 3301·2 units; at this level of earnings, an increase in earnings of £1 yields an increase of 0·2 units of utility (approximately), a smaller sum. The unit of measurement used is arbitrary, only the relative change in utility as earnings change at different levels is uniquely significant. We could increase, reduce, multiply or divide the right hand side of equation 1 by any positive number without altering any of the results of the intended uses of the model. The precise mathematical relationship between earnings and utility may vary from individual to individual. Provided that the relationship has the general property that marginal utility falls but remains positive as earnings increase the same general implications for attitudes to risk will hold good.

The maximization of expected utility

Let us now assume that individuals follow the decision rule that they will accept a project if the expected value of its utility is positive (or greater than the expected utility from some alternative). Expected utility is to be calculated as the weighted average of the utilities of possible outcomes, using their probabilities as weights, i.e. the calculation is the same as that of expected money values (illustrated above on page 207) – but measurements are now based on the effect on total utilities rather than on net cash receipts.

Consider an illustration of the implementation of this decision rule. Suppose Mr Cepheus has earnings of £6000 per annum which he regards as virtually certain. He is considering adopting an additional activity, for which he has prepared the estimates of likely outcomes given in Table 43.

The project has a positive expected money value. It would be expected to yield a surplus on the average, if it were undertaken a large number of times. However, Mr Cepheus would accept the activity only once. The affect of his doing so on his total earnings and their utility is given in Table 44.

These calculations indicate that, if Mr Cepheus follows the

decision rule of maximizing the expected utility of his activities, the project will be rejected even though it has a positive expected money value.

Table 43 Calculation of expected money value for Cepheus' project

Surplus or deficit (£) s	Probability p	£ps
−4000	0·15	−600
−2000	0·15	−300
0	0·25	0
+2000	0·30	+600
+4000	0·15	+600
	1·00	
Expected money value		300

Our assumed model of utility can now be seen to have described one way in which risk aversion may arise. If an individual's satisfaction at given increases in earnings dimin-

Table 44 Calculations of expected utility for Cepheus

Surplus or deficit (£) s	Total earnings (£) $Y = 6000 + s$	Total utility $U = 1000 \log_{10} Y$	Probability p	pU
−4000	2 000	3301·0	0·15	495·15
−2000	4 000	3602·1	0·15	540·32
0	6 000	3778·2	0·25	944·55
+2000	8 000	3903·1	0·30	1170·93
+4000	10 000	4000·0	0·15	600·00
expected utility of earnings if project is accepted				3750·95
earnings if project is rejected: £6000−utility				3778·20
Loss of utility from accepting project				27·25

ishes as the level of earnings increases, and if he attempts to maximize expected satisfaction (utility), he may prefer earnings with a low expected money value and low risk to earnings with a high risk and high expected money value. If expected money value is large enough, however, the greater risk may still be accepted; there is a 'trade-off' between risk and expected money value.

The rationale of maximizing expected utility

The assumption that extra satisfaction or utility from extra money decreases as the basic level of earnings gets larger seems plausible, and to accord with the feelings of most of us about our money resources. Most of us would not risk losing £1000 per annum for an equal chance of gaining £1000 per annum. The rule that one should maximize the expected value of a given measure of utility is less obviously justified. We must consider, further, the role of this type of analysis.

The main purpose in developing a model for predicting an individual's utility from cash earnings would be to guide him in taking consistent decisions about the worthwhileness of various activities available to him. It makes it possible to detect a common structure in complex problems. If an individual can develop a mode] of his utility from different financial results, and if he applies it to decisions on various projects in the form of analysis described above, he will achieve consistency in the sense that each time a given money effect is anticipated with a given probability it would be given the same weight in appraisal. Utility is not significant in itself, however. It has no natural interpretation. It is rather a concept invented – a kind of coding of actual money values – for the specific purpose of explaining observed decisions and providing a basis for consistency in future decisions (rather in the way that natural scientists have invented concepts of gravity).

More fundamentally, utility models achieve consistency in the way that they relate the values attributed to various sums of money. Implicitly they involve the calculation of a sum of money for certain which is valued equally with a specified probability distribution, i.e. a sum of money which an individual would exchange for the 'lottery' of an uncertain project without sense of gain or loss. For example, using the utility model $U = 1000 \log_{10} Y$, the utility of project P, a 50 per cent chance of £2000 and a 50 per cent chance of £4000, is

$$0.5(1000)(\log 2000) + 0.5(1000)(\log 4000) = 3451.6,$$

the same as the utility of the certain receipt of a sum x, such that $1.0(1000)\log x = 3451.6$, thus x is £2829. Similarly the utility of project Q, a 50 per cent chance of £1500 and a 50 per cent chance of £4500, is

$$0.5(1000)(\log 1500) + 0.5(1000)(\log 4500) = 3414.7,$$

the same as the utility of the certain receipt of £2598. If we were choosing between the certain sums, we should prefer £2829 to £2598. If we behave consistently, we should prefer the distribution of project P to that of project Q. Such consistency would be secured by maximizing expected utilities. Utility analysis also secures consistency in evaluation of more complex distributions. For example if:

project P, £2000 ($p = 0.5$) + £4000 ($p = 0.5$)
is valued equally with   £2829 ($p = 1.0$)
and project Q, £1500 ($p = 0.5$) + £4500 ($p = 0.5$)
is valued equally with   £2598 ($p = 1.0$)
then project R, involving   £1500 ($p = 0.25$) + £2000 ($p = 0.25$) + £4000 ($p = 0.25$) + £4500 ($p = 0.25$)
should presumably be valued equally with $\frac{1}{2}$ project P and $\frac{1}{2}$ project Q;
i.e. at x where $1.0 (1000) \log x = 0.5 (1000) \log 2829$ $+0.5 (1000) \log 2598$,
thus $x =$ £2710.

Again, utility analysis would secure such consistency.

An individual could, perhaps, take optimal decisions simply by considering subjectively the probability distribution of a project and deciding whether he liked it – for ultimately the decision is a matter of personal taste. However, the complexity of the analysis makes this unlikely.

Our discussion assumes that an individual wishes to take decisions that are consistent – that if he took a decision at variance with utility analysis and we pointed out the inevitable inconsistency, he would agree that he had been mistaken. If an individual does not wish to behave consistently, his decisions can hardly be guided by systematic analysis. He would simply accept the projects which he wanted to accept. We could define a different decision model for each decision such that the model would explain his decision. However there would be no useful purpose in such models.

Our analysis started by assuming a utility model for an individual, and its applicability depends on the possibility of developing such a model. No general arguments will indicate the precise nature of an individual's utility model – it must be a matter for specific investigation, clearly one of considerable difficulty. Some writers have suggested that utility models may be inferred from decisions recorded on the worthwhileness of a number of hypothetical projects.

The estimation of utility models

Let us consider how this process of inference might be undertaken. We might base the analysis on the hypothetical purchase of lottery tickets, which have known probabilities of specified winnings. The objective is to find the maximum purchase price which our subject, whom we will call Miss Algol, would be willing to pay for a lottery ticket – the certain sum of money which she values equally with the lottery ticket. Suppose we begin by considering a lottery ticket which secures a ·5 chance of winning £5000 and a ·5 chance of no winning. We ask Miss Algol whether she would prefer – say – £500 or the lottery ticket and learn that the lottery ticket is preferred. Accordingly we increase the price until we find a sum such that she is at the point of indifference between the direct payment and the lottery ticket. Suppose we discover by these questions and a series of similar ones that Miss Algol values equally the sums of money and lottery tickets as in Table 45. Each lottery ticket after the first is chosen to include two values which have featured in our previous enquiries.

We can now build up a utility model for Miss Algol. We begin by assigning arbitrarily utility values to the two money values associated with the first lottery ticket. Suppose we assign 800 'utils' to £5000 and 0 'utils' to £0. We can choose these numbers quite freely. We shall use them to assign consistent utility values to the other sums dealt with by our enquiry. The choice will affect the absolute number of utils given to other money values but the relative values will be unaffected. In graphical terms the shape of the money–utility relationship will be independent of our initial choice – only the scale will vary. It is the relative values which are important for decisions.

Table 45

	Certain sum	Lottery ticket for
1	£600	£0 ($p = 0.5$) or £5000 ($p = 0.5$)
2	£1100	£600 ($p = 0.5$) or £5000 ($p = 0.5$)
3	£2100	£1100 ($p = 0.5$) or £5000 ($p = 0.5$)
4	£3000	£2100 ($p = 0.5$) or £5000 ($p = 0.5$)

The intention in computing utilities is that we should be able to calculate expected utilities for any course of action and base a decision directly on the resulting magnitude; if alternative A is preferred to alternative B, it should be assigned the greater expected utility and if we are indifferent between them they should have the same expected utility. Hence, for Miss Algol, £600 for certain should have the same utility as a lottery ticket having a 50 per cent chance each of winning £0 and £5000. Our initial assignment of utils gives the lottery ticket an expected utility of $(.5 \times 0) + (.5 \times 800) = 400$ utils and we should therefore assign 400 utils to £600 for certain. Using the same procedure and our second piece of information we assign the value $(.5 \times 400) + (.5 \times 800) = 600$ utils to £1100 and so on. This procedure yields the utility/money relationship for Miss Algol shown in Table 46.

This information, and similar more extensive information, could be plotted on a graph like Figure 19 and the whole utility/money relationship derived by interpolation. Utility values for any money sum could then be read from the graph for use in decision analysis; alternatively it may be possible to fit a mathematical equation to the information so that we can proceed as we did for Mr Cepheus.

Table 46

Money value (£)	Utility value (utils)
0	0
600	400
1100	600
2100	700
3000	750
5000	800

The sense in which utility analysis achieves consistency in decisions can now be illustrated further. Suppose Miss Algol is offered a choice between £1100 for certain, and a 50 per cent probability of each of £600 and £3000. We have a value of 600 utils for £1100 and expected utility of $(\cdot 5 \times 400) + (\cdot 5 \times 750) = 575$ utils for the uncertain result; £1100 would be preferred as it has the higher expected utility. Since Miss Algol has told us that she values equally £1100 for certain and a lottery ticket with a 50 per cent probability of each of £600 and £5000, the preference of £1100 to a 50 per cent probability of £600 or £3000 is a logical necessity, given consistency and the preference for larger rather than smaller money sums. Utility analysis will always secure consistency in this sense.

The derivation of utilities is subject to many difficulties in practice, however, which have prevented the process from becoming operational. Individuals are likely to give inconsistent answers to the questions required to establish their utility models because of the complexity of the process. Miss Algol might have told us later, after much questioning, that she preferred a certain receipt of £1000 to a lottery ticket with a 50 per cent chance of winning £600 or £5000, contradicting her previous statement (2 in Table 45).

Such inconsistencies may be capable of resolution by further questioning although it is not clear how reliable the results would be. More serious is the difficulty in knowing whether responses to questions on hypothetical projects (gambles which may be the subject of special pleasure or aversion) would yield information which could validly be applied to real business decisions. Moreover a study of attitudes in actual business decisions would involve the equally serious difficulty that the projects studied might have special – strategic – features which would not be reflected in the estimate of possible money outcomes. When one adds that utility values may change rapidly over time as wealth and tastes change and that it is often difficult to question the people whose utilities are important (shareholders as well as managers), the extent of the difficulties becomes clear. Nevertheless the analysis given above may be useful for the insight it gives into the general rationale of attitudes to risk.

We should note that some individuals may prefer risk to certainty. This possibility has not been illustrated, because it seems to be quite unusual. However, such tastes could be catered for in a similar way to those of risk aversion using a different form of utility model. The prevalence of gambling – e.g. on horse racing or football pools – also calls for some comment. The gambler in such situations is undertaking an activity with a negative expected money value, otherwise book-makers and pools companies would not make profits; if the utility of an increase in wealth falls as wealth grows larger, i.e. if the gambler is risk averse, the activities would also have a negative expected utility. We should not, however, conclude that this, the acceptance of the gamble in spite of its negative expected utility, necessarily represents an argument against the assumed commonness of risk aversion. We may explain gambling by assuming that the excitement of the activity provides a satisfaction, like consumption, which outweighs the loss of other utility; or we may assume that our model is invalid for the very small stakes which are usually involved in gambling.

The variance reconsidered

When we first discussed the meaning of risk, we introduced the statistical measure of variance and related concepts to explain the basic principles. We noted the possibility of characterising a project in terms of its expected value and its variance although we also noted the limited usefulness of such characterization for decision purposes. We now emphasize this statement. Suppose we consider a choice between two projects having the same expected value but different variances. A decision-taker using utility analysis will not necessarily choose the project with the smaller variance, even if he is a risk averter. The choice will depend on the shape of the money/utility relationship and on the pattern of the probability distributions. If the probability distributions are symmetrical, i.e. if outcomes of a given amount above and below the expected value have equal probabilities, the risk averter will prefer the project with lower variance. He will not necessarily do so in other cases.

14 Risk and Uncertainty: The Portfolio Effect

The mutual dependence of uncertain projects

When we analyse projects subject to uncertainty, using utility models, it is important to consider the impact of the project on the individual's total cash earnings. The total would be taken for the period under review or for each of several periods in the case of investment decisions. A project should not be appraised independently; it may be acceptable at one level of earnings and not at another, i.e. acceptable in conjunction with one set of projects but not with another. Let us consider the case of Mr Cepheus again and alter just one assumption – let the certain earnings level be £14 000. The revised appraisal is given in Table 47. The project has the same

Table 47 Calculation of expected utility for a richer Mr Cepheus

Surplus or deficit (£) s	Total earnings (£) $Y = 14\,000 + s$	Total utility $U = 1000 \log_{10} Y$	Probability p	pU
−4000	10 000	4000·0	0·15	600·00
−2000	12 000	4079·2	0·15	611·88
0	14 000	4146·1	0·25	1036·53
+2000	16 000	4204·1	0·30	1261·23
+4000	18 000	4255·3	0·15	638·30
expected utility of earnings if project is accepted				4147·94
earnings if project is rejected: £14 000 — utility				4146·10
gain of utility from accepting project				1·84

expected money value as before, but now it increases expected utility (by a small amount) and so, presumably, should be accepted. The analysis demonstrates one reason why it is desirable to appraise projects in the light of their effects on aggregate results. The decision-taker should ideally consider each possible combination of projects for a particular period and estimate the probability distribution of aggregate receipts and payments for each one; he should then estimate the aggregate utility for each set and select the one with the highest utility overall. The need to consider the effects of combining projects adds a further dimension to our study of appraisal under risk and uncertainty. The combination of one risky project and a certain earnings stream, as assumed in the case of Cepheus, is a simple matter; the estimation of the aggregate probability distribution for the combination of several uncertain projects is more complex.

Portfolio theory – the effects of aggregation

We will consider the general effects of aggregation using a numerical example. Suppose Mr Cetus is considering an activity which he could undertake once, many times or not at all. We might imagine, for example, that he is considering the installation of whisky vending machines, which cost £250 and have operating lives of one year, in Ruritania – where such machines are legal. He could install machines in one location or in many similar locations. He estimates that each machine has a 50 per cent chance of earning net cash receipts of £500 and a 50 per cent chance of earning £100. Suppose, further, that the amounts earned from each machine would depend on whether the location was good or bad and each location would be assumed *a priori* equally likely to be good or bad. Knowledge of the yield of machine A would not affect the estimate that machine B is equally likely to yield £100 or £500, i.e. the results of each machine are statistically independent. Hence, from two machines, there would be a 25 per cent ($\cdot 5 \times \cdot 5$) of getting £100 from each, a 25 per cent chance of getting £100 and £500, a 25 per cent chance of £500 and £100 and a 25 per cent chance of £500 from each. The probability distributions for aggregate yields from installing up to four machines are given in Table 48.

Table 48 Probability distribution for portfolios

Number of machines installed	Distribution of results		Expected value (£)	Standard deviation (£)	Standard deviation/ expected value
	Net receipts	Probability			
1	100	0·5	300	200	0·677
	500	0·5			
		1·0			
2	200	0·5 × 0·5 = 0·25	600	282.8	0·471
	600	2(0·5 × 0·5) = 0·50			
	1000	0·5 × 0·5 = 0·25			
		1·00			
3	300	0·5 × 0·5 × 0·5 = 0·125	900	346.4	0·385
	700	3(0·5 × 0·5 × 0·5) = 0·375			
	1100	3(0·5 × 0·5 × 0·5) = 0·375			
	1500	0·5 × 0·5 × 0·5 = 0·125			
		1·000			
4	400	0·0625	1200	400	0·333
	800	0·25			
	1200	0·375			
	1600	0·25			
	2000	0·0625			
		1·0000			

It can be seen that the relative level of risk, as measured by the ratio of standard deviation to expected value, falls as the number of machines installed is increased, whilst the expected earnings per machine remains constant. The installation of one machine would give an expected surplus of £50 but a high level of risk. Mr Cetus may prefer to instal several machines (depending upon the characteristics of competing opportunities and his attitude to risk). Indeed, if a very large number of machines could be installed, the risk might be assessed as being negligible and the decision might be based on expected value alone.

Relationships between results of individual projects

The earnings of various activities may not be independent as assumed in our example, however; they may be related because they are influenced by common factors. Let us consider the types of relation possible by considering the example of the vending machines further. Suppose the machines will earn £500 or £100 according to whether the present environment continues unchanged (earning £500) or the Government introduces legislation prohibiting the sale of whisky in vending machines – in which case the machines would have to be converted to sell orange squash (earning £100). The probability of introduction of the legislation is assessed at 50 per cent. In such a case each machine would yield £100 or £500 according to government policy; two machines would give a 50 per cent chance of £200 and a 50 per cent chance of £1000 and so on. The ratio of standard deviation to expected value would remain constant, regardless of how many machines were installed; the level of risk could not be reduced by purchasing many machines.

The results of different activities may also be inversely related. Suppose Mr Cetus were considering the installation of machines selling iced drinks and machines selling hot drinks. The yield of each machine might be subject to a good deal of uncertainty because sales would depend on average weather conditions during the year, changes in tastes and so on; the yield of two machines combined – one of each type – might be subject to less uncertainty because it is thought that a certain level of expenditure on drinks (from vending machines) is very likely, even though it is not known which drinks will be preferred. In an extreme case, it might be predicted that if one machine were to yield £100, the other would be virtually certain to earn £500 and vice versa. Mr Cetus would then be certain to earn the expected value of £300 per machine (£600 on each pair of machines). The risk attached to the results of individual machines would be eliminated on aggregation. Such exact counterbalancing of results from different activities is not likely to be found in actual business activities. However, there may be an association between good results on some activities and bad results on others, with the result that aggregate risk is reduced when the activities are combined.

Portfolio theory suggests that in assessing risk it is important to consider the aggregate distribution of results (results for the whole portfolio of projects) taking account of the association between different results possible from different projects. Our discussion has been based on the possibility of repeating many times, identical or similar activities. We now give some general conclusions which may be applied to all activities.

Consider any two activities, project x and project y, which might be undertaken by an individual (or a firm). Imagine (for purposes of exposition) that we write out a list of possible net cash earnings from each activity. We will use the shorthand notation x_i to denote the outcomes of project x ($x_1, x_2, ..., x_n$) and y_i to denote the outcomes of project y ($y_1, y_2, ..., y_n$); we also denote the expected values $\bar{x}$ and $\bar{y}$, the variances $\text{Var}(x)$ and $\text{Var}(y)$ and the standard deviations s_x and s_y. We choose come convenient number n for the number of possible results to include in the list, the same for each project, and we include each possible result several times in the list, a number of times in proportion to its probability of occurrence. Suppose, for example, that we estimate the probability distributions for the two projects to be those shown in Table 49.

We might decide to list one hundred possible results for each project, in which case for project x, we should include £100 forty times, £300 twenty times and £500 forty times.

The main purpose of portfolio theory is to estimate the effect of combining projects. We wish to estimate what relationship there would be between the possible results of different projects. We might approach the task by considering what independent influences would affect the outcomes – the general economic climate, actions of competitors, changes in taste and

Table 49

Project x		Project y	
Probability	Surplus (£)	Probability	Surplus (£)
0·40	100	0·40	200
0·20	300	0·20	500
0·40	500	0·40	800

so on – and whether the projects would be affected in the same way by a given influence; for example, suppose we are considering a seaside hotel and a city cinema as the two projects; a general rise in incomes might affect both projects favourably whereas a wet summer might affect the hotel unfavourably and the cinema favourably.

We would represent the results of our deliberations by pairing the results of the two projects to represent likely combinations. If we thought the projects subject to completely different influences, we would assign results for y in association with a given result for x in proportion to the probabilities of different results for y; for example the forty listings of £100 for x would be paired with £200 sixteen times ($40 \times 0·4$), £500 eight times ($40 \times 0·2$) and £800 sixteen times and so on. This is the case of statistical independence. Alternatively, we might think x and y subject to similar influences which would tend to cause both to do well or both badly. We would then pair the surplus of £100 on x with £200 on y more than sixteen times; in an extreme case, we might expect the two worst outcomes always to be associated, in which case we should have forty pairs of £100 and £200. This possibility is known as positive correlation. It is also possible for the good results of one project to be associated with poor results for the other – the case of negative correlation.

The aggregate expected value for combining project x and project y is simply the sum of their separate expected values, $\bar{x}+\bar{y}$: this may be written as $\frac{1}{n}\sum x_i+\frac{1}{n}\sum y_i$ where $\sum x_i$ is shorthand for the sum of all possible results of project x. As we have noted, the variance of a project is defined as the average of the squares of differences between each possible outcome and the expected outcome, i.e. for project x it is $\frac{1}{n}\sum(x_i-\bar{x})^2$. To find the variance for the combination of x and y, we consider the aggregate result from each pair of results in our list. We obtain the following expression:

$$\text{Var }(x+y) = \frac{1}{n}\sum\{(x_i+y_i)-(\bar{x}+\bar{y})\}^2 \qquad \textbf{1}$$

$$= \frac{1}{n}\sum(x_i-\bar{x})^2+\frac{1}{n}\sum(y_i-\bar{y})^2+$$

$$+\frac{2}{n}\sum(x_i-\bar{x})(y_i-\bar{y}). \qquad \textbf{2}$$

The last term in expression **2** is a product of an important statistical measure, the covariance, equal to $\frac{1}{n}\sum(x_i-\bar{x})(y_i-\bar{y})$ and written $\text{Cov}(x,y)$. We may therefore write expression **2**:

$$\text{Var}(x+y) = \text{Var}(x)+\text{Var}(y)+2\,\text{Cov}(xy). \qquad \textbf{3}$$

The covariance provides the key to the potential for risk reduction by combining projects. The first step in its calculation involves considering each pair of results and finding the amount by which the result for each project differs from the expected value for that project: results below the expected value give negative differences; the differences are then multiplied together (to give 'cross-products') and the cross-products are averaged. If poor results for one project are paired with poor results for the other and good results are also paired, the covariance will have a large positive value and (see expression **3**) the aggregate variance will be relatively large. If good results for one project are paired with poor results for the other, the covariance will have a large negative value and the aggregate variance will be relatively small. If the projects are statistically independent (the pairs good–good, good–bad, bad–bad arise at random), positive and negative cross-products cancel out, the covariance is zero and the aggregate variance has an intermediate value.

In chapter 7, we noted the use of the coefficient of correlation r, as a measure of the association of two variables. It can be shown that

$$r = \frac{\text{Cov}(x,y)}{s_x s_y}. \qquad \textbf{4}^1$$

The coefficient of correlation, i.e. the covariance divided by the product of the standard deviations, has a maximum value of $+1$ (perfect positive correlation corresponding to a strictly ordered good–good, bad–bad sequence of pairings) and a minimum value of -1 (perfect negative correlation corresponding to a strictly ordered good–bad pairing). Rearranging expression **4** and substituting in **3** we have

$$\text{Var}(x+y) = \text{Var}(x)+\text{Var}(y)+2r(s_x s_y). \qquad \textbf{5}$$

Taking square roots, to obtain the aggregate standard deviation:

$$\text{If } r = +1, \; s_{x+y} = s_x+s_y. \qquad \textbf{6}$$

$$\text{If } r = -1, \; s_{x+y} = s_x-s_y. \qquad \textbf{7}$$

1. From footnote on page 92;

$$r^2 = \frac{\{n \Sigma xy - \Sigma x \Sigma y\}^2}{\{n \Sigma x^2 - (\Sigma x)^2\}\{n \Sigma y^2 - (\Sigma y)^2\}} \text{ (writing } y \text{ for } T),$$

hence

$$r = \frac{\Sigma xy - \dfrac{1}{n} \Sigma x \Sigma y}{\sqrt{\left\{ \Sigma x^2 - \dfrac{1}{n} (\Sigma x)^2 \right\}} \sqrt{\left\{ \Sigma y^2 - \dfrac{1}{n} (\Sigma y)^2 \right\}}}$$

$$= \frac{\Sigma (x_i - \bar{x})(y_i - \bar{y})}{\sqrt{\Sigma (x_i - \bar{x})^2} \sqrt{\Sigma (y_i - \bar{y})^2}}$$

$$= \frac{\text{Cov}(x,y)}{s_x s_y}.$$

We can now see the effect of combining projects on the aggregate risk as measured by the variance or standard deviation (for a given expected value). There are three possibilities:

1 Positive correlation, r, between 0 and $+1$: aggregate variance is relatively large and there is little risk reduction; in the extreme case of perfect positive correlation, there is no risk reduction in the sense that aggregate standard deviation equals the sum of the standard deviations on the two projects (expression 6).

2 Negative correlation, r, between 0 and -1: aggregate variance is relatively small and there is considerable risk reduction; in the extreme case of perfect negative correlation, aggregate standard deviation is equal to the difference in standard deviations and could even be zero (denoting the elimination of risk) if the standard deviations are equal (expression 7). (Note s_y cannot exceed s_x if $r = -1$ and negative aggregate standard deviation is impossible.)

3 Zero correlation, $r = 0$: this is an intermediate position in which there is some reduction of risk.

These results can be generalized for any number of projects and exploited in the decision-making process. An individual who dislikes risk may make a particular search for activities which are negatively correlated. The avoidance of too many projects which are positively correlated is the essence of the strategy of diversification described in chapter 5.

The relative size of individual projects is a material factor in assessing the overall risk. If a portfolio comprises a large number of small projects with independent outcomes, the aggregate risk may be relatively small and appraizal may concentrate on the expected values of outcomes. On the other hand, if there are just a few large projects available (not negatively correlated) or if there are many small projects, all likely to be affected by a common factor, it will usually be important to consider aggregate risk explicitly.

The estimation of the correlation between the results of different projects is a matter of considerable practical difficulty. Nevertheless, the planning procedures should take some account of the portfolio effect. A practicable procedure would be to evaluate several plans in relation to various assumptions about critical uncertainties in the state of the economic environment – the rate of economic growth, availability of supplies of resources and so on. Such an analysis would at least provide some insight into the association between the results of different activities.

Decisions under uncertainty in the firm

The foregoing completes our short survey of the analysis of uncertainty from the viewpoint of the individual. We must now consider the implications of our conclusions for decisions in the firm.

We continue to assume that firms wish to take decisions which are optimal, judged by the interests of their shareholders. As noted in the introduction, shareholders derive benefits from the activities of a firm by the medium of holding shares, and shareholding has substantial long-term (investment) aspects. However, we shall continue to restrict our attention to activities with mainly short-term effects in accordance with the scope of this book.

In discussing individuals' decisions under uncertainty, we noted the possibility of securing consistency in different decisions by the device of identifying probability distributions for available activities, estimating an earnings/utility model and selecting the activities leading to maximum expected utility. We acknowledged the difficulties in making earnings/utility relationships explicit; the best that can be hoped for may well be that the individual will estimate probability distributions and reach a decision, taking implicit account of his attitude to risk (hence his earnings/utility relationship) with a knowledge of the conceptual issues involved.

Individuals may hold shares in a large number of firms and the choice of activities by those firms is in some senses part of the individual's decision problem. An ideal (but impracticable) decision process for the firm might be designed along the following lines. Each firm would estimate probability distributions of results for all activities available. It would send to shareholders details of these and the constraints restricting their acceptance. Shareholders would then consider probability distributions for all possible combinations of activities available to them as individuals; they would count in such combinations proportions of possible activities of firms in which they might hold shares, e.g. if a firm was considering an activity which would give a ·60 probability of £100 and a ·40 probability of £50, and the shareholder was contemplating a 10 per cent shareholding, he would count a ·60 probability of £10 and a ·40 probability of £5 in his personal plans. Shareholders would derive an estimated aggregate probability distribution of results for each possible combination of activities and choose the best in the light of their attitude to risk (implicitly or explicitly taking account of the earnings/utility relationship). They would then notify firms of their decisions and firms would undertake the activities chosen by their shareholders.

It is hard to believe that such a procedure could ever become operable. There would be a large educational gap to be overcome in the first place – all participants would have to understand what was going on. Even if the educational difficulty could be overcome, the operation would be prohibitively expensive. Furthermore a firm might receive conflicting advice from different shareholders and it would have no convincing means of deciding how to choose which to follow; there is nothing in economic theory to tell us how to combine conflicting utility models.

Economic theory does suggest that a firm need not enquire into the tastes of its shareholders in great detail provided it sets some satisfactory minimum standards for its activities. Shareholders consider whether the holding of shares in a particular firm is worthwhile by relating expected values and covariances (with other activities) to the market price; if they are not satisfied they can switch their holdings to other firms – provided that different firms have an adequate range of different characteristics – and the market price of shares will adjust to an equilibrium position. Shareholders presumably have diversified portfolios and have chosen to hold shares in a particular firm partly because they assess the risk of its ongoing activities to be satisfactory in the context of their total portfolio. This suggests that a firm should attempt to maintain a similar level and type of risk on its aggregate activities to that which has prevailed in the past. It should not accept activities which would alter total risk materially – as measured by the aggregate probability distribution for results; and it should not take a decision which would alter materially the correlation between its expected results and the expected results of other firms, e.g. by entering a completely new line of business.

Such lines of argument do not seem to deal with the difficulties satisfactorily, however. The suggestion that the market will adjust to a firm's activities supposes a more complete flow of information about these activities than is actually available. Moreover if a firm restricts its new activities to ones which are similar to existing activities, many good opportunities may be lost. A means of assessing new activities in relation to shareholders' tastes is required.

If a firm cannot rely on market adjustment and cannot communicate with shareholders, it must develop all the decision criteria internally. The suggested ideal process indicates that it must develop two main assumptions if it wishes to promote the well-being of its shareholders. The firm must form a view of the attitudes to risk of shareholders – e.g. by estimating a model of their earnings/utility relationships – and it must have some indication of its role in shareholders' total portfolios of activities, i.e. of the association between the results of its activities and the other activities in the portfolio.

Some investigators, as noted above, have attempted to measure earnings/utility relationships by asking people to indicate how they would react to each of a large number of hypothetical activities. Such means have been used to investigate the attitudes of managers to uncertainty; they have not yet been applied to the measurement of shareholders' attitudes. There would be many difficulties in measuring shareholders' attitudes in this way. There would be the same problems of cost, educational gaps and conflicts of interest described in relation to the suggested 'ideal decision process'. There would be similar difficulties in getting information about the role of shares in a particular firm in the shareholders' total portfolios.

This discussion indicates that the actual treatment of uncertainty in a firm's decision procedures must fall a long way short of the ideal, given the present state of knowledge. To deal with the problem satisfactorily, managers require insight into the minds of the shareholders. They can only fall back on some generalized assumptions, consistent with attitudes which seem reasonable in the light of theories about individual behaviour.

There are some grounds for arguing that risk aversion should be a relatively minor consideration for a firm seeking to act in shareholders' interests. We have noted above that an individual who includes in his portfolio activities with perfectly negatively correlated results, could, in an extreme case, eliminate risk in the aggregate and would then base his decisions solely on expected results in money terms. Such an extreme is unlikely to prevail in reality. However, many shareholders will have diversified portfolios and the more fully diversified a portfolio, the less the aggregate risk and the better the approximation to expected utility obtained by calculating expected money results. In taking decisions, a firm should be concerned not with the total risk of an activity but with the part of the risk which cannot be eliminated in aggregate.

The divergence between expected utility and expected money value also depends on the range of total income 'at stake'. If a large part of a shareholder's income is relatively certain and only a small part at risk from firms' decisions, money values will give a close approximation to relative utilities. For example, consider the earnings/utility relationship assumed in the case of Mr Cepheus:

$$U = 1000 \log_{10} Y. \qquad \text{(1 from chapter 13)}$$

It can be shown (using differential calculus) that marginal utility, i.e. the relative satisfaction derived from the Yth £ of cash earned, is given by U' in:

$$U' = \frac{1000}{Y} \log_{10} e.$$

Substituting in this expression for various values of Y, we find the following marginal utilities at different levels of earnings (Table 50). Hence if firms' decisions influence earnings only

Table 50

Earnings (£)	Marginal utility $U' = \dfrac{1000}{Y} \log_{10} e$ units
1 000	0·4343
5 000	0·0869
5 200	0·0835
10 000	0·0434

in the range of £5000 to £5200, utilities per £1 vary only between 0·0869 units and 0·0835 units. These absolute values are arbitrary – they depend on the scale we have chosen for the measurement of utility. However, in relative terms, we can see that the use of money values rather than utilities would lead to error, at the extremes, of less than 4 per cent $\left(\dfrac{0·0869 - 0·0835}{0·0869} \right)$. If an individual had a very large part of his earnings at stake – e.g. the range between £1000 and £10 000 – and did not want the risk reduction achieved by diversifying his portfolio, the position would be quite different. His attitude to risk would have a critical relevance for a firm's decisions. Many people in such a position, i.e. having a very large stake in a firm, may be involved in the management of those firms and hence able to bring their views on risk to bear directly.

In the discussion of decisions under uncertainty in the firm, it is assumed that all appraisals consider the effect of various courses of action on aggregate risk. The portfolio effect operates for projects within the firm in the same way as for the individual.

It is noteworthy that many managers profess to be greatly concerned to avoid risk – perhaps more concerned than the above analysis would lead us to expect. One reason for this may be that a firm's objectives are not centred exclusively on the shareholders. Decisions in the firm may seek to promote the well-being of managers and other employees as well, and such objectives may imply the overriding desire to perpetuate the existence of the company at some minimum level of activity and hence to avoid risk. The bankruptcy of a firm might be much more of a disaster for an employee than for a shareholder, and it might be said to be implicit in a manager's contract with a firm that he be allowed to endeavour to keep the company in existence at almost any cost, even rejecting potentially profitable but risky projects.

The strategy of diversification

One attitude that managers of a firm may adopt towards risk is of particular interest in view of the virtual impossibility, noted above, of implementing a theoretically satisfactory policy. The view may be taken that risk is so difficult to analyse explicitly that it would be regarded as a strategic consideration and made the subject of proxy goals. A firm may attempt to measure the riskiness of a project and simply exclude from consideration projects which, by reason of their size and distribution of results, appear to be too risky. Furthermore, a firm may seek to pursue a policy of diversification. It may seek to engage in activities, the results of which are affected by different influences or which respond in opposite ways to given influences. The aggregation effect may then reduce the risk of the total plan.

15 Risk and Uncertainty: Sensitivity Analysis

There is, as we have noted, considerable practical difficulty in estimating a probability distribution for the results of an activity and in estimating an earnings/utility relationship which reflects attitudes to risk. Firms have accordingly sought simpler methods of appraising projects subject to uncertainty, avoiding explicit estimates of these matters. Some of the methods developed are known collectively as sensitivity analysis. They involve a detailed study of the range of possible results of an activity, breaking it down into parts where appropriate and including, in particular, a consideration of extreme possibilities. In this way a profile of the activity is developed. A decision on the worthwhileness of the activity would be reached by studying the profile and weighing, perhaps implicitly, the probabilities of different outcomes and managers' attitudes to the level of risk indicated. Sensitivity analyses may be carried out in various ways. The following are examples:

1 The activity under investigation may be analysed according to various aspects of its results, e.g. in the case of a product, the quantity which can be sold, cost–volume relationships and so on. Estimates are made of the most likely result and of the range of extreme possible results (the range might be estimated in such a way that the probability of a value higher or lower than the extremes would be, say, ·05 – it would then be called a 95 per cent confidence interval). The estimates for individual aspects are combined to form estimates of the range and expected value of results for the whole activity; a decision is based on these aggregate estimates.

2 The analysis may start with estimates of the most likely results of various aspects of the activity. Calculations are then

made of what variations can take place in the most likely results without destroying the worthwhileness of the activity. A decision would take account of the likelihood of variations of this magnitude.

3 Calculations might be made directly of the combinations of results (volume of sales, cost per unit and so on) which would lead to a break-even position on the activity, i.e. no gain or loss. A decision would be reached by considering the likelihood of results better and worse than these.

Attitudes to risk may be reflected in various ways in decisions based on sensitivity analysis. If the extreme outcomes of an activity are undramatic or the activity is small in relation to the size of the firm's operations, a decision may simply be based on most likely results. In the case of large projects or activities which could involve large losses, however, managers who are risk-averters might take the decision which would give the best result if things go wrong. For example, a project with an expected surplus might be rejected if it could lead to a large loss.

Sensitivity analysis may be useful in many short-term decision problems, for example, in appraising contracts offered to a firm and in developing an optimal plan when resources are scarce and the level of their supply and the worthwhileness of their uses are uncertain. However, we will restrict ourselves to a relatively simple illustration concerning a pricing decision on a product, having uncertain sales price–volume and cost–volume relationships.

Auriga Ltd is considering whether the manufacture of a new product is worthwhile and, if so, at what price it should be sold. It is thought, with considerable confidence, that introduction of the product would cause fixed costs to increase by £90 000. Variable costs of manufacture would be a constant amount per product unit; managers estimate their most likely amount at £17 per unit but they are very uncertain about their estimate – they believe that variable costs might fall in the range £15 to £20 per unit (the 95 per cent confidence interval). There is similar uncertainty about the sales price–volume relationship. The managers begin by estimating how many units would be sold at a price of £50; they agree on a most likely quantity of 3750 units and a range of 3000 to 4000 units. There is uncertainty concerning both the level and the elasticity of demand. It is decided to study the implications of three price–volume relationships, model B being the one considered most likely to give good predictions:

(A) $q = 9000 - 100p$,
(B) $q = 10\,000 - 125p$,
(C) $q = 10\,500 - 150p$.

Price would be fixed for the whole of the planning period and the firm would, as a matter of policy, attempt to fulfil all orders received.

Optimal price and output levels, for possible combinations of price–volume and cost–volume relationships, are calculated in Table 51, by equating marginal cost and marginal revenue. If the most likely situation prevails, marginal cost £17 and price–volume model B, the best plan will be to set price at £48.5. However, if other situations prevail, the optimal price may be anywhere in the range £42.5 to £55. Managers may therefore decide to investigate further the possible consequences of setting various prices. We restrict our analysis to three prices, the extremes, £42.5 and £55, and the likely optimum, £48.5.

Table 52 gives predicted results if each of these prices is adopted and various price–volume and cost–volume relationships prevail. The level of uncertainty in the result differs strikingly according to which price is set. The price of £48.5 will give the best net surplus (£34 031) in the most likely conditions (cost £17, price–volume model B). The price of £55 would give the largest possible surplus (£50 000) in certain conditions but it would fail to earn a surplus if model C applied; it may be ruled out for that reason, depending on attitudes to risk. If the worst likely conditions prevail – cost £20 per unit and model C – the price of £42.5 gives the best result, a surplus of £2812; however, the likely optimum price of £48.5 would then give a surplus of £1912, only a little worse.

Table 51 Optimal price and output levels

Price–volume relationship	Model A	Model B	Model C
sales volume, q =	$9000 - 100p$	$10\,000 - 125p$	$10\,500 - 150p$
thus p =	$90 - \dfrac{q}{100}$	$80 - \dfrac{q}{125}$	$70 - \dfrac{q}{150}$
total revenue, pq =	$90q - \dfrac{q^2}{100}$	$80q - \dfrac{q^2}{125}$	$70q - \dfrac{q^2}{150}$
marginal revenue (see chapter 9)	$90 - \dfrac{q}{50}$	$80 - \dfrac{2q}{125}$	$70 - \dfrac{q}{75}$
if marginal cost is £15, optimal quantity is	$50(90-15) = 3750$	$62\cdot5(80-15) = 4062\cdot5$	$75(70-15) = 4125$
if marginal cost is £17, optimal quantity is	$50(90-17) = 3650$	$62\cdot5(80-17) = 3937\cdot5$	$75(70-17) = 3975$
if marginal cost is £20, optimal quantity is	$50(90-20) = 3500$	$62\cdot5(80-20) = 3750$	$75(70-20) = 3750$
optimal (quantity, price) found by substituting optimal quantity in above price model.	(3750, £52·5) (3650, £53·5) (3500, £55)	(4062·5, £47·5) (3937·5, £48·5) (3750, £50)	(4125, £42·5) (3975, £43·5) (3750, £45)

Managers might well decide that the product was worth manufacturing and selling at a price of £48.5, a course unlikely to produce a loss and likely to produce better results on the whole than a price of £42.5. They would have reached this decision without making explicit estimates of probabilities or putting any numerical values on attitudes to risk; they would have investigated a range of possible outcomes, however, and they would have dealt with attitudes to risk implicitly.

The managers of Auriga might have adopted a less sophisticated approach, either instead of the above, or to supplement it. They might have started by calculating the likely contribution, using the optimal price of £48.5 derived from the likely price–volume and cost–volume relationships:

Price per unit (£)	48.5
Cost per unit (£)	17.0
Contribution per unit (£)	31.5
Total contribution from likely volume of 3937.5 units (£)	124 031
Fixed costs (£)	90 000
Net contribution (£)	34 031

The total contribution which would enable the product to break even is £90 000. The level of costs per unit which would yield a break-even result, given the volume of 3937·5 units, would be £C in:

$$3937.5\,(48.5-C) = 90\,000,$$
thus $C = £25.6.$

Costs could be 50 per cent higher than the estimated level of £17 before the product would make a loss. Similarly, the volume of sales which would lead to a break-even position, given the unit costs of £17, would be q in:

$$q(48.5-17) = 90\,000,$$
thus $q = 2857$ units.

Table 52 Estimated earnings from product

Price set at:	£55			£48.5			£42.5		
Price–volume relationship	A	B	C	A	B	C	A	B	C
Predicted sales volume:	3500	3125	2250	4150	3937·5	3225	4750	4687·5	4125
contributions per unit:									
if marginal cost is £15,		£40			£33.5			£27.5	
if marginal cost is £17,		£38			£31.5			£25.5	
if marginal cost is £20,		£35			£28.5			£22.5	
total contributions (£):									
if marginal cost is £15,	140 000	125 000	90 000	139 025	131 906	108 037	130 625	128 906	113 437
if marginal cost is £17,	133 000	118 750	85 500	130 725	124 031	101 587	121 125	119 531	105 187
if marginal cost is £20,	122 500	109 375	78 750	118 275	112 219	91 912	106 875	105 468	92 812
net surplus after fixed costs (£):									
if marginal cost is £15,	50 000	35 000	0	49 025	41 906	18 037	40 625	38 906	23 437
if marginal cost is £17,	43 000	28 750	(4500)	40 725	34 031	11 587	31 125	29 531	15 187
if marginal cost is £20,	32 500	19 375	(11 250)	28 275	22 219	1912	16 875	15 468	2812

Sales volume could fall $1080/3937 = 27 \cdot 4$ per cent below its estimated level before the product would make a loss. The percentage deviations between the estimated position and the break-even position, indicate how sensitive the outcome is to various errors of estimation. A decision would depend on whether managers judged these 'safety margins' to be adequate in relation to their confidence in the estimates. In our example, the margins seem ample; in some cases, however, it might be clear that certain features of the estimates were critical (had low safety margins) and special attention might then be given to the estimates in question. This approach to analysis gives a less complete picture of the likely results from an activity than that described first; it is preferable, however, to an approach which goes no further than an estimation of the likely results.

16 The Accounting Information System: An Historical Perspective

In previous chapters, we have studied characteristics of relevant information for various types of decision and methods of analysing that information to estimate the best decision. We have not discussed means of obtaining the required information but our analysis has perhaps suggested the need to undertake a special study to obtain the information for each decision. Special studies will normally be an important part of a firm's decision processes, particularly for some important, nonroutine decisions. However, a firm normally has a large number of routine decisions for analysis and considerations of cost effectiveness suggest the desirability of some routine system for collecting the information required for such cases. The design of the information system may impose some restrictions on the type of information available; however, it may be desirable to accept the provision of information which is less than ideal in the interest of keeping the costs of collecting the information at a reasonable level. Indeed, as we shall see in chapter 19, the choice of the optimal information system is itself a decision which may be analysed in terms of the relative costs and benefits of different systems, using the general principles described earlier in this book.

Various types of accounting record form the basis for the provision of information for business decisions. It is customary to distinguish financial accounting – the provision of information mainly for use outside the firm by shareholders and others – from cost accounting which provides information for decisions and control within the firm. Both types of accounting record may be associated with a budgetary control system under which future results are systematically estimated and subsequently compared with actual results in order to identify and enquire into differences; such enquiry is intended to promote a learning process which will make it possible to improve the quality of estimates. However, although they may be distinguished, all these types of accounting record have been developed in a single continuous historical process.

The purpose of this chapter is to identify the main practices which are used in deriving accounting information; this will provide a basis for judging its aptness for decision purposes. It is hard to understand the rationale of accounting practices if one studies them as part of a system especially designed to satisfy some single, well identified, purpose. In fact accounting has come to attempt to satisfy several purposes, using the information provided by one basic system subject to only a few special modifications. The resulting practices are a compromise, having regard to the conflicting needs for the various purposes. If one wishes to understand how accounting practices came to be adopted, it is most rewarding to study the historical development of the subject. And since the developments of financial and cost accounting are inextricably mixed, each influencing the methods of the other, we shall study them concurrently.

The history of accounting is a story of the development of financial records in response to the needs of a changing business environment. The needs changed slowly; there was no dramatic revolution. In consequence accounting progressed by the gradual adapting of the existing system; at no point was the total process thought out afresh. There was no inevitable reason why the basic method used in accounting systems – that of double-entry book-keeping – should have endured. No doubt it seemed to work well and it has the merit of facilitating accuracy. In some respects the nature of the method may seem relatively unimportant. Double-entry book-keeping offers great flexibility and could have been the means of applying many different practices. However, as we shall see in this chapter, it is hard to escape the conclusion that the method did shape the development of practice, at least partly. The practices adopted seem, of all the possibilities, to arise naturally within the system. Subsequently, attempts have been made to give them a rationalization in their own right; such attempts rarely seem to go to the heart of the matter.

Accounting in the classical world

Some of the earliest documents known today, dating from classical Greece, Rome and Middle-Eastern civilizations, give primitive accounting information. They give the kind of records needed to enable a man to keep track of his rights and possessions, notes of debts and inventories of property, usually in terms of physical quantities rather than money values. There are also records of communal activities, records of receipts and payments associated with particular projects, for example, and simple budgets giving estimates of payments required for particular purposes. However, as far as we know, ancient accounting did not progress beyond the preparation of various unconnected statements for particular purposes.

Accounting in the Middle Ages
The stewardship function

The first important development of accounting arose out of the practice of men of property of employing agents or stewards to manage some aspects of their affairs. The principals wanted some means of ensuring, as far as possible, that their stewards accounted honestly for the proceeds of property in their charge. An accounting form of control was devised, a statement of personal indebtedness between principal and steward drawn up on the so-called charge and discharge system. The account would record particulars of money or goods which the steward collected on behalf of his principal (charges) and authorized expenditures out of the collections and remittances from steward to principal (discharges). The account would thus disclose any balance still to be accounted for and the entries could be checked against independent evidence as to what amounts should have been collected and what expenditures were properly made. This type of account is an early example of records serving what is now called the stewardship function of accounting.

Suppose, for example, that Lord Ceres employs a steward to

collect rents from his tenants. Rents collected should total £2625 per annum but some tenants are unable to make payments on time. At the start of the year, rents outstanding amounted to £55 and at the end of the year to £40. The steward made authorized payments for the maintenance of buildings amounting to £350 and he made an interim payment to Lord Ceres of £1000. The steward is authorized to retain 10 per cent of amounts collected as his remuneration. The statement of account might run as in Table 53.

Table 53 Record of Lord Ceres of account with steward

Charges	£	Discharges	£
outstanding rents at start	55	outstanding rents at end	40
rents due for year	2625	expenditure on maintenance	350
		steward's remuneration 10% of £2640	264
		interim payment by steward	1000
			1654
		balance due from steward	1026
	2680		2680

The choice of which side of the account to use for charges and which for discharges is arbitrary: only consistency is important. It may be noted that stewardship accounts did not involve important difficulties in choosing the prices at which items should be valued. If the stewardship related to the collection of goods rather than cash, records of quantities served the purpose as well as values; and if money values were attributed to the goods, various methods of valuation, consistently applied, would serve the purpose equally well.

The stewardship function is still important in accounting today. The managers of a large public company are commonly looked on as 'stewards' of the property entrusted to them by the shareholders of the company. One of the functions of financial accounting is to control the honest fulfilment of the stewardship, i.e. the proper use of shareholders' funds; and to the extent that shareholders' funds are held in assets other than cash, various systems of valuation will meet the control needs quite well.

Venturing in partnership

It was common business practice in the Middle Ages to form *ad hoc* partnerships to undertake special ventures or projects. A venture was normally clearly identified as a separate undertaking and of fairly short duration – for example a voyage of a ship to buy merchandise overseas and sell it in the home country.

Ventures were one of the earliest situations in which it was necessary to produce a computation of profit; for the profit computation would be the basis for determining how the proceeds of the venture were to be divided between partners. Because of the short duration of most ventures, however, it was normally sufficient to prepare one profit statement after all transactions had been completed. This would be a simple matter. It was necessary, simply, to compute the difference between cash receipts and cash payments associated with the undertaking, excluding cash introduced by way of finance or withdrawn on account of anticipated profits by the partners. Hence profit would be equal to net cash earnings.

In modern business undertakings, profit calculation is much more difficult. It is desired to produce statements of profit at regular intervals; it is not practicable to wait for the winding-up of the business, because the timing of the winding-up is normally uncertain and very far distant (indeed it may never happen). If interim calculations of profit are made, according to the intuitively appealing definition that profit is the net increase earned in the value of all assets over the period, it is necessary to put some value on assets held in a form other than cash. The choice of method of valuation is one of the central problems of modern accounting. It did not arise in early profit calculations, however, because such calculations were made only when all assets had been converted into cash.

The control of resources under the domestic system

Under the domestic system, an entrepreneur would require a supply of raw materials and issue them to independent workers who carried out the processes of production in their own homes. The outworkers returned finished goods for sale. Under such a system, the entrepreneur had several control needs. He needed to control the stocks of raw materials and finished goods held in his own warehouse; he needed to ensure that materials issued by him were not wasted carelessly or stolen by out-workers; and if he did not restrict himself to sales for cash, he needed to control the proper collection of amounts due to him for sales.

We have already noted that early accounting records were mainly concerned with simple control purposes – the need of an owner to keep track of his property and the need of a principal to secure the proper behaviour of a steward. Let us now attempt to invent an accounting system to meet the control needs of the domestic system.

The use of the domestic system spanned a long period of history. It originated with the earliest manufacturing processes and continues, on a minor scale, at the present time. It is convenient for us to discuss it at this point because it provides a means for illustrating the processes which led to the development of double-entry book-keeping. Our invention will produce a method which was not applied in the earliest uses of the domestic system; indeed the method is a refined version of systems which developed much later – double-entry book-keeping probably developed first in much simpler, trading businesses. To that extent, we are taking the historical sequence out of order and must claim pedagogic licence. However, the historical process itself was not neatly ordered. Poor communications prevented the prompt dissemination of double-entry methods and various versions of the methods probably developed independently at different times. Our description is presented as an accurate reflection of the type of thought processes which led to the development of double-entry – and there is evidence of actual use of procedures similar to those described. We may also note that the accounting methods appropriate to the domestic system may be seen as the forerunners of costing records.

A simple adaptation of the accounting statement suggested as a means of stewardship control would satisfy the needs of the domestic system. It would be necessary to keep a separate account for raw materials in each possible location and for finished goods, e.g. for material in the warehouse, finished goods in the warehouse, material in the hands of each outworker and so on; it would also be necessary to keep an account of indebtedness by customers to whom sales were made.

The accounts for stocks held by outworkers present a particular difficulty. The outworkers received payment for the work which they undertook in manufacture. In consequence, the raw materials which they received were less valuable, relatively, than the finished goods returned to the entrepreneur – it would have cost more to replace the loss of finished goods than the raw materials used in their manufacture. It may be desirable for control purposes to reflect this difference in value in the accounting records. The need can be met by including payments to outworkers in the accounting records and including the value of labour in the record of stocks on hand.

Let us consider a numerical illustration. Mr Hamal is an entrepreneur dealing in shoes. He buys hides for £2.40 and issues them to outworkers. Each hide contains enough material for twenty shoes. Mr Hamal pays the outworkers 16p for their labour on each finished shoe. He sells shoes on credit for 35p per shoe (70p per pair). During his first year in business he buys 680 hides and issues 610 to outworkers; the outworkers finish and receive payment for 11 800 shoes, 11 620 of which are collected by Mr Hamal. Mr Hamal sells 11 460 shoes during the year and collects £3570 from his customers. At the end of the year stocks are counted. There are 67 hides and 155 shoes in the warehouse and 18 hides and 173 shoes held by outworkers.

Accounting records designed for control purposes might run as shown in Tables 54 and 55. In practice a separate account might be kept for each outworker, but for simplicity we restrict ourselves to one total account, giving the same result in aggregate.

Table 54

Hides in warehouse					
	Quantity	Value (£)		Quantity	Value (£)
purchases	680	1632.00*	issues to outworkers	610	1464.00
			losses during year	3	7.20
	680	1632.00		613	1471.20
			balance – closing stocks	67	160.80
	680	1632.00		680	1632.00

Hides held by outworkers					
	Quantity	Value (£)		Quantity	Value (£)
issues	610	1464.00*	11 800 finished shoes	590	3304.00
payments for work		1888.00*	losses during year	2	4.80
	610	3352.00		592	3308.80
			balance – closing stocks	18	43.20
	610	3352.00		610	3352.00

The significance of the asterisks is explained below. Each account shows on the left-hand side, items which have to be accounted for – stocks brought into existence in the given location by purchase, issue, manufacture and so on. Entries on the right-hand side explain what has happened to the stocks – some are accounted for by use, including the standard allowance of one-twentieth of a hide per shoe in the case of hides held by outworkers, others are accounted for by stocks still held. However these explanations are insufficient in every case; there is a residue lost. Mr Hamal will exercise control by considering whether these losses are reasonable in the light of rates of spoilage, pilfering and so on that he is prepared to accept. If he decides that any of the losses are unreasonable he must consider what preventative action he can take and weigh the likely cost and likely saving.

Each account includes a record of quantities (except in the

case of debtors, for which £s are the natural measure of quantities) and these alone are useful for control purposes. We also include value columns which give a better indication

Table 55

Shoes held by outworkers					
	Quantity	Value (£)		Quantity	Value (£)
finished shoes	11 800	3304.00*	shoes collected	11 620	3253.60*
			losses during year	7	1.96
	11 800	3304.00		11.627	3255.56
			balance – closing stocks	173	48.44
	11 800	3304.00		11 800	3304.00

Shoes in warehouse					
	Quantity	Value (£)		Quantity	Value (£)
collected from outworkers	11 620	3253.60*	sales at cost	11 460	3208.80
			losses during year	5	1.40
	11 620	3253.60		11 465	3210.20
			balance – closing stocks	155	43.40
	11 620	3253.60		11 620	3253.60

Debtors			
	Value (£)		Value (£)
sales 11 460 at 35p	4011.00	cash collected	3570.00*
	4011.00		3570.00
		balance – outstanding	441.00
	4011.00		4011.00

of the seriousness of the losses. Hides are valued at their cost price of £2.40. The account for hides held by outworkers transforms the value of the raw material by the addition of labour costs; finished shoes are valued at 28p each, 12p for the cost of material (£2.40 per hide divided by twenty, the number of shoes per hide) plus 16p for labour. As we shall see, these values arise naturally in the recording process. It is also natural that when information was required about the costs of different activities, for decision purposes, reference should be made to records like these to obtain it.

The development of double-entry techniques

The detailed history of the development of double-entry book-keeping is obscure. It seems certainly to have originated before the publication, in 1494, of the first book on the subject. For the author, Paciolo, refers to a manuscript circulated privately, the ideas of which he used. There is some reason to believe that businessmen had been using double-entry in practice over a period of about two hundred years previously. It seems likely that the method was evolved by several people independently, as the natural end-product of a series of refinements of more primitive systems of records, rather than that some one person developed the whole system at one time and communicated his ideas to others.

We can only speculate on the mode of evolution of double-entry techniques, but some speculation is relevant to our theme of explaining modern accounting practices. Let us speculate, making further use of Mr Hamal's business for purposes of illustration. It seems likely as noted above that double-entry actually developed in simpler businesses, perhaps the business of traders rather than manufacturers. However, in this respect and a few others we use some licence for purposes of exposition.

Mr Hamal would presumably have at least one property which he would wish to control, other than the stocks and debtors referred to previously: cash. An account to control this would have the same form as the control accounts described previously. It would record receipts on one side (cash to be accounted for) and payments on the other, leaving a balance to be checked by counting the amount held at the year end. Suppose Mr Hamal's cash account runs as in Table 56, using the data given above and the additional information that he provided £600 to start the business, spent £370 on general business expenses and withdrew £260 for personal living expenses.

We have now established six different accounts for Mr Hamal, each compiled independently, recording the history of his property. If we study the records, however, as we may assume they were studied by the pioneers of double-entry book-keeping, we notice that the different accounts are linked. There are several matching entries. The issues to outworkers on the right-hand side of 'Hides in warehouse' account is matched by an entry on the left-hand side of 'Hides held by

Table 56

Cash on hand			
	(£)		(£)
provided by Mr Hamal	600.00	purchases of hides	1632.00*
collected from debtors	3570.00*	payments to outworkers	1888.00*
		business expenses	370.00
		living expenses	260.00
	4170.00		4150.00
		balance – cash on hand	20.00
	4170.00		4170.00

outworkers' account. The entry 'Purchase of hides' on the right-hand side of 'Cash on hand' account is matched by an entry on the left-hand side of 'Hides in warehouse' account. Indeed, all the entries marked by an asterisk have matching counterparts and may be thought of as representing a flow of activities: cash converted to hides, hides issued to outworkers, goods manufactured by outworkers, returned to the warehouse and sold. The process of invention of double entry may have begun at an even earlier stage, when stock records were kept only in terms of quantities. It might then have been noticed that transactions had paired effects, that a fall in cash was linked with an increase in stocks, a fall in one stock with an increase in another and so on. This observation would have suggested that the exploitation of the concept of matching entries required the valuation of stocks at their 'actual costs' as we have assumed in our illustration – the cash payment of £1632 for hides would be matched with a debit entry in stock of hides of the same value and so on.

We may imagine that the record-keepers noticed this matching of entries and saw in it a possible scheme for improving the accuracy of their records. In practice each account would have contained a large number of individual entries (rather than the totals we have used) and errors would have abounded, diminishing the value of the records for control purposes. As the records stand, only some of the entries are matched. Suppose a system were to be invented for recording every entry twice, once on the left-hand side of an account and once on the right-hand side. It would then be possible to incorporate an arithmetic check into the records. The totals of entries in each account could be entered on a summary sheet, with separate columns for the left-hand side (debits as they were called) and the right-hand side (credits), and the two columns should give the same total. If they did, the arithmetic accuracy of the records could be taken as proven – excepting the relatively unlikely possibility that two errors would exactly compensate. If the two columns did not give the same total a search would have to be made to find and correct the errors. Moreover the differences between debits and credits (the balances) could also be listed and should also give an arithmetic 'proof', i.e. the net debits should equal the net credits.

The invention of matching entries for the remaining transactions of Mr Hamal presents little difficulty. We simply create additional accounts (see Table 57).

The matching entries are now complete. There is no need to invent matching entries for the closing stocks – they can be left as balances on the accounts. The summary sheet, giving the check on arithmetic accuracy, would run as Table 58.

At this point, our inventor of double-entry book-keeping might well rest, having achieved his goal of improving his arithmetical accuracy. His system had further development potential, however. Some of the balances in the summary sheet would be required for further use. Stocks, debtors and cash on hand would be required to start off the accounts for the next year – they represent available resources, the use of which must be controlled. In other words, the accounts for property of various kinds must be kept running from year to year to

Table 57

Losses of stock (£)			
hides in warehouse	7.20		
hides held by outworkers	4.80		
shoes held by outworkers	1.96		
shoes in warehouse	1.40		
	15.36		—
		balance	15.36
	15.36		15.36
Sales at cost (£)			
shoes in warehouse	3208.80		
	3208.80		—
		balance	3208.80
	3208.80		3208.80
Sales (£)			
		debtors	4011.00
	—		4011.00
balance	4011.00		
	4011.00		4011.00
Cash provided by Mr Hamal (£)			
		cash on hand	600.00
	—		600.00
balance			
	600.00		600.00
Business expenses (£)			
cash on hand	370.00		
	370.00		—
		balance	370.00
	370.00		370.00
Living expenses (£)			
cash on hand	260.00		
	260.00		—
		balance	260.00
	260.00		260.00

Table 58

	Totals		Balances	
	Debits (£)	Credits (£)	Debits (£)	Credits (£)
hides in warehouse	1632.00	1471.20	160.80	
hides held by outworkers	3352.00	3308.80	43.20	
shoes held by outworkers	3304.00	3255.56	48.44	
shoes in warehouse	3253.60	3210.20	43.40	
debtors	4011.00	3570.00	441.00	
cash on hand	4170.00	4150.00	20.00	
losses of stock	15.36		15.36	
sales at cost	3208.80		3208.80	
sales		4011.00		4011.00
cash provided by Mr Hamal		600.00		600.00
business expenses	370.00		370.00	
living expenses	260.00		260.00	
	23 576.76	23 576.76	4611.00	4611.00

maintain continuous control. Other balances have served their
purpose of completing the arithmetical check, however, and
can now be disregarded. We might divide our summary sheet
on this basis (see Table 59).

Although the balances in our revised summary statement
were derived in the process of checking arithmetical accuracy,
their nature invites economic interpretation. Such economic
interpretation probably developed many years after the origins
of double-entry when the need was felt for an indication of the
progress of a business, perhaps by investors who were not
involved in its management; at this time the original purposes
for which double-entry developed were probably forgotten.
The balances in the first section of Table 59 *appear* to represent
the net worth of Mr Hamal's business property; the balances
in the second section, apart from the provision of cash and
living expenses, are all items aptly described as revenues and
costs, the net amount of which could be called 'profit' (though
its economic significance is not clear from its derivation).

Table 59

Balances of continuing interest	Debits (£)	Credits (£)
hides in warehouse	160.80	
hides held by outworkers	43.20	
shoes held by outworkers	48.44	
shoes in warehouse	43.40	
debtors	441.00	
cash on hand	20.00	
	756.84	—
Net total	756.84	
Balances of 'no further interest'	Debits (£)	Credits (£)
losses of stock	15.36	
sales at cost	3208.80	
sales		4011.00
cash provided by Mr Hamal		600.00
business expenses	370.00	
living expenses	260.00	
	3854.16	4611.00
Net total		756.84

Moreover, the linkage of the two sections, through their net totals, suggests that we can explain where the net worth came from in terms of the second section – profits plus cash provided less living expenses.

Table 60 Profit and loss account

	(£)	(£)
sales		4011.00
less cost of sales		3208.80
		802.20
less business expenses	370.00	
less stock losses	15.36	
		385.36
net profit		416.84

Hence, via a process of evolution, which was lengthy in historical terms, we obtain primitive versions of the modern profit and loss account and balance sheet (see Tables 60 and 61).

Table 61 Balance sheet

Source of net worth	(£)	(£)	Net worth	(£)	(£)
Cash introduced	600.00		Hides in warehouse	160.80	
add net profit	416.84		hides held by outworkers	43·20	
	———		shoes held by outworkers	48.44	
	1016.84		shoes in warehouse	43.40	
less living expenses	260.00			———	
	———	756.84			295.84
			debtors		441.00
			cash on hand		20.00
		———			———
		756.84			756.84

Such, we may imagine, was the beginning of the development of the accounting system which provides some of the information to guide decisions in modern business. Its usefulness for this purpose is a matter we must consider further.

The development of valuation conventions

Our speculations about the way in which double-entry bookkeeping developed provide a basis for explaining the origins of two conventions of current accounting practice.

First, the convention of basing asset valuations on their cost prices in normal circumstances (departures from the cost valuation are made in some cases but are exceptions rather than the general rule). Cost-based valuation would have come into practice naturally, in the development of double-entry processes. The double-entry comprised the linking of the cash payment representing the cost price of an asset with the matching entry for the increase in asset value.

Secondly, the so-called realization convention – the convention that profits are not recognized until they are represented by cash or a firm contractual right – follows the cost-based valuation convention. A profit arises under the double-entry system when an increase in the value of an asset is recognized (without compensating decrease in another asset) or one asset is replaced by another having higher value. In the example of Mr Hamal, stocks were recorded at their cost until they were sold and replaced by debtors accorded a higher value; at that point a profit was recorded equal to the difference between sales value and cost. The value of stock could have been increased earlier and a profit recognized earlier. The recording would have presented no great difficulty; but accounting conventions do not normally admit the possibility.

If accounting had been designed originally to inform interested parties of the economic progress of a business, it is possible that some other conventions for asset valuation and profit recognition would have been adopted. However, early accounting evolved in the small businesses of owner-managers who did not need special information about its progress. They had – or thought they had – all the information they needed from personal experience. As we have noted, accounting was developed for control purposes and these purposes would be served quite well by almost any valuation system. There was no need to depart from the simple cost-based convention.

Early cost accounting

The initial impetus to the development of the techniques which now comprise cost accounting – the provision of information on the costs of various activities – was to come from the need to identify the cost of finished goods held by concerns which had manufactured them. A simple example of this need was given in the valuation of Mr Hamal's shoes. The convention of valuing assets at cost had become firmly established by the time this need became widespread; but the identification of the cost of manufactured stock involved special difficulties of definition and accounting organization.

The manufacture of goods may be regarded as involving two main types of cost. On the one hand, materials and labour, known as direct costs, are easy to identify with particular products and are generally regarded as part of their cost. On the other hand, other manufacturing costs, indirect items such as factory rent, supervisory labour and the cost of machinery

are hard to identify with particular products and there is scope
for disagreement about the desirability of attempting to do so.
If indirect costs are regarded as part of the cost of manufactured
stock, they must be divided between the units produced by
some rule of thumb method, for there is no obvious physical
link between the products and the costs.

Such costing problems received little attention in early
applications of double-entry, however. The major enterprises
were trading concerns and the cost of their stock was readily
identifiable from payments to suppliers. Manufacturing was
mainly carried out by craftsmen, operating on a small scale,
and having little need for elaborate accounting records. Their
methods of production were very simple and their indirect
costs accordingly small; even if they had kept formal accounting records, the decision on whether or not to include indirect
costs in the value of stock would have seemed immaterial. One
or two cases are known, dating from the sixteenth century, of
manufacturers who calculated costs of production, including
an allowance for indirect costs. The calculations took the
form of special statements, however, not integrated in a formal
double-entry system. Early accounting was concerned mainly
with simple control purposes, and, for such purposes, it
matters little whether indirect costs are included in stock values
or not.

Accounting in the nineteenth century

Increase in the scale of business enterprise

The main developments in nineteenth-century accounting
were brought about by increases in the size and complexity of
business firms. Machines had been developed which enabled
manufacturing processes to be carried out more efficiently;
they could be exploited, however, only if goods were produced
on a large scale and production processes were broken down
into separate, small operations, undertaken by different
employees. In consequence, firms needed larger amounts of
finance to enable the purchase of machinery and the holding of
larger stocks; they also needed more complex organization

with more effort devoted to supervision. These developments influenced both financial accounting and cost accounting.

The main influences on financial accounting were associated with developments in the legal form of business organization. Small groups of individuals in partnership were often unable to provide the large amounts of finance required for manufacturing business. The joint-stock company developed as a means of tapping new sources of finance. It involved a large number of individuals (stockholders or shareholders) in subscribing finance. Most of them took no direct part in the management of the firm – they elected a group of directors to manage affairs on their behalf. The return for the use of their capital was the payment of a dividend (of variable amount) out of company profits. However, under the existing law, if a company became bankrupt, its shareholders would be liable to settle the debts of the company out of their personal property. Such a liability was naturally a considerable deterrent to the large-scale investment of funds in the new form of organization. The Government encouraged the growth of the number of joint-stock companies, in due course, by giving shareholders the privilege of limited liability – creditors of the company could then no longer look to shareholders' private assets for satisfaction in the event of business failure.

The significance for accounting of the development of joint-stock companies with limited liability was two-fold. First, it increased the importance of the stewardship function – it was desirable that directors should account to shareholders for the honest management of the property entrusted to them. As we have noted, almost any system of asset valuation would be suitable for this purpose.

Secondly, a new significance was given to calculations of profit. Because shareholders had limited liability, it was thought right to give creditors some new measure of protection. Means were sought to ensure that shareholders did not receive too large sums as dividends and thereby expose creditors to greater risk. The method adopted was to restrict dividends to the amount of profits earned by the company. The value given to assets was an important determinant of the profit calculation: the higher the value given to assets, the higher the profit would be. The convention of basing asset values on their original cost was quite firmly entrenched by this time. Whereas it seems to have developed accidentally in the first place, it was now argued to be desirable in principle compared to the alternative of some higher value. It implied that profits would be recognized only on realization, and recognition of profits at an earlier time might encourage higher dividend payments and hence prejudice the interests of creditors. The protection of creditors also promoted the adoption of the supporting convention of conservatism. If asset values are thought to have fallen below cost, they are immediately reduced and the loss is accordingly recognized immediately in the profit computation. This convention gained general acceptance in the nineteenth century because of its value in protecting creditors from the after-effects of excessive dividends.

It might be expected that the increase in absentee business owners (shareholders) would have put another pressure on accounting. Shareholders would require information from which they could form good estimates of the future results of their company, as a guide to personal decision taking; some system of reporting for this purpose might have been expected to develop. None did, however. Shareholders received only the traditional profit and loss account and balance sheet, originally by-products of a system designed for the stewardship function and the protection of creditors. They seem to have been satisfied with these statements although they were not demonstrated to be apt to their needs. The accounting conventions on which they were based had acquired the status that goes with long usage and were accepted as leading to 'correct' computations of profit. Their economic significance for decisions seems hardly to have been questioned. Furthermore they have not changed significantly up to the present time (although shareholders are now given more detailed information).

The increased scale of business activity in the nineteenth century also had implications for cost accounting. It led to a large growth in the proportionate significance of indirect costs and hence added urgency to the need to develop an agreed treatment of such costs in the valuation of manufactured stock. The growth in the size of business also made it impossible for senior managers to have first-hand knowledge of the technology and costs of the process applied in manufacturing all the firm's products. It became increasingly important to develop some routine system to provide information for the estimation of costs, information on which pricing and output decisions could be based. Even so there was little progress with such problems until the last quarter of the century.

Competition and the quest for accurate costs

The development of cost accounting on a large scale seems to have started in the engineering industry in the last quarter of the nineteenth century. Competitive pressures on pricing provided a fresh stimulus. At these times, there was little sophistication in the procedures by which a firm set its prices. The model-building approach described in chapter 9 was not used (nor is it today on any large scale). A manager would simply try to obtain a selling price which would cover costs and allow a sufficient margin for him to earn a reasonable aggregate profit. However, even this process required information about product costs. Previously, firms had been able to charge prices which allowed generous profit margins – so generous that, on the average, any likely error in calculating the cost of a product could be absorbed easily. Then competition led to a reduction in profit margins and prompted a search for a system which would yield 'accurate' estimates of the cost of various activities.

The search for accuracy did not imply a careful consideration of which costs were relevant for particular decisions (in the manner of our discussion in chapter 5). Moreover the focus of attention for decision purposes was on accounting profits rather than the net cash receipts which we have argued to be relevant. The objective was to spread the total costs of a firm over its outputs so that if an output was priced at the cost attributed to it plus a percentage for profit, there seemed to be reasonable certainty of earning a satisfactory profit overall. The system required would not only identify the direct costs of each output; if total costs were to be covered, indirect costs had to be brought into the calculations.

Methods developed for allocating indirect costs to outputs involved the selection of some characteristics that could be measured for each output and used as a basis for allocation. For example, the cost of direct labour might be chosen as a basis. If it were estimated that total direct labour costs for a period would be £10 500 and that total indirect costs would be £6300, it might be assumed that $£\dfrac{6300}{10\,500} = £0.60$ of indirect cost would be incurred for each £1 of labour cost. The cost of a particular product might be built up as follows:

	(£)
Raw materials – cost of actual materials used	72
Direct labour – actual time, 140 hours at £0.75 per hour	105
Indirect costs – 60 per cent of direct labour cost	63
Total cost	240

We shall discuss the methods adopted for the allocation of indirect costs in more detail in chapter 17, and we shall discuss the limitations of indirect cost allocation as a means of pricing and product selection in chapter 18.

The integration of financial and costing records

Originally, the costing information was provided by separate calculations, apart from the main double-entry system of financial accounting. A second significant development near the end of the nineteenth century was the integration of costing records into the main double-entry book-keeping system. The method seems to have been described in the literature firstly by Garke and Fells in 1887 – though it may have been used in practice at an earlier time. One advantage of the method was that it secured for the costing records, the arithmetic checks implicit in double-entry systems. The integration also had the effect of consolidating into costing practice, the valuation conventions used in stewardship accounting. For example, the convention of valuing assets at cost led to the crystallization of the normal costing practice of costing materials used from stock at their original cost, rather than the possible alternative of replacement cost. It would have been possible to change the conventions and still operate a system of double-entry recording; established practice was so strong, however, that no change was seriously considered. Some costing practices were similarly absorbed into stewardship accounting. The method of allocating indirect costs to identify the costs of product units was consistent with cost-based valuation conventions and many firms used this method for valuing their stocks of finished goods in their balance sheets.

Costing normal activity

The method of allocating indirect costs over actual production seemed to work well in times of normal business activity. However, its effects, in times of unusual variation in the volume of production, were seen to be strange. If the volume of output was reduced, the cost attributed to each unit increased, even though there was no change in the time taken over production and there was, normally, no ground for charging a higher price. In order to overcome this anomaly, it became usual to attribute to each product unit the proportion of indirect costs which would be appropriate at normal output levels. If the level of activity was low, some indirect costs would not be attributed to individual products; if it was high, the total amounts attributed to products would exceed the costs incurred.

The development of standard costing

The next stage in the development of costing practice may be seen partly as a change in emphasis from cost ascertainment to cost control. The development may also be seen as a natural outgrowth of the use of 'normal' levels of activity as a basis for the allocation of indirect costs.

The idea behind the development was that costing could be used for other purposes than as a guide to pricing and output decisions. It was not sufficient simply to accept measurements of actual cost figures for various activities. It was probable that some jobs were carried out less efficiently than possible and that the costing system could be used as a means of tracing such inefficiency. Moreover, the system of recording actual costs for each business activity was an insufficient basis for the assessment of efficiency. If a manager tried to assess the level of efficiency simply by reading the reported costs for various activities, his judgement would be biased by the figures actually reported. He needed a standard of efficiency for purposes of comparison. The chosen remedy was to develop a standard cost estimate for each activity, an independent estimate of what a product should cost to manufacture if operations were carried out with reasonable efficiency. Actual costs were then compared with the standard costs and substantial differences were analysed and investigated. The investigation would lead to action designed to improve future performance or to an admission that the standards were unreasonable and should be revised.

Standard costing, as this system of control is called, may be seen as the beginning of a more scientific approach to management. Its introduction coincided with a time of rapid technological progress. Manufacturing operations were studied and often reorganized in a more efficient manner. Changes were stimulated by competitive pressures and their implementation was assisted by standard costing. Although standard costing was intended primarily as an instrument of control, it is significant that it involved independent and systematic predictions of future results. In this, it anticipated the requirements of information for decision purposes, analysed in this book. Much (though not all) of standard costing information is more directly relevant for decisions than costing records of past results. However some time had to pass before the influence of operational research methods brought to bear on this financial information the analytical techniques required to exploit it; and the process of development is far from complete today.

17 The Nature and Value of Cost Accounting

Cost accounting is a system of record keeping which seeks to identify the results of individual activities carried on by a business (the manufacture of various products and so on). It seems to have grown out of accounting statements intended to control business assets and to facilitate the valuation of stocks in the preparation of financial accounts. More recently, the complexity and competitiveness of business caused managers to seek systematic information to guide their decisions. They wanted estimates of the cost of various activities so that they could judge whether those activities were worthwhile, given a prevailing or offered price; and they wanted estimates of costs as a basis for determining their own pricing policy when prices were not dictated by external factors. They often used for these purposes, the information on actual costs of past activities readily available in the cost accounts.

It is widely accepted in the academic literature and in the best practice that the application of conventional costing methods may fail to yield the best information for business decisions. There are two main reasons for this. First, costing gives information about past activities (and is often called historical costing in consequence), whereas direct estimates of the results of future activities are required for decisions (possibly guided by a study of past results). Secondly, estimates on which decisions will be based should indicate how costs will *vary* according to the various alternative decisions that might be taken; in attributing costs to particular activities, costing often implies an inappropriate model of their variability. In many businesses, particularly the larger ones, a system of standard costing has displaced historical costing as the means of providing information for decisions; standard costing at least uses explicit estimates of future results even though it does not generally incorporate improved models of cost variability.

The uses and limitations of various types of costing information are still not appreciated in business as widely as seems desirable. We therefore consider some of the practices of cost accounting in more detail in order that their output may be contrasted with the information required for decisions, described in the early chapters of this book.

The unit of costing

One of the first questions that has to be settled in setting up a costing system is the choice of a basic unit of activity for the analysis of costs. The appropriate unit will vary from one type of business to another. If a business carries out a number of independent jobs or contracts, it will probably decide to calculate the cost of each one. On the other hand, if it has a standard line of products, it may decide to calculate the cost per unit of each product; or, if a number of product units are processed at the same time, a 'batch' of units may be a preferred basis. Some manufacturing operations involve processing operations on some material, e.g. liquids, chemicals, metals and so on. In such cases, individual units may not be physically identifiable and the natural costing base may be the unit of each type of output, a gallon of liquid, a ton of material and so on.

Costing methods are often used by firms which provide a service rather than a product of a physical nature. In some such firms individual contracts or jobs may provide the best basis for costing – professional firms often fall in this category. In others, something more akin to process costing may be appropriate; a transport undertaking may calculate the average cost of carrying a passenger or a ton of freight for one mile.

Direct costing versus full costing

We noted, in chapter 16, that early costing systems were mainly concerned with so-called direct costs, costs such as materials and labour which can be identified reasonably easily with individual jobs or other activities. More remote costs, known as indirect or overhead costs, were only brought into costing systems at a later date, mainly because they were originally immaterial in amount. The question of whether overhead costs should be apportioned to individual activities in a costing system is today the subject of controversy.

Some firms restrict their costing information to an analysis of direct costs; such systems are known as direct or marginal costing systems. Proponents of this approach argue that many overhead costs are not altered by the acceptance of an additional unit of activity. Decisions should be based on estimates of cost variability. The inclusion of some proportion of overhead costs in the cost of an activity may lead to confusion about the amount of variable costs whereas direct costs represent good estimates of variable cost.

Firms which use a full costing system, i.e. which allocate overhead costs to individual activities, counter with the argument that a firm has to cover its overhead costs if it is to make a profit overall; if they are excluded from the costing system, it is argued, this requirement may be overlooked.

There are also differences in practice concerning which overhead costs, if any, should be dealt with in a full costing system. Some firms restrict themselves to a consideration of manufacturing overheads, i.e. costs which are closely related to production (e.g. factory rent, cost of machinery). Such costs normally account for the major part of overhead costs. Other firms also allocate office and administration costs to individual activities. It is rare for selling and distribution costs or finance costs to be allocated however. Selling and distribution costs are excluded because a major use of costing information is to put a value on the stock of finished goods for the firm's balance sheet, and selling and distribution costs normally arise only when an item has ceased to be held in stock.

Finance costs comprise interest on capital employed by a firm. Some of the capital bears an explicit interest cost, for example, long-term loans at a fixed rate of interest and bank overdrafts. A major part of business capital, however, is provided by ordinary shareholders who do not receive a contractual rate of interest. The traditional accounting view is that the treatment of costs should be consistent and hence that interest should be included on all the capital or not at all; and it is preferred to omit the item altogether rather than impute a cost that does not appear in the records explicitly. Such a view does not meet the economic argument that there is an opportunity cost in the use of all capital (interest sacrificed in an alternative use) which must be covered if the actual use is to be justified.

We shall consider further the relative merits of direct and full costing later. Firstly, however, let us consider the application of the methods in more detail.

Direct costing

We begin by considering direct costs. We noted above that proponents of direct costing systems base their arguments on an assumed identity between the costs allocated to activities under a direct costing system and the increase in total costs, caused by the activity. This identity holds good only approximately, however.

One important difference between direct costs and variable costs arises because of essentially practical considerations. The accountant has to organize a record-keeping system that traces individual costs to particular activities. The operation of such a system does not present especial difficulty in the case of materials and labour costs and these costs are normally large enough to make the operation seem worthwhile. In essence it is necessary simply to keep a record of all materials issued from store, including a note of the activity they will be used on, and to have all employees keep a record of how they spend their time. Many other costs are variable in nature, e.g. fuel and power – and it is possible to conceive of systems for identifying such costs with individual activities. The difficulty (and hence the cost) of tracing such items individually, however, normally persuades the accountant that it is not worthwhile. Direct costs are therefore restricted to those costs which can be identified with activities within a routine system without excessive cost.

On the other hand, some costs, treated in practice as direct costs, may not be variable. Accounting practice is strongly influenced by convention and it has become customary to classify certain labour and materials costs as direct costs without considering the particular circumstances of each case. Labour costs may sometimes arise at a fixed level, independent of the volume of activity carried on by a firm. Suppose, for example, that a firm employs a skilled workforce. If some employees were dismissed when business was slack, it might prove extremely costly to re-assemble a skilled team when business revived. In consequence, the firm might decide to retain its workforce at full strength during slack times, provided business was expected to revive. In such a case, the alternative to using an employee on a particular job might be to keep him idle, or, at least, to employ him on work which would not cover his wage. Acceptance of an additional job might not cause any increase in the firm's total labour cost; but the labour cost would normally still be included as a direct cost. Let us now consider costing practices relating to materials and labour costs in turn.

Costing for materials

It is not difficult to identify the physical quantities of material used on a particular activity. In order to build up a record of the cost of a job, however, it is necessary to put a value on the material – and this gives rise to one or two problems. In settling the value, it might be thought that the first question would be to debate the relative merits of bases such as actual (historical) cost, replacement cost, opportunity cost, realizable value and so on. However, such a debate has not taken place; as we noted in chapter 16, cost accounting has adopted, from financial accounting, the practice of basing asset values on actual costs – and the cost attributed to the use of the asset has followed suit. The problems that have been debated have been at a lower level, concerning, for example, the identification of actual cost. The identification of the cost of a material may be difficult because a firm has in stock identical supplies, purchased at different prices. It might be possible to apply some system whereby different items were marked with their actual prices – but such a system is not normally thought to be worth the effort. Instead cost accounting identifies cost by assuming some standard pattern in the flow of goods through stores. At least three different assumptions are accepted in practice. They are (a) FIFO – the assumption that goods purchased earliest (first in) are the first to be used (first out), (b) LIFO – the assumption that goods purchased most recently (last in) are the first to be used (first out), and (c) Average Cost – a compromise which involves valuing all items of a particular type at an average cost, the average being recomputed each time a new purchase is made. A simple example will illustrate that the use of different methods of cost identification can lead to significant differences in the cost of material attributed to an activity. Altair Ltd has 3000 tons of a certain material in stock, 1000 tons having been purchased on 5 January at £10 per ton and 2000 tons on 8 January, after a price increase, at £13 per ton; 2000 tons are issued for a job on 10 January. For costing purposes, the value given to this material would be under

(a) FIFO: 1000 at £10+1000 at £13 = £23 000,

(b) LIFO: 2000 at £13 = £26 000,

and

(c) Average Cost: 2000 at £12

$$\left(\text{i.e. } \frac{1000 \times £10 + 2000 \times £13}{3000}\right) = £24\,000.$$

Under all three methods, the amounts eventually attributed to jobs will equal the total costs actually incurred in purchasing materials, provided stocks fall to zero at some time; however, the distribution of the cost between different activities will vary. In a period of rising prices, FIFO will attribute a relatively low value to materials used and a relatively high value to stocks remaining on hand (and hence future jobs); LIFO will give a relatively high value to materials used and a relatively low value to stocks remaining on hand; and the average cost method will achieve an intermediate position. A consideration of the relative merits of the methods for reporting to shareholders is beyond the scope of this book. Each method is satisfactory for keeping track of materials owned. The discussion in chapter 5 suggests that none of them is strictly satisfactory for decision making. Replacement cost is probably the value of stock most usually relevant for decision purposes and the LIFO method would normally give the closest approximation of replacement cost.

The assumption that all three methods for the costing of materials will involve the eventual allocation of all costs of materials to various activities depends on the assumption that there is no wastage or loss by deterioration or evaporation in the store. If such a loss takes place, and no adjustment is made, the accounting records will disclose a larger stock of materials on hand than actually exists. In adjusting for such losses, it is customary to distinguish between normal losses (which are an unavoidable consequence of normal operation) and other losses. It is argued that normal losses are an inevitable cost of a firm's activities. Consequently, if it is normal to lose, say, 10 per cent of a material, the basic charge for materials to each activity should be inflated in the proportion $\frac{10}{9}$ to allow for the losses. If the estimate of the rate of loss is exactly correct, the quantity of stock remaining on hand, as recorded in the accounts, will exactly match the quantity ascertained by physical count. If an accurate count of stock on hand is taken, however, it may well give a different value from that given in the accounting records, even though allowance has been made for normal losses. Any such remaining difference would be excluded from activity costs; it would be eliminated from the stock of materials account and treated as a reduction or increase in profit on account of abnormal losses or savings.

Costing for labour

The costing of labour is somewhat simpler than the costing of materials. Costing records are based on summaries of employees' time records, analysed by activities; each activity is allocated the cost of the time it has absorbed, priced at the wage rates of the employees concerned. The time that can be identified with individual jobs will probably be less than the total time paid for by the firm. There will probably be some normal idle time (time spent in changing jobs, waiting for the issue of materials, dealing with clerical tasks and so on) and there may be some abnormal idle time (time lost because of prolonged machine breakdown, for example) or possibly some abnormal saving of time (implying over-allowance for normal idle time). Idle time is dealt with in the same way as wastage of material. An inflated wage rate would be charged to jobs to cover normal idle time; and any remaining difference would be excluded from the activity costs and included in the profit account.

The costing of overheads

We have noted that many firms also include an allowance for factory overhead costs in computing the costs of individual activities. This process raises some difficult questions. Whereas, in the case of direct costs, it is simple to identify resources used with individual activities, in the case of overhead costs there is no natural unit that can be used as a basis for identification. There is no obvious method, for example, for identifying what part of the cost of renting a factory should be related to each job undertaken. The essence of the method adopted by accountants to overcome this difficulty is to link the overhead costs with some other measure that can be identified with individual activities; for example, it might be assumed that overhead costs attributed to each activity should be proportional to labour hours spent on the activities.

Bases of overhead allocation

Four main base measures are used for factory overhead allocation, either singly or in combination; materials costs, labour costs, labour hours and machine hours. The first two were often used in early costing practice, presumably because of their simplicity, but they are not greatly favoured in current practice. Materials cost is sometimes used as a basis for the allocation of storage costs (warehouse rent and wages and so on), but rarely for general factory overheads; labour cost, if it is used, is normally justified only on the grounds that it gives a simple approximation to the labour hour method, an approximation which is close if all employees receive similar rates of pay. We shall therefore concentrate our attention on the use of machine hours and labour hours as bases of allocation.

Identification of cost centres

Normally, the first step in a system of overhead allocation is to split the overhead costs for the whole firm between a number of subsidiary divisions of the firm – cost centres, as they are called. Cost centres are usually chosen as the smallest natural units, fulfilling a homogeneous function, into which the firm may be divided. If a firm comprises a number of departments (or divisions), costs would be allocated between these in the first place; and, indeed, the departments may, in some cases, be regarded as cost centres. More usually however, cost centres are chosen as smaller units. If the machine hour method is used for overhead allocation, the cost centres may be single machines or groups of associated machines; similarly if the labour hour method is used, an individual employee or group of employees may be chosen as a cost centre.

Overheads are divided between cost centres on bases which are rule of thumb, yet have superficial appeal because of some physical significance. Rent, for example, may be divided between cost centres in proportion to the floor area occupied by departments, machines or men; heating in proportion to the volume of space occupied; supervisory labour according to an estimate of the proportion of the supervisor's time taken up in each cost centre. Depreciation – a proportion of the acquisition cost – of machinery would normally be calculated separately for each machine and attributed to the cost centre in which the machine was used; machine running costs, e.g. fuel and power, might be measured separately for each machine or divided between machines in proportion to their operating hours, weighted to allow for the rate of power input requirements of each. The list of allocation methods could be extended considerably with various other examples, but enough has been said to indicate the general nature of practice; the list would finish with a category for general costs which might be allocated between cost centres in equal amounts or in proportion to other costs because no more appropriate basis could be found.

Hour rate computations

An overhead rate per machine hour is defined, for a cost centre, as the total overhead costs allocated to that cost centre divided by the number of hours of operating time for machines in that centre; the labour hour rate is similarly defined. If an hour rate method is used for the allocation of overhead costs, each activity would bear a charge for each cost centre which contributed to its completion; the charge for each cost centre would be the hourly rate for the centre times the number of hours of machine or labour time used by the activity in that centre.

The exact calculation of a machine hour rate or a labour hour rate for a period, according to the definitions given, could only be carried out at the end of an accounting period, when cost and operating hour details were known. A firm would normally wish to be able to calculate the cost of an activity as soon as it is finished, however, or even to keep a running record of the cost accumulated on an activity at any time. In order to be able to do this, it is usual to calculate hourly rates for overheads at the start of a period, using estimates of costs and operating hours. If the estimates are exactly correct, the total of the overhead costs allocated to individual activities will be exactly equal to the total costs incurred by the firm. If either estimate is incorrect, however, there will be an under-allocation or an over-allocation of actual costs.

We noted in chapter 16, that the use of estimates of actual activity levels in the allocation of overheads may cause considerable variation over time in the total costs allocated to similar activities. In slack times, when the firm may be operating a good deal below its capacity level, the hourly rates for overheads based on an estimate of actual operating time, and, hence, the total costs attributed to each activity, may be a good deal higher than usual. For the reasons given in chapter 16, it is normally preferred, in practice, to avoid such variations in overhead rates by basing their calculations on estimates of normal operating hours rather than estimates of actual hours. In times of reduced levels of activity, therefore, there will normally be an under-allocation of actual overhead costs.

Choice between different bases of allocation

In choosing between different bases for overhead allocation, an accountant will seek a basis which seems to him to be 'equitable' in the particular circumstances of the case on hand. Accountants often use the word 'equitable' in discussing the choice of bases though they do not usually explain who is the person whose interests they have in mind nor do they explain how the entitlements of different people are affected by their choice. They judge a basis to be equitable if it satisfies a set of conditions such as the following.

They argue fundamentally that overheads appear normally to accrue with the passage of time; hence some basis of allocation that takes time into account is to be preferred to others. For this reason the methods using hourly rates are preferred to the methods based on materials or labour costs. In choosing between the two main hourly rate methods, weight is normally given to what seems to be the dominant factor of production. If production is highly mechanized, the machine hour rate method would be preferred; otherwise the labour hour rate method might well be chosen.

It is not clear precisely how one can identify the dominant resource in production; accounting theory has offered no firm definition, preferring to leave the matter to individual judgement in each particular case. It would not be hard to construct an example in which the dominant factor was unclear intuitively; for example, the total depreciation of a firm's machinery might slightly exceed the total wage bill whilst the number of labour hours worked slightly exceeded the number of machine operating hours. However in many cases the dominant factor will be intuitively clear and in other cases there is the possibility of using the two methods alongside each other, allocating some costs by a labour hour rate and others by a machine hour rate. A more fundamental objection is that accounting theory has not demonstrated the relevance of dominance for the choice of an allocation base or contrasted it with alternative criteria such as relative scarcity.

A study of the above brief description of traditional cost accounting procedures indicates that the cost assigned to individual activities has the characteristic of an average cost. The overhead cost allocated to an activity is the average cost per activity, weight being given for the time spent on it. The costing characteristic of averaging is even more apparent in some special systems of activity costing.

Batch costing and process costing

Consider, for example, the batch costing system, in which cost is calculated, not for each individual product but for a batch of units manufactured together. The total cost of manufacturing a batch may comprise the cost of time for setting up a machine at the start of the operation as well as the cost of direct materials and labour for the units manufactured and an allocation of overhead costs (if a full costing system is used); furthermore the labour cost of manufacturing each successive unit in the batch may fall as the employees 'warm' to their task. Hence the total cost of a batch may not increase proportionally with the number of units in the batch. This fact tends to be obscured in a batch costing system. The cost per product unit tends to be thought of as the total cost for the batch divided by the number of units in the batch – an average of direct costs as well as overhead costs; the pattern of variation in unit costs as output increases is obscured.

The position is somewhat similar in process costing systems, which are designed to calculate the cost of processing a unit of output, e.g. a gallon of some liquid chemical. In such a system, all costs are allocated to processes in the first place. The cost per unit processed is found by dividing the total cost allocated to a process by the number of units processed during the relevant period, due allowance being made for quantities partly finished at the start and end of the period. The result again is clearly an average.

The depreciation of equipment

Decisions concerning the investment of resources with a view to long-term benefits are beyond the scope of this book. In consequence, we have not discussed the relevant cost of using machinery and other items of equipment having long lives; the methods discussed cater only for equipment user costs arising from relatively short-term leasing contracts. However, conventional cost accounting attributes an annual cost – called depreciation – to the use of machinery, and processes it in much the same way as other overhead costs. It may therefore be appropriate to give a few comments on depreciation at this point.

The difficulty in dealing with outlays on machinery, from a costing point of view, is the need to allocate the costs over time before deriving an amount for allocation to activities. Several rule of thumb methods are available for this purpose. The most common in the United Kingdom are the straight-line basis – which apportions the total cost of the asset equally between each year of its estimated life – and the fixed percentage of reducing balance method – which assumes the cost in any year to be a fixed percentage of that part of the cost of the asset which has not been allocated as depreciation in previous periods. Suppose, for example, that a machine is purchased for £1000 in the expectation that it would be used for three years and then sold for £216. Depreciation for each year of the asset's life would be calculated as shown in Table 62. The two methods give significantly different results but accounting theory does not give a clear indication of how we should choose between them.

The straight line method of depreciation gives the impression that the purchase of the machine would be worthwhile if the machine could be used to produce a product yielding a total annual contribution (sales proceeds less variable costs) of £261. This view is mistaken, however, because it ignores the interest cost in having capital tied up in the machine. Let us assume that the asset is purchased by borrowing at 10 per cent per annum (or that interest of 10 per cent per annum is sacrificed because the cash is not available for some alternative use)

Table 62

	Straight line method	Reducing balance method
percentage rate	26·1%	40%
	(£)	(£)
cost of asset	1000	1000
depreciation – year 1	261	400
undepreciated cost – end of year 1	739	600
depreciation – year 2	261	240
undepreciated cost – end of year 2	478	360
depreciation – year 3	262	144
expected sales proceeds	216	216

and that net cash receipts arise at the end of each year; it can be shown that annual contributions of £337 are required to break even (see Table 63).

A strict analysis of the relevant cost of using a machine already owned on some specified activity may require quite complex mathematical analysis. Some indication of the considerations can be given, however. The analysis should start from the question: What difference will the use of the machine make to cash receipts and payments? If the machine has some spare capacity and the extra use will not cause it to wear out more quickly and bring forward the time for replacement, the use will have no effect on cash flows and hence be costless. In other cases, use of the machine will require the provision of extra capacity or bring forward the time at which replacement is necessary. In such a case, the use of the machine has a step-like cost function, rather like the case of the employee discussed in chapter 6; if the steps are small, the cost may aptly be treated as a variable cost. Suppose the machine in our above example can be used for 1000 hours per annum. Its use will be justified if it can earn $£\frac{337}{1000} = 33.7$p per hour and this may be regarded as a good approximation of the cost of use; such a cost may be regarded as a break-even rental for the machine if it were hired from an organization requiring a return of 10 per cent per annum on capital. Finally we may note that our discussion of cost estimation (chapter 5) showed that the original cost of a resource was irrelevant for decision purposes and that replacement cost was the relevant cost for a resource

Table 63

	(£)
cost of machine – borrowed at 10%	1000
end year 1 – interest	100
	1100
– cash contributions	337
	763
end year 2 – interest	76
	839
– cash contributions	337
	502
end year 3 – interest	50
	552

– cash contributions	336	
– sale of machine	216	
		552
balance of indebtedness		0

in common use. The calculation of the break-even rental should accordingly normally take account of estimated replacement cost and not just the original cost of the asset.

Non-manufacturing overheads

We have noted that non-manufacturing overheads, notably office and administrative costs, are often allocated to individual activities in costing systems. The method of allocation applied to such costs is usually less sophisticated than that applied to manufacturing overheads. Commonly an estimate is made of the percentage relationship between relevant non-manufacturing overheads and direct costs plus manufacturing overheads. This percentage relationship is then assumed to apply to each individual activity; the total cost for each activity is found by increasing other costs assigned to the activity by the standard percentage.

Cost accounting: an illustration

We now give an illustration of the application of the techniques described above. Milky Way Ltd is preparing a cost statement for Job 72937. The firm uses twenty-five machines in its factory which has a floor area of 5000 square feet; each is regarded as a separate cost centre. The job under consideration required twenty-eight lbs of material BG, twenty hours of Grade 3 labour, fifteen hours of the time of machine 7 and five hours of the time of machine 23. The following additional information is available:

1 1000 lb. of material BG were in stock when issues were made for Job 72937; 600 lb., purchased first, cost £1.25, the remainder £1.40. The FIFO system is used for costing materials. There is no normal wastage of materials.

2 Grade 3 labour is paid £1.92 per hour; idle time is normally 4 per cent of the total time paid for.

3 Machine 7 costs £2000 and has an expected life of eight years; machine 23 cost £5000 and has an expected life of ten years; neither machine is expected to have any scrap value at the end of its life. The straight line method of depreciation is used. Both machines are normally operated for 2000 hours per annum.

4 Factory rent and other building costs are estimated at £32 000 per annum. Machine 7 occupies 100 square feet and machine 23 occupies 250 square feet.

5 Running costs, maintenance and so on are estimated at £100 per annum for machine 7 and £500 per annum for machine 23.

6 Supervisory labour costs are estimated at £10 000 per annum; supervisors divide their time equally between each machine in the factory.

7 Miscellaneous factory overheads amount to 10 per cent of total factory overheads.

8 Administrative overheads amount to 8 per cent of direct costs plus factory overheads.

The machine hour rate computations would run as in Table 64.

Table 64

Costs per annum	Machine 7 (£)		Machine 23 (£)
depreciation $1/8 \times £2000$	250	$1/10 \times £5000$	500
factory rent (floor area basis) $£\dfrac{32\,000 \times 100}{5000}$	640	$£\dfrac{32\,000 \times 250}{5000}$	1600
running costs	100		500
supervisory labour – each $£\dfrac{10\,000}{25}$	400		400
sub-total	1390		3000
miscellaneous $\dfrac{10}{90}$ times sub-total	154		333
total per annum	1544		3333
rate per hour $£\dfrac{1544}{2000}$	£0.772	$£\dfrac{3333}{2000}$	£1.667

The charge per hour for grade 3 labour, allowing for normal idle time, is $£\dfrac{1.92}{0.96} = £2$. The cost for Job 72937 may now be assessed as in Table 65.

Table 65

	(£)
material BG – 28 lbs at £1.25	35.00
labour (grade 3) – 20 hours at £2	40.00
machine time – cost centre 7 – 15 hours at £0.772	11.58
cost centre 23 – 5 hours at £1.667	8.34
	94.92
administrative overheads – 8 per cent	7.59
Total cost	£102.51

The usefulness of cost accounting

We have noted that few large businesses today calculate historical costs for their activities in isolation. Historical costs are calculated as a part of a standard costing system in which they are compared with costs estimated in advance. The principles of cost allocation used in standard costing are, however, the same as those described in this chapter. A detailed discussion of standard costing is beyond the scope of this book.

Cost accounting information has two main uses in decision taking, as opposed to the routine control of the efficiency of activities. It may be used as a basis for price determination and to judge the cost of activities in assessing their worthwhileness. We shall discuss the uses and limitations of cost accounting information for pricing in chapter 18.

Many of the earlier chapters of this book discussed the information on costs required to guide decisions in a firm. The essence of our conclusions was that estimates were required of how costs would vary in the future according to what courses of action were selected by the firm. Cost accounts provide one possible source of evidence on which the estimates might be based. They do at least list some of the resources required for various activities; and they have the advantage of providing information at a relatively low cost as part of a routine system. They are not an ideal indication of likely costs in themselves, however, for several reasons:

1 They deal with past results whereas explicit estimates of future results are required, taking account of any changed circumstances.

2 They do not provide the required information about variations in the total costs of a firm, resulting from accepting a new activity or altering the level of an existing activity; indeed they can be positively misleading unless interpreted carefully because:

(a) Some overhead costs are variable and others are fixed. Methods of overhead allocation in costing do not respect the distinction and therefore fail to identify marginal cost;

(b) They give averages of direct costs over batches or other aggregates of output; they do not disclose how direct costs vary with output levels;

(c) They price resources used at historical, actual cost rather than at replacement cost or realizable value and they ignore opportunity cost;

(d) Direct costs are not differentiated adequately as between fixed and variable costs.

We shall explore the significance of some of these limitations further in chapter 19. However, it does seem that a minimum requirement for the establishment of a costing system useful for decisions is that a preliminary study should be undertaken to distinguish fixed and variable costs and that the costing system should be restricted to the latter.

18 Pricing Strategy

In chapter 9, we approached the estimation of optimal pricing policy and output levels using analytical techniques developed from those of economic theory; our approach emphasized, particularly, the need to take account of the mutual dependence of price and the quantity that can be sold. It was argued that this relationship should be considered explicitly, in spite of the difficulties of estimation; it is relevant to the setting of optimal output and the chance of error is increased if assumptions about demand remain implicit or as a vague qualitative statement.

However, we must note the widespread practice of other approaches to the setting of price and consequently output, all, like the method described in chapter 9, now subject to any restrictions imposed by government control.

One method, the cost-plus method of pricing, is based on calculations which use accounting data. Its starting point is that price should be set equal to full cost, calculated according to cost accounting conventions plus an allowance for profit, possibly expressed as a standard percentage.

Cost-plus pricing

We may study cost-plus pricing with the help of a numerical example: Juno Ltd sets prices using a cost-plus formula. It manufactures a single product and regards its normal output level as being 1200 units per annum. Costs comprise fixed overhead costs of £18 000 per annum plus a variable cost of £17 per unit covering materials, direct labour and variable overheads, i.e. the cost–volume relationship is the simple linear expression $T = 18\,000 + 17q$. The pricing calculation might run as follows:

Variable cost per unit	£17
Fixed cost per unit £$\dfrac{18\,000}{1200} = 15$	
Total cost per unit	32
Add profit (say) $12\frac{1}{2}$ per cent	4
Selling price	£36

Such an approach to pricing makes some implicit assumption about the relationship between price and volume of sales. It is assumed that a firm will reach a decision in which price and volume are compatible – in the case of Juno Ltd, that the 1200 units assumed for purposes of overhead allocation can be sold at £36. A cost-based price will not invariably have this property – demand may be less than assumed volume at the cost-plus price; but we may suppose that a firm will adapt its formula over a period of years until a decision consistent with actual price–volume relationships is achieved. Its concept of normal volume and desired profit percentage may alter in the process. However, because it neglects the elasticity of demand, the method gives no reason to suppose that an optimal level of activity will be found. Let us consider the case of Juno Ltd further. Suppose that the price–volume relationship may be estimated as

$$q = 1920 - 20p.$$

This relationship suggests that a volume of 1200 units and a price of £36 are compatible. At a selling price of £36, the firm's operations may be expected to yield a net cash surplus of £4 × 1200 = £4800 per annum (the profit per unit times sales volume). Using the arguments given in chapter 9, we may estimate the optimal output level by setting marginal revenue ($R' = 96 - q/10$) equal to marginal cost:

$$96 - q/10 = 17$$

thus $q = 790$, and optimal price $= 96 - \dfrac{q}{20} = $ £56.50.

Cash surplus at this level of operation would be substantially better than that from the original plan:

Sales 790 at £56.5		£44 635
Variable costs 790 at £17	£13 430	
Fixed costs	18 000	
	———	31 430
Cash surplus		13 205

In a multi-product firm the fixed overhead costs would be
allocated to each product by one of the methods described in
chapter 17 (the labour hour rate and so on) with similar
results. Our illustration shows that the cost-plus formula does
not necessarily lead to the adoption of an optimal price and
suggests that it does not normally do so.

The long-run effects of pricing

In defence of the cost-plus method of pricing, it is often argued
that it leads to a traditional or fair price, one that will be
accepted as reasonable by the customers of a firm. It is pointed
out that it is unsatisfactory to consider the sales price–volume
relationship for one period in isolation. Pricing policy may
have a delayed effect, i.e. the price set for one period may
affect sales volume in subsequent periods. For example, a
'high' price may cause some loss of volume in the current
period because some customers obtain their supplies of the
product elsewhere or go without; other customers may take
longer to adjust to the price level and (say) find alternative
sources of supply only during a subsequent period. The current
'high' price would then cause a further loss of sales volume in
subsequent periods. The single period analysis of optimal output level, such as we have considered, fails to take this factor
into account and may therefore lead to error.

This type of argument assumes that the cost-plus pricing
method will yield a price that avoids a delayed loss of business
because the price is seen as being reasonable. It may yield a
price in line with that charged by competitors; for competitors
may have a similar average cost of production and they may

use a similar pricing system. It may therefore amount to a method of tacit collusion. The method is also simple to operate. It is possible, in principle, to formulate a model which deals with several decision periods and reflects the effect of price in one period on volume in the current and several later periods. This process is complex, however, both computationally and, more importantly, because it involves difficult problems of estimation. Cost-plus pricing may be viewed as a strategic decision rule, of the type discussed in chapter 4, designed to deal implicitly with considerations subject to great uncertainty. The setting of a 'fair' price, in accordance with the cost-plus formula, would then be regarded as a proxy goal, adopted because it is believed to be consistent with appropriate long-run aims.

It must be admitted that there is some force in these arguments. Any pricing decision should take account of all consequences, long-run as well as immediate. One might have some confidence in a price-fixing system that involved estimating an optimal price in the light of estimated short-run price–volume effects and then amending it in the light of other (qualitative) arguments touching on long-run considerations. The drawback of the cost-plus pricing method is that it appears to ignore altogether any consideration of the trade-off between price and quantity.

The practical application of cost-plus pricing

If one investigates the practice of cost-plus pricing more fully, however, it appears that it is not so much at variance with the economist's approach to pricing as the above description implies. Many businessmen profess to set prices mechanically, according to the simple cost-plus formula; and yet an examination of actual prices charged indicates that the target price – the one calculated by the cost-plus formula – is rarely adopted without amendment. The price is shaded upwards or downwards in the light of such considerations as how much work the firm has on hand in relation to its capacity (the 'length' of the order book), the extent of competition from other firms, policy relating to the development of customer relations and so on. There is an adjustment process which takes account of some of the factors which influence the relationship between the cost model and the sales price–volume model. However, an informal adjustment process does not fully answer the criticisms of the cost-plus method. The explicit use of a model still seems worthwhile because it directs attention to the fundamental considerations involved in the decision process; moreover, the relationships are complex and informal adjustment may well not deal with them adequately.

Cost-plus pricing and budgeting

It may help to put the cost-plus pricing method in better perspective if we consider further its role in a firm's system of

Table 66 Earnings–output relationships under full-cost pricing

	Output volume	
	1200 units (£)	*1100 units* (£)
variable costs at £17 per unit	20 400	18 700
fixed costs	18 000	18 000
	38 400	36 700
sales at £36 per unit	43 200	39 600
surplus	4 800 (12½ per cent of £38 400)	2 900
reconciliation of surplus: standard profit at £4 per unit	4 800	4 400
fixed costs not covered by output 100 at £15	—	1 500
	4 800	2 900

financial planning and control. First, consider the analysis of the results of Juno Ltd, provided in Table 66. This calculates the surplus that the company will earn for the year if price is set at £36 and sales volume is either 1200 units or 1100 units (and other results accord with the estimates). If sales volume is 1200 units, as assumed in the original calculation of average costs, the surplus will equal 1200 times the standard profit allowed per unit. If actual volume differs from the estimate, the calculation of average fixed costs will be incorrect. Suppose actual volume falls short of the estimate. Actual surplus will differ from the expected surplus, not only because fewer units of profit are earned but also because fewer slices of fixed cost are recovered, in total sales revenue; if the strict cost-plus price is maintained, actual surplus will equal:

Actual volume times standard profit less volume shortfall times allocated fixed cost per unit.

It has been suggested that cost-plus pricing should be seen not as a method of optimal pricing so much as a basis for budgeting and controlling results. As a financial period elapses a business manager needs a running index of how results are progressing, i.e. he needs a continuously updated indication of the likely level of net cash earnings for the period; the cost-plus formula provides a basis for obtaining such an indication.

It may be easier for a firm to predict directly its total costs than its total revenues for a period, based on some normal level of activity, particularly if it does not sell a standard product line but rather undertakes a number of special jobs or contracts which are priced individually. As is illustrated in Table 65, if the cost-plus pricing formula is followed precisely and the assumed activity volume is correct, earnings may be predicted simply as the standard profit percentage, used in the formula, times estimated total cost. Moreover, if the prices actually charged are more or less than the target prices indicated by the cost-plus formula, a revised estimate of earnings may be obtained by estimating the standard percentage on cost and applying some adjustment for 'overs' and 'unders'. Similarly a running adjustment may be made to correct the estimated surplus for the effect of errors in the assumed volume of activity. Imagine a firm which undertakes special contracts. At the start of a year, it estimates a volume of activity such that direct (variable) costs will be D. Fixed overhead costs are estimated at F; using the cost-plus pricing rule, therefore, the percentage $r = \dfrac{F}{D}$ may be added to the direct costs for each contract. Total costs will be increased by the percentage p to provide a profit margin. Hence estimated profit will be:

Estimated receipts less estimated costs

$$
\begin{aligned}
&= D(1+r)(1+p) - (D+F) \\
&= pD(1+r).
\end{aligned}
$$

Suppose that actual direct costs are $D+D'$, that actual fixed overhead costs are $F+F'$ and that actual receipts exceed the strict cost-plus prices by S. Then actual profit will be:

Actual receipts less actual costs

$$
\begin{aligned}
&= (D+D')(1+r)(1+p)+S-(D+D'+F+F') \\
&= (D+Dr+D'+D'r)(1+p)+S-(D+D'+Dr+F') \\
&= p(D+Dr)+p(D'+D'r)+(D+D'+Dr)+D'r+S \\
&\quad -(D+D'+Dr)-F' \\
&= p(D+Dr)+S+D'(p+pr)+D'r-F',
\end{aligned}
$$

i.e. actual profit equals estimated profit, plus or minus:

Differences between actual prices and cost-plus prices;
The under- or over-estimate of direct costs times the mark-up for fixed costs and profit, $D'(p+pr)$;
The over- or under-allocation of fixed overheads, $D'r$;
Any over- or under-estimate of fixed overhead costs.

Although such a financial control procedure may have a useful role in a firm's decision procedures, it does not remove the need for preliminary pricing studies using the analysis discussed in chapter 9.

Product design

In describing the process by which firms decide what products to sell and at what prices, particularly in relation to new products, some writers suggest that the price is taken as fixed at an early stage in each round of preparing plans and is not sub-sequently regarded as a decision variable. They suggest that the problem is viewed in the form of a search for a product of suitable design, and hence cost characteristics, for sale at a particular price; and that it is not viewed as the estimation of the best price at which to sell a particular product of given characteristics. The price, it is supposed, may be fixed in line with prices that are traditional in certain types of business, or it may be chosen because a marketing department has suggested that there would be a demand for a particular type of product at a specified price.

It is useful to consider the pricing problem in such a frame-work. It emphasizes that any basic product may be designed in many different ways, so that the number of strictly different products that could be offered for sale is very large. Somehow a decision process must be evolved to reduce the theoretical possibilities to a relatively small number of actual products. We have ignored this dimension of the decision in our previous discussion; we assumed that we had a product of given design and needed to select a price. The alternative approach now suggested is to regard the design as more or less continuously variable over a range of possibilities and consider the selection of the design, given the price.

The relationship between price and design as decision variables

Such a perspective on the decision problem does not suggest the need for a fundamentally different procedure. It remains necessary to estimate cost and sales price–volume relation-ships for the products with a view to maximizing the overall cash surplus. Strictly, it is desirable to look at design and price as independent variables and consider all possible combina-tions. Considerations of practicability make it necessary to restrict the scope of the analysis somewhat; but it will normally be desirable for a firm to consider several possible designs for each product and a range of possible selling prices for each design.

The Glacier Metal Company project

Yet another approach to price decisions has been developed in the Glacier Metal Company. The analysis starts from specifications of a number of desirable qualities that a price fixing system should have. It assumes that financial control in an organization will best be served if one individual, perhaps the chief executive, is able to control pricing policy personally, an assumption which may be justified in view of possible inter-dependencies between prices for one set of products and demands for others. It is noted that the chief executive has insufficient time to consider the price for each of a large number of products individually. Hence it is argued that some general formula is needed by which the chief executive may adjust the whole level of prices or alter the relationship between prices of different products or groups of products, whilst retaining an overall structure which appears consistent to the market.

The cost-plus method of pricing was rejected by the Company because it fails to take account of market demand factors, and may fail to produce a structure of prices which appears consistent in terms of the attributes of products. An alternative system was developed, based on the assumption that each product is comprised of a number of measurable properties, for example its content of raw material and components, and physical and design properties such as size, weight, finish, operating accuracy and so on. Each of these properties is assigned a value which is assumed to be reasonable from the viewpoint of consumers – we shall denote the values £v_a per unit for property a and so on; that value may be partially independent of cost even in those cases where cost is separately identifiable. The target price for each product is then expressed as the sum of the values of properties possessed by that product – the sum of terms like $q_a v_a$ where q_a is the quantity of a property that the product is assumed to possess. The price obtained may be adjusted by a percentage addition or subtraction which is constant for a group of products to give additional flexibility in dealing with particular characteristics of product groups. Target prices for each product may be described by the following series of equations:

$$P_1 = r_1(v_a q_{1a} + v_b q_{1b} + v_c q_{1c} + \ldots + v_m q_{1m}),$$
$$P_2 = r_2(v_a q_{2a} + v_b q_{2b} + v_c q_{2c} + \ldots + v_m q_{2m}),$$
.
.
.
$$P_n = r_n(v_a q_{na} + v_b q_{nb} + v_c q_{nc} + \ldots + v_m q_{nm}),$$

where r represents the percentage adjustment, the numerical subscript denotes the product number, n is the number of products and m is the number of different properties identified. The process of assigning initial values to the various product properties would be one of trial and error. Properties would be measured for a number of products and tentative prices assigned to the products (based on previous marketing experience). In this way, it is possible to derive a series of equations, with the property values as unknowns. For example, if we substitute imaginary values for prices $P_1, \ldots, P_n$, and quantities of the properties, $q_a, \ldots, q_m$ in the above equations, we obtain the series:

$$51 = r_1(v_a 20 + v_b 36 + v_c 18 + \ldots + v_m 6),$$
.
.
.
$$22 = r_n(v_a 26 + v_b 5 + v_c 12 + \ldots + v_m 4).$$

If we assign values to the percentage factors, $r_1, \ldots, r_n$, presumably $1 \cdot 00$ in the first place, we may analyse the equations to discover what set of property values gives the best fit to the tentative prices, using multiple regression techniques (see chapter 7). The analysis may suggest that some of the tentative prices are out of line in the sense that they imply different values for given properties and we may wish to revise them and repeat the process until we are satisfied.

This short description of the Glacier pricing project begs some difficult questions concerning the measurement of product properties. We restrict ourselves to noting that some properties may vary continuously over a range, e.g. weight, whereas others either do or do not exist, e.g. the property of being made of brass. The latter possibility can be dealt with by assigning the value one to the existence of the property and zero to its non-existence.

An example of the Glacier pricing methods

Let us consider an illustration of the Glacier method of pricing. Pallas Ltd produces a range of screws and prices are to be calculated in 'Ruritanian' cents per 100 screws. The product properties described in Table 67 have been chosen to represent

Table 67

	Product property	Property value per 100
q_a	the length of the screw in millimetres	8 cents per millimetre (based on the length per screw)
q_b	the diameter of the head in millimetres	25 cents per millimetre
q_c	the fineness of the thread, three grades: one, two and three.	45 cents times number of grade
q_d	quantity of steel in grammes	1·6 cents per gramme (based on the total weight per 100 screws)
q_e	quantity of brass in grammes	10 cents per gramme (based on the total weight per 100 screws)
q_f	having rounded head, 1 = yes; 0 = no	30 cents if yes, 0 cents if no

the main features which contribute to the value of the products. Values for the properties are given per 100 screws. Some of the properties are physically interdependent, i.e. quantity of metal is influenced by length and diameter of head, but it is assumed that such properties contribute independently to the worth of the article and hence may be treated independently in the pricing formula.

The firm manufactures many types of screw; we will consider five by way of illustration:

Type 1, 20 mm long, flat head diameter 4 mm, 400 grammes of steel per 100, thread grade 3;

Type 2, 10 mm long, flat head diameter 3 mm, 125 grammes of steel per 100, thread grade 2;

Type 3, 30 mm long, flat head diameter 4 mm, 300 grammes of brass per 100, thread grade 1;

Type 4, 20 mm long, round head diameter 3 mm, 175 grammes of brass per 100, thread grade 3;

Type 5, 10 mm long, flat head diameter 2 mm, 75 grammes of brass per 100, thread grade 2.

If we assume that no percentage adjustment is applied in the pricing formula for these products, we may calculate target prices as follows:

$$
\begin{aligned}
P_1 &= 20v_a + 4v_b + 3v_c + 80v_d + 0v_e + 0v_f \\
&= 20 \times 8 + 4 \times 25 + 3 \times 45 + 400 \times 1 \cdot 6 + 0 \times 10 + 0 \times 30 \\
&= 1035, \\
P_2 &= 10 \times 8 + 3 \times 25 + 2 \times 45 + 125 \times 1 \cdot 6 + 0 \times 10 + 0 \times 30 \\
&= 445, \\
P_3 &= 30 \times 8 + 4 \times 25 + 1 \times 45 + 0 \times 1 \cdot 6 + 300 \times 10 + 0 \times 30 \\
&= 3385, \\
P_4 &= 20 \times 8 + 3 \times 25 + 3 \times 45 + 0 \times 1 \cdot 6 + 175 \times 10 + 1 \times 30 \\
&= 2150, \\
P_5 &= 10 \times 8 + 2 \times 25 + 2 \times 45 + 0 \times 1 \cdot 6 + 75 \times 10 + 0 \times 30 \\
&= 970.
\end{aligned}
$$

Such a framework for pricing might be used by a manager in various ways. He could alter the overall level of prices, e.g. he might direct that all price equations should have a factor of 1·10 introduced, representing an increase of 10 per cent. He could also alter relative prices, e.g. if he felt that market conditions favoured an increase in the price of brass products (only), he could achieve this simply by directing that the price associated with brass should be raised, e.g. to 12 cents per gramme. The formula would readily yield a 'consistent' price for a new product in the same range, e.g. a screw 20 mm long, with flat head diameter 3 mm, thread grade 2, requiring 175 grammes of brass.

The economist's approach versus the Glacier approach

Although the Glacier method of pricing has some desirable features, it suffers from the drawback that it does not allow scope for an explicit consideration of the effect of alternative pricing policies on sales volume in relation to costs. The method implies that there is only one price worth considering given the qualities of a product. Market demand considerations may be taken into account partially and implicitly if demand is related to the product properties measured. However, the Glacier method would indicate an optimal price only by chance unless it was supplemented by some further analysis which took the target price as a base point and estimated the impact of changes on the volume of sales.

Sales promotion strategy

We have noted that, in practice, pricing procedures adopted by firms are often designed to avoid the difficult problem of estimating explicitly a sales price–volume relationship. The pricing procedure is presumably chosen as being likely to yield a satisfactory result, compatible with the existing price–volume relationship, but it is preferred to leave the details of the relationship implicit. Such procedures may therefore be regarded as 'strategies' attuned to proxy goals.

Similar procedures are generally used to set levels of sales promotional expenditure; indeed advertising expenditure is generally set by some rule that is even more clearly arbitrary, e.g. equal to a fixed percentage of sales revenue. We may again regard such practice as an example of responding to extreme uncertainty by reaching a decision with reference to a proxy goal – the maintenance of a firm's reputation, product image and so on by a certain rate of expenditure. It is difficult to improve on this procedure by formulating a decision model which includes advertising although the attempt to do so seems worthwhile. At the least, some estimate might be made of the marginal effect of variations in advertising on sales volume or price, taking as a base point the level indicated by the strategic decision rule.

19 The Optimal Information System

As we have already noted, the accounting system of a firm is an important and economical source from which managers may obtain information about the likely outcomes of activities which they may undertake. It has many deficiencies for the purpose. In particular, it provides results of activities which have taken place in the past whereas managers require predictions of what is likely to take place in the future.

However, systematic analysis is possible in any field of human endeavour involving practical applications only if observations of past results tell us something about likely future results. Some relationship between past and future is universally assumed, in business as in the natural sciences. An accounting system gives records of some of the past events that may be relevant for predicting future results. Accounting systems therefore have a claim to be considered as useful sources of information for managerial decisions. In this chapter, we consider the case for establishing some routine systems for the collection of information to guide decisions; and we discuss the criteria for judging what is the best system we could design to meet these needs, with particular reference to the merits of traditional accounting systems.

The information required by managers

Let us begin by reviewing the information needs of managers. They are implied by our analysis of considerations relevant to decisions given in previous chapters. The main needs are for estimates of the following, ideally in the form of probability distributions and including at least, the most likely values:

The cost–volume relationship for all activities which the firm might undertake, including estimates of the resources required

and the costs of those resources;
The sales price–volume relationships for all activities which the firm might undertake;
The quantities of various resources available to the firm.

The concepts of information theory

We may now consider how we might judge the merits of a particular system for providing the information required. A system should be considered only if it has some relevance and accuracy. These are not easy qualities to measure. Recent literature, however, has developed concepts on which the measurements may be based, building upon the mathematics of communication theory. The basic concept is that the quantity of information conveyed by a system may be measured by a mathematical expression, incorporating the probabilities of events which are the subject of prediction. Concepts such as 'noise' and 'loss' are used to measure the efficiency with which the information provided by the system is transmitted to the decision taker.

The worthwhileness of information

If an information system is to be useful, there must be some chance that it will influence a decision. Suppose a manager wishes to predict the cost of a particular activity. If he is in a state of *complete* uncertainty, he will presumably assign an equal probability to each of a very large number of cost levels (literally an infinite number). However a state of complete uncertainty will almost never prevail. Even without the guidance of systematic information, a manager will have some ill-structured expectations, distilled from casual observations, which will lead him to have some *a priori* probability distribution for the cost levels. An information system will provide him with indications which may lead him to modify the *a priori* probability distribution. Following this line of thought, we may define information more strictly as a message which causes a manager to alter his probability distribution of results for some particular event. An information system may be worthwhile if it may lead managers to alter their subjective probability distributions for an event. In some cases, the messages from a system may simply confirm managers in their initial expectations; if they always do so, the system is not useful.

The value of information depends not only on its intrinsic merits, but also on the way it is interpreted by managers. A system that would improve the decisions of one manager may cause a deterioration in the decisions of another because he imparts a consistent bias to the information he receives; e.g. he may be over-cautious and assume that actual costs of an activity will be some percentage greater than the level indicated by the information. In judging the value of a system we consider its potential value, assuming no systematic bias in interpretation. In practice, it may be important to study means of interpretation, e.g. by correlating information received with actual results for activities undertaken. It may also be helpful to monitor managers' interpretation by having them formulate estimated probability distributions for the results of an activity before and after receiving information from the system, and relating those estimates to actual results for activities undertaken; then managers' interpretation might be improved by an iterative learning process.

The foregoing assumptions and definitions indicate that if information were costless, we should wish to arrange for managers to receive all possible messages which might alter their estimated probability distributions for results of available activities. We should merely exclude messages which we believed to be irrelevant. However, information is costly to acquire and to process, both directly and because a manager may receive more information than he can absorb and hence take refuge in some irrational decision mechanism. In choosing an information system, we should weigh the cost of information against its benefits. Useful information will enable a manager to formulate better plans, i.e. plans which have a larger value than those he would otherwise have made. Information may be judged worthwhile if it increases the value of plans by more than its cost. The ideal information system may be thought of as one derived by providing for the addition of various types of information as long as the value of the additional information exceeds the additional cost of providing it.

The value of information

Let us consider an illustrative calculation of the value of information. Suppose Rigel Ltd is considering whether or not to accept a contract which it has been offered at a fixed price of £4500. The firm bases decisions on the expected money value of projects, i.e. it is indifferent to the risk of the individual projects. The contract would involve the use of an untried technique. If the new method is successful, it is estimated that the cost of completing the contract would be £3200; if the new method fails, however, Rigel would have to fall back on old-established methods and total cost would then be £5600. If the contract were accepted, the new method would be tried initially; its success or failure would not become apparent until part of the work was completed and a switch to the established method might be necessary at that point. The cost of the established method would be the same whether it was applied from the start or when the project was part completed. The estimated probability of success with the new method is 60 per cent. The contract would yield a surplus of £1300 or a deficit of £1100, depending on the success of the new method; its expected value is £340.

		(£)
Contract price		4500
Expected costs:		
0·6(3200) =	1920	
0·4(5600) =	2240	
		4160
Expected surplus		340

If no further information is available, the project would be judged worthwhile, because its expected value is positive. Suppose, however, that we could carry out some test to discover practically for certain whether the new technique would be successful. We should assess the probability that the test would indicate success at 60 per cent, consistently with our previous estimate. However, the expected value of the contract would now be higher, for we could eliminate the possibility of a deficit; if the test indicated failure of the new method, Rigel would not accept the contract. The expected value would now be £780, before allowing for any cost of carrying out the test:

	(£)
Test indicates success; accept contract and earn surplus £1300. Expected value (0.6×1300)	+780
Test indicates failure; reject contract and earn surplus of £0. Expected value (0.4×0)	0
	+780

Rigel has a choice as to whether it will carry out the test or not. We can look upon the overall decision as a choice between two mutually exclusive projects, the contract with the test or the contract without the test. The former will be preferred if it has the greater expected value, that is, if £780 less the cost of the test is greater than £340. Hence the test will be carried out if it costs less than £440 and the value of the information it provides may be said to be £440.

We may illustrate the calculation of the value of information further, by supposing that Rigel's test will not yield a definite conclusion on the viability of the new technique. Suppose we estimate that there is a 60 per cent chance of a favourable test result and that, following a favourable result, chances of successful implementation of the new technique would be assessed at 80 per cent in favour and 20 per cent against. On the other hand, if the test result is unfavourable, the chances are 30 per cent in favour of successful implementation and 70 per cent against. Success may follow a favourable test or an unfavourable test; its overall probability is still 60 per cent $\{(0.6 \times 0.8) + (0.4 \times 0.3)\}$. The new expected value of the contract with the test is calculated as follows:

If the test is favourable ($p = 0.60$): (£)

Chance of success 80 per cent; success yields surplus
of £1300. Expected value $(1300) \times 0.8$ +1040

Chance of failure 20 per cent; failure yields deficit
of £1100. Expected value $-(1100) \times 0.2$ −220

Expected value following favourable test   +820

Contract would be accepted following favourable test;

If the test is unfavourable ($p = 0.40$): (£)

Chance of success 30 per cent; success yields surplus
of £1300. Expected value $(1300) \times 0.3$ +390

Chance of failure 70 per cent; failure yields deficit
of £1100. Expected value $-(1100) \times 0.7$ −770

Expected value following unfavourable test   −380

Contract would be rejected following unfavourable test.

Thus there is a 60 per cent chance of an expected value of £820
and a 40 per cent chance of an expected value of £0 (following
rejection). Overall expected value is $(820)0.6 + (0)0.4 = £492$.
In the revised circumstances, the possibility of carrying out
the test increases the expected value of the contract from the
original value of £340 to £492. The value of the information
provided by the test is now only £152. Similar principles could
be applied in the situation where a firm was not indifferent to
risk, by using an analysis based on utility measurements.

Sources of information

A firm will wish to draw on various sources to obtain the basic
data it must analyse in the process of taking decisions. We
noted in chapter 4 the importance of a deliberate effort to
search for new activities that the firm could undertake. Re-
ports on new activities available may be received from research and development departments, special forward planning teams, marketing departments and from many functional
areas within the firm. Various people within the firm will be

assigned the tasks of predicting the supply of various resources; e.g. available labour might be estimated by the personnel department.

Much of the remaining required information could be supplied by traditional accounting systems with some supplementation. If the records have been kept in an appropriate form, they may give a good deal of information on which statistical analysis of cost–volume relationships for on-going activities may be based. The cost–volume relationship may be estimated in two stages, the first identifying the relationships between output volume and physical quantities of resources used and the second adding in prices of resources. Estimates of prices of resources may be derived from accounting records of recent prices, possibly supplemented by information from market sources. Information on quantities of resources required to produce various output volumes may be supplemented by test operations under controlled conditions. The accounting system will also convey a certain amount of information about sales prices–volume relationships for a firm's products. This information is somewhat sparse, however, and deals with only a few possible prices; it will probably require supplementation by market surveys or by knowledge possessed by managers about the qualities of the product, attitudes of customers, potential of competitors and so on.

The relevance of accounting information

Conventional accounting records do not provide all the information required by a business for taking decisions. They do provide information which has some relevance for particular decisions. We must *question* their usefulness, however, even in a limited role. We have noted in our previous discussions, particularly in chapter 17, a number of respects in which accounting systems fail to provide ideal information for decision purposes. In some cases, the deficiency may be remedied simply by ignoring part of the information which is not relevant. For example, a costing system may include allocations of fixed overhead expenses to individual activities; most decision purposes would be served better by ignoring this calculation. There may be greater difficulty with some costing calculations, however, because we do not wish to ignore the information but rather have it calculated in a different way. We would wish, for example, to have a good estimate of how total costs vary as a result of changes in activity levels, rather than the uncertain approximation to cost variations, given by direct costs, computed in accordance with costing practice.

Accounting, however, at least provides an operational system for the routine gathering of information; and the information it provides is by no means totally irrelevant. Questions of practicability restrict the amount and type of information it provides. In spite of its limitations, it might be optimal, judged in the light of a proper weighing of the costs and benefits of information having more direct relevance.

For example, it may be possible to obtain better estimates of the future cost of resources by consulting current price lists and similar data rather than using accounting records of the cost of similar resources in the past. However, there may be a reasonably stable relationship between past costs and current costs and the extra cost of the routine search for and recording of the current information may be considerable. The benefit of the updated information may be outweighed by the extra cost of getting it.

An illustration of the value of accounting information

This point may be illustrated in a simplified example. Early in December, Spica Ltd publishes its selling prices for each of its three products and plans output for the three months ending 31 March on the basis of orders received. A similar timetable is followed each quarter. The firm uses three types of raw material, one for each product. It has storage space only for small quantities of material. Suppliers review their prices on 1 January and at three monthly intervals.

The managers believe that they could introduce a programme of research which would give almost perfect predictions of suppliers' prices at a cost of £300 per quarter. It wishes to know whether the cost would be justified by the value of improved decisions.

There is currently a world shortage of the materials used by Spica. On the basis of past experience, modified by their assessment of current economic conditions, but without special investigation, the managers estimate that on 1 January, suppliers will increase their prices

by 10 per cent with probability 0·2
by 5 per cent with probability 0·5
and by 0 per cent with probability 0·3
_____
1·00

Product costs for the current quarter are given in Table 68. Labour costs are expected to be unchanged during the coming year. The cost–volume relationship for each product is linear.

Table 68 Costs of production, quarter ending 31 December

Product	A	B	C
	(£)	(£)	(£)
materials – actual cost	45	20	36
labour	20	25	30
	65	45	66

It is assumed for simplicity that it is known with certainty that the volume of orders for the coming quarter will satisfy the following price–volume relationships:

Product A; $p_a = 100 - \dfrac{q_a}{50}$.

Product B; $p_b = 80 - \dfrac{q_b}{100}$.

Product C; $p_c = 120 - \dfrac{q_c}{120}$.

The firm is indifferent to risk, i.e. decisions will be taken in a way that optimises expected values.

Consider, first, what price the firm should set for its products if it does not ascertain the actual market prices of materials for

Table 69 Expected value of optimal plan with imperfect information

Product	A	B	C
costs per unit:	(£)	(£)	(£)
expected cost of material	45	20	36
cost last quarter			
cost next quarter			
– increase 0 per cent (p = 0.30)	45	20	36
– increase 5 per cent (p = 0.50)	47.25	21	37.8
– increase 10 per cent (p = 0.20)	49.5	22	39.6
expected cost this quarter	47.025	20.9	37.62
labour cost	20	25	30
	£67.025	£45.9	£67.62
sales price–volume relationship	$p = 100 - \dfrac{q}{50}$	$p = 80 - \dfrac{q}{100}$	$p = 120 - \dfrac{q}{120}$
total revenue	$100q - \dfrac{q^2}{50}$	$80q - \dfrac{q^2}{100}$	$120q - \dfrac{q^2}{120}$
marginal revenue	$100 - \dfrac{q}{25}$	$80 - \dfrac{q}{50}$	$120 - \dfrac{q}{60}$
optimal quantity – q in	$100 - \dfrac{q}{25} = 67.025$ $q = 824$	$80 - \dfrac{q}{50} = 45.9$ $q = 1705$	$120 - \dfrac{q}{60} = 67.62$ $q = 3143$
optimal price	$p = 100 - \dfrac{824}{50}$ $= £83.52$	$p = 80 - \dfrac{1705}{100}$ $= £62.95$	$p = 120 - \dfrac{3143}{120}$ $= £93.80$
contributions from optimal plan	$(83.52 - 67.025)824$ $= £13\,592$	$(62.95 - 45.9)1705$ $= £29\,070$	$(93.8 - 67.62)3143$ $= £82\,284$
total contributions: £124 946			

Table 70 Expected value of plan with perfect information

Product	A	B	C
costs per unit (no increase in cost of materials)	£65	£45	£66
marginal revenue	$100 - \dfrac{q}{25}$	$80 - \dfrac{q}{50}$	$120 - \dfrac{q}{60}$
optimal quantity (cost = m.r.)	875	1750	3240
optimal price	82.5	62.5	93
contributions from optimal plan	$(82.5-65)875 = 15\,313$	$(62.5-45)1750 = 30\,625$	$(93-66)3240 = 87\,480$
costs per unit (5 per cent increase in cost of materials)	£67.25	£46	£67.8
marginal revenue	$100 - \dfrac{q}{25}$	$80 - \dfrac{q}{50}$	$120 - \dfrac{q}{60}$
optimal quantity (cost = m.r.)	819	1700	3132
optimal price	83.62	63	93.9
contributions from optimal plan	$(83.62-67.25)819 = 13\,407$	$(63-46)1700 = 28\,900$	$(93.9-67.8)3132 = 81\,745$

(10 per cent increase in cost of materials)

	$100 - \frac{q}{25}$	$80 - \frac{q}{50}$	$120 - \frac{q}{60}$
marginal revenue			
optimal quantity (cost = m.r.)	762	1650	3024
optimal price	84.76	63.5	94.8
contributions from optimal plan	$(84.76 - 69.5)762$ $= 11\,628$	$(63.5 - 47)1650$ $= 27\,225$	$(94.8 - 69.6)3024$ $= 76\,205$
expected value of plan			
situation (1), probability – 30 per cent	$0.3 \times 15\,313 = 4\,594$	$0.3 \times 30\,625 = 9\,188$	$0.3 \times 87\,480 = 26\,244$
situation (2), probability – 50 per cent	$0.5 \times 13\,407 = 6\,703$	$0.5 \times 28\,900 = 14\,450$	$0.5 \times 81\,745 = 40\,873$
situation (3), probability – 20 per cent	$0.2 \times 11\,628 = 2\,326$	$0.2 \times 27\,225 = 5\,445$	$0.2 \times 76\,205 = 15\,241$
	13 623	29 083	82 358

Total expected contributions £125 064

the coming quarter. The plan with the largest expected value is obtained by setting marginal revenue equal to expected marginal cost for each product.[1] Calculations are given in Table 69.

If Spica could obtain perfect information about cost levels for the coming quarter, its plan would have the expected value calculated in Table 70. The calculations give the contributions for the optimal plan if each of the three possible cost levels prevails. The expected value of the plan in this situation is derived as the weighted average of the three plans, using the probabilities of each cost level as weights.

The calculations demonstrate that improved information about market prices of material would make it possible to improve the expected value of the optimal plan – from £124 946 to £125 064, i.e. by £118. The assumed cost of obtaining the information, £300, outweighs the benefit that it brings in this case.

The example of Spica demonstrates that a firm's optimal policy may be to use relatively poor information (compared to the best available) for decisions in order to economise on information costs. The example was over-simplified in many ways: normally some prices would have changed at various times during the last accounting period and they would have some probability of changing at various times during the coming period; the assumed probability distribution for price changes was simple; the assumption that other cost and demand conditions were known with certainty was unrealistic;

---

1. Price of a product, $p = f(q)$; total revenue $= q f(q)$. There are three possible unit cost levels, C_1, C_2, C_3, with probabilities S_1, S_2, S_3. It is required to maximize the expected value of net receipts, which for any price, p, is

$$R = S_1(q f(q) - q C_1) + S_2(q f(q) - q C_2) + S_3(q f(q) - q C_3)$$
$$= q f(q) - q(S_1 C_1 + S_2 C_2 + S_3 C_3)$$

since $S_1 + S_2 + S_3 = 1$

Setting the first derivative equal to zero, we have

$$\frac{dR}{dq} = f(q) + q f'(q) - (S_1 C_1 + S_2 C_2 + S_3 C_3) = 0,$$

i.e. marginal revenue less expected marginal cost equal zero.

and it would normally be possible to adjust the plan as further information becomes available during the year. None of these simplifications, however, would affect the main principles illustrated. Calculations of greater complexity could be applied to a set of more realistic assumptions in a similar manner, and the possibility would remain that the optimal plan might involve using data which is less perfect than the best available. A similar example, for a firm using a wide range of materials, might have demonstrated the optimality of using past cost data even though replacement cost was relevant and published.

Our example deals with the prediction of future costs from past costs. Similar conclusions might hold for other examples of uses of imperfectly relevant information, derived from cost accounts. The approximation to variable costs given by direct costs is another example.

Our purpose in the above discussion, is not to give a general defence of uncritical uses of data from traditional accounting systems. It is simply to emphasize that information is not costless and that the best information available is not required at any price.

20 Conclusion

This book has attempted to describe shortly the main principles involved in applying the best modern methods of decision taking in business. The reader will notice that in many respects there are loose ends. The present state of our knowledge is quite imperfect for handling business decisions. In part this is because of the intrinsic difficulty of business decisions due to the uncertainty of the future events on which they depend. In part, it is because the best decisions depend on personal tastes, and tastes are extremely hard to measure even if they may be assumed to be consistently applicable in different situations. Only a small beginning has been made in trying out the techniques in practice. Little experience has been gained in their application and relatively little time has been spent in the development of theoretical refinements.

It is evident, however, that the rationale of decision taking has changed substantially in the past few years, or at least has received more explicit consideration. Decision taking has become more scientific. We may expect to see further rapid developments in applications and theory over the next few years.

Further Reading

Chapter 2

The reader who wishes to study some features of cost accounting practice in greater detail may refer to one of the following text books:

N. Dopuch and J. G. Birnberg, *Cost Accounting: Accounting Data for Management's Decisions*, Harcourt Brace & World, 1969, especially Part 4.

M. J. Gordon and G. Shillinglaw, *Accounting: A Management Approach*, 4th edition, Irwin, 1969.

C. T. Horngren, *Cost Accounting: A Managerial Emphasis*, 2nd edition, Prentice-Hall, 1967.

The nature of business objectives is discussed in:

R. Marris, 'A model of the managerial enterprise', *Quarterly Journal of Economics*, vol. 77, no. 2, 1963.

H. A. Simon, 'Theories of decision-making in economics and behavioral science', *American Economic Review*, vol. 49, no. 3, 1959.

J. Williamson, 'Profit, growth and sales maximization', *Economica*, 1966, pp. 1–16.

On the resolution of conflicting goals, see:

R. M. Cyert and J. G. March, *A Behavioral Theory of the Firm*, Prentice-Hall, 1963.

The analysis of investment decisions is discussed in:

J. Hirshleifer, 'On the theory of optimal investment decision', *Journal of Political Economy*, vol. 66, 1958, pp. 329–72. Reprinted in B. V. Carsberg and H. C. Edey (eds.), *Modern Financial Management*, Penguin, 1969.

J. T. S. Porterfield, *Investment Decisions and Capital Costs*, Prentice-Hall, 1965.

J. C. Van Horne, *Financial Management and Policy*, Prentice-Hall, 1971.

Chapter 3

S. Beer, 'Operational research and accounting', *Operational Research Quarterly*, vol. 5, 1954, pp. 1–12. Reprinted in D. Solomons (ed.), *Studies in Cost Analysis*, Irwin, 1968.

J. Boot, *Mathematical Reasoning in Economics and Management Science*, Prentice-Hall, 1967.

C. W. Churchman and R. L. Ackoff, 'Operational accounting and operations research', *Journal of Accountancy*, vol. 99, 1955, pp. 33–9. Reprinted in D. Solomons (ed.), *Studies in Cost Analysis*, Irwin, 1968.

C. C. Herrmann and J. F. Magee, 'Operations research for management', in F. C. Bursk and J. F. Chapman (eds.), *New Decision-Making Tools for Managers*, Mentor, 1965.

A. Schuchman (ed.), *Scientific Decision Making in Business*, Holt Rinehart & Winston, 1963, pp. 63–144.

Chapter 4

The main development of the analysis of business strategy is in:

H. I. Ansoff, *Corporate Strategy*, McGraw-Hill, 1965.

H. I. Ansoff, 'A quasi-analytic method for long-range planning', *Organizational Decision Making*, Prentice-Hall, 1967. Reprinted in B. V. Carsberg and H. C. Edey (eds.), *Modern Financial Management*, Penguin, 1969.

P. Drucker, 'Long-range planning, challenge to management science', *Management Science*, vol. 5, 1959, no. 3.

R. A. Johnson, F. E. Kast and J. E. Rosenzweig, 'Systems theory and management', *Management Science*, vol. 10, 1964, pp. 367–84. Reprinted in B. V. Carsberg and H. C. Edey (eds.), *Modern Financial Management*, Penguin, 1969.

A survey of work on cost–benefit analysis is given in:

A. R. Prest and R. Turvey, 'Cost–benefit analysis: a survey', *Economic Journal*, 1965, pp. 683–735.

On search procedures adopted in practice, see:

R. M. Cyert and J. G. March, *A Behavioral Theory of the Firm*, Prentice-Hall, 1963.

The problem of sub-optimization is discussed in:

J. Hirshleifer, 'On the economics of transfer pricing', *Journal of Business*, vol. 29, 1956, pp. 172–84. Reprinted in B. V. Carsberg and H. C. Edey (eds.), *Modern Financial Management*, Penguin, 1969.

D. Solomons, *Divisional Performance: Measurement and Control*, Financial Executives Research Foundation, 1965.

Examples of well-structured problems, including the transportation scheduling problem, are given in:

A. Henderson and R. Schlaifer, 'Mathematical Programming: better information for better decision making', in E. C. Bursk and J. F. Chapman (eds.), *Decision-Making Tools for Managers*, Mentor, 1965.

Chapter 5

B. V. Carsberg, *An Introduction to Mathematical Programming for Accountants*, George Allen & Unwin, 1969, chapter 2.

J. R. Gould, 'The economist's cost concept and business problems', in W. T. Baxter and S. Davidson (eds.), *Studies in Accounting Theory*, Sweet & Maxwell, 1962.

C. T. Horngren, *Cost Accounting: A Managerial Emphasis*, Prentice-Hall, 1967, chapter 13.

D. Solomons, 'Economic and accounting concepts of cost and value', in M. Backer (ed.), *Modern Accounting Theory*, Prentice-Hall, 1966.

Chapter 6

N. Dopuch and J. Birnberg, *Cost Accounting: Accounting Data for Management's Decisions*, Harcourt Brace and World, 1969, chapter 2 and pp. 71–5.

C. T. Horngren, *Cost Accounting: A Managerial Emphasis*, Prentice-Hall, 1967, chapter 7.

Chapter 7

Expositions of statistical methods are given in:

J. Freund, *Elementary Statistics*, Prentice-Hall, 1964.

J. Johnston, *Econometric Methods*, McGraw-Hill, 1960.

A. A. Walters, *An Introduction to Econometrics*, Macmillan, 1968.

Applications to problems of cost analysis are discussed in:

G. J. Benston, 'Multiple regression analysis of cost behavior', *Accounting Review*, vol. 41, 1966, pp. 657–72. Reprinted in D. Solomons (ed.), *Studies in Cost Analysis*, Irwin, 1968.

N. Dopuch and J. G. Birnberg, *Cost Accounting: Accounting Data for Management Decisions*, Harcourt Brace & World, 1969, chapter 3.

J. Johnston, *Statistical Cost Analysis*, McGraw-Hill, 1960.

Chapter 8

General descriptions of economic models of market situations are given in:

W. J. Baumol, *Economic Theory and Operations Analysis*, 2nd edition, Prentice-Hall, 1972, chapters 9, 10 and 14.

G. J. Stigler, *The Theory of Price*, Macmillan, 1952.

A simple exposition of the use of mathematical models is given in:

R. G. D. Allen, *Mathematical Analysis for Economists*, Macmillan, 1938, chapter 5.

On the kinked demand curve see:

G. J. Stigler, 'The kinky oligopoly demand curve and rigid prices', in *Readings in Price Theory*, Irwin, 1952.

Chapter 9

R. G. D. Allen, *Mathematical Analysis for Economists*, Macmillan, 1938, chapter 8.

W. J. Baumol, *Economic Theory and Operations Analysis*, 2nd edn, Prentice-Hall, chapters 13 and 14.

G. J. Stigler, *The Theory of Price*, Macmillan, 1952, chapters 9 and 10.

Chapter 10

Economists Advisory Group, *The Economics of Advertising*, The Advertising Association, 1970.

W. J. Baumol, *Economic Theory and Operations Analysis*, Prentice-Hall, 3rd edition, 1972, pp. 246–251 and pp. 327–8.

Chapter 11

B. V. Carsberg, *An Introduction to Mathematical Programming for Accountants*, George Allen & Unwin, 1969, chapters 3, 4 and 5.

N. Dopuch, 'Mathematical programming and accounting approaches to incremental cost analysis', *Accounting Review*, October ,1963.

G. Hadley, *Linear Programming*, Addison-Wesley, 1962.

L. A. Rapoport and W. P. Drews, 'Mathematical approach to long-range planning', *Harvard Business Review*, 1962, pp. 75–87. Reprinted in B. V. Carsberg and H. C. Edey (eds.), *Modern Financial Management*, Penguin, 1969.

J. H. Samuels, 'Opportunity costing: an application of mathematical programming', *Journal of Accounting Research*, Autumn, 1965.

The simplex method of solving linear programming problems is described in:

W. J. Baumol, *Economic Theory and Operations Analysis*, Prentice-Hall, 1965, chapters 5 and 6.

Uses of dual prices in divisional control are discussed in:

N. Dopuch and D. F. Drake, 'Accounting implications of a mathematical programming approach to the transfer price problem', *Journal of Accounting Research*, Spring, 1964.

D. Solomons, *Divisional Performance: Measurement and Control*, Financial Executives Institute, 1965.

Chapter 12

W. J. Baumol, *Economic Theory and Operations Analysis*,
Prentice-Hall, 1965, chapters 7 and 8.

B. V. Carsberg, *An Introduction to Mathematical Programming for
Accountants*, George Allen & Unwin, 1969, chapter 7.

G. Hadley, *Nonlinear and Dynamic Programming*, Addison-Wesley,
1964.

Chapter 13

Two useful general books on decisions under uncertainty are:

R. D. Luce and H. Raiffa, *Games and Decisions*, Wiley, 1957.

R. Schlaifer, *Probability and Statistics for Business Decisions*,
McGraw-Hill, 1959.

The path-breaking work in this area was by:

J. Von Neumann and O. Morgenstern, *Theory of Games and
Economic Behavior*, Princeton University Press, 2nd edition, 1947.

For an account of an attempt to apply utility analysis in practice
see:

C. J. Grayson, *Decisions under Uncertainty*, Boston, 1960.

For a discussion of the rationale of gambling, using utility analysis,
see:

M. Friedman and L. J. Savage, 'The utility analysis of choices
involving risk', *Journal of Political Economy*, August, 1948.
Reprinted in S. H. Archer and C. A. D'Ambrosio, *The Theory of
Business Finance*, Macmillan, 1967.

See also

W. J. Baumol, *Economic Theory and Operations Analysis*,
Prentice-Hall, 3rd edition, 1972, chapter 22.

Chapter 14

H. Markowitz, 'Portfolio selection', *Journal of Finance*, March,
1952.

W. F. Sharpe, 'Capital asset prices: a theory of market equilibrium under conditions of risk', *Journal of Finance*, September, 1964.

(The two above articles are reprinted in S. H. Archer and C. A. D'Ambrosio, *The Theory of Business Finance*, Macmillan, 1967.)

H. Markowitz, *Portfolio Selection, Efficient Diversification of Investments*, Wiley, 1959.

The strategy of diversification is discussed in:

H. I. Ansoff, 'A model for diversification', *Management Science*, 1958, pp. 392–414.

H. I. Ansoff, 'Strategies for diversification', *Harvard Business Review*, 1957, pp. 113–24.

Chapter 15

D. B. Hertz, 'Risk analysis in capital investment', *Harvard Business Review*, 1964, pp. 95–106.

R. K. Jaedicke and A. A. Robichek, 'Cost–volume–profit analysis under conditions of uncertainty', *Accounting Review*, October, 1964. Reprinted in D. Solomons (ed.), *Studies in Cost Analysis*, Irwin, 1968.

Chapter 16

The historical development of accounting is described in:

A. C. Littleton and B. S. Yamey (eds.), *Studies in the History of Accounting*, 1956.

A. C. Littleton, *Accounting Evolution to 1900*, 1933.

D. Solomons, 'The historical development of costing', in D. Solomons (ed.), *Studies in Cost Analysis*, Irwin, 1968.

For introductory expositions of double-entry book-keeping and budgetary control and standard costing see:

H. C. Edey, *Introduction to Accounting*, Hutchinson, 1963.

H. C. Edey, *Business Budgets and Accounts*, Hutchinson, 1959.

Full titles of historical works mentioned in the text are:

E. Garke and J. M. Fells, *Factory Accounts*, 1887.

L. Paciolo, *Summa de Arithmetica, Geometria, Proportioni et Proportionalita*, first published in Venice, 1494.

Chapter 18

Discussions of pricing practice appear in:

R. S. Edwards, 'The pricing of manufactured products', *Economica*, vol. 19, 1952, pp. 298–307. Reprinted in B. V. Carsberg and H. C. Edey (eds.), *Modern Financial Management*, Penguin, 1969.

R. L. Hall and C. J. Hitch, 'Price theory and business behaviour', in T. Wilson and P. W. S. Andrews, *Oxford Studies in the Price Mechanism*, Clarendon Press, 1951.

I. F. Pearce, 'A study of price policy', *Economica*, vol. 23, 1956, pp. 114–27. Reprinted in B. V. Carsberg and H. C. Edey (eds.), *Modern Financial Management*, Penguin, 1969.

The suggestion that cost-plus pricing is best viewed as a budgetary control device is made in:

W. T. Baxter and A. R. Oxenfeldt, 'Approaches to pricing: economist versus accountant', *Business Horizons*, vol. 4, 1961, pp. 77–90. Reprinted in B. V. Carsberg and H. C. Edey, (eds.) *Modern Financial Management*, Penguin, 1969.

The Glacier Metal Company's approach to pricing is described in:

W. Brown and E. Jaques, *Product Analysis Pricing*, Heinemann, 1964.

Chapter 19

M. M. Alexis and C. Z. Wilson (eds.), *Organisational Decision Making*, Prentice-Hall, 1967.

G. J. Stigler, 'The economics of information', *Journal of Political Economy*, June, 1961, pp. 213–225, in D. Needham (ed.), *Economics of Industrial Organisation*, Holt, Rinehart & Winston, 1971.

H. Theil, *Economics and Information Theory*, Chicago, 1967.

Index

More about Penguins and Pelicans

Penguinews, which appears every month, contains details of all the new books issued by Penguins as they are published. From time to time it is supplemented by *Penguins in Print*, which is our complete list of almost 5,000 titles.

A specimen copy of *Penguinews* will be sent to you free on request. Please write to Dept EP, Penguin Books Ltd, Harmondsworth, Middlesex, for your copy.

In the U.S.A.: For a complete list of books available from Penguins in the United States write to Dept CS, Penguin Books, 625 Madison Avenue, New York, New York 10022.

In Canada: For a complete list of books available from Penguins in Canada write to Penguin Books Canada Ltd, 2801 John Street, Markham, Ontario L3R 1B4.

A Dictionary of Economics

Graham Bannock, R. E. Baxter and Ray Rees

A Dictionary of Economics is addressed to both the student and the general reader who wants to be able to follow economic discussions in the press and elsewhere, or whose daily work demands some familiarity with economic terms. It aims to provide a comprehensive companion to support other reading in a discipline which employs remarkably similar terminology in Britain and the United States.

This new dictionary, prepared by three practising economists, contains over 1,500 entries on economic terms and theory, the history of economics, and individual economists where they have made a definable contribution to contemporary economic thought. An elaborate system of cross-referencing makes the dictionary easy to use and extremely informative.

Health Economics

Edited by M. H. Cooper and A. J. Culyer

How much should a country spend on health services?
How should its expenditure be financed? Is health expenditure
an investment or is it consumption? What is the output of
health-care institutions? What is the demand for health and
what determines that demand? What contribution does better
health make to the growth of GNP and the quality of life?

This book of Readings attempts an economic analysis of these
questions. Part One contains some of the major theoretical
contributions in the field, including Kenneth Arrow's classic
examination of the US health-care system in relation to a
hypothetically ideal market. Empirical questions such as the
measurement of the contribution of health services to
national output are presented in Part Two, while Part Three
analyses the hospitals, with regard to costs and the
maximization of utility. The last part examines the important
problem of bringing concern for human lives into the decision-
making process.

The Economics of the Common Market

Dennis Swann

This clearly written book describes the social and political origins of the Common Market, traces its evolution through the practical decisions that have been taken since 1958, and indicates the possibilities of future development.

The attitudes of the member states towards central issues such as the Common Agricultural Policy, movements of labour and the coordination of social security are clearly brought out. The reader is given real insights into the decision-making functions of the Council of Ministers on such matters as the attainment of economic and monetary union, the methods of achieving the objectives of the Rome Treaty in the face of tremendous difficulties, and the spur to integration that the American challenge affords.

This thoroughly revised edition is written in the context of Britain's membership of the EEC and has a postscript on the changed situation since the return of a Labour Government committed to important negotiations.

'This is an excellent text to put in the hands of university students of economics and should satisfy also the wider public' *Economic Journal*

Economic Systems and Society: Capitalism, Communism and the Third World

George Dalton

It is less useful today to group economic systems under the traditional headings of capitalist or communist, because both kinds continue to change structurally and ideologically in unforeseen ways.

In this historical account of changing systems, George Dalton has traced the development of these economies, from the Industrial Revolution to the present. He deals first with nineteenth-century capitalism, the contrasting responses of utopian, Marxian and democratic socialism, the welfare-state capitalism of the 1930s and 1940s, and the policies and practices of Stalin's Russia. Later chapters explore recent change in both developed and developing economies: the author shows in particular how the Industrial Revolution is being relived today in Africa and Asia.

This book very clearly shows how the policy goals, policy instruments and economic institutions of each country are shaped by its historical and political traditon. It is intended for students just starting an economics course as well as others involved with political science or social history.

Self-Management:
Economic Liberation of Man

Selected Readings
Edited by Jaroslav Vanek

Is an answer to our industrial problems to encourage workers' control and will this have a liberating effect on their attitude to work? In this age of increasingly depersonalized business enterprises, the cry of workers for more control over their destiny has been increasing. This selection of Readings examines one way out.

Professor Vanek provides a long introduction outlining the large variety of schemes that can be considered as 'labour-managed', especially in the light of the economic environment in which they operate. The selection of Readings is then divided into four parts. Part One considers the growth of the doctrine of labour management from the ideas of Buchez in the 1830s to the present day. Part Two describes actual cases of self-management beginning with a European survey and continuing with examples from Peru, America, Israel, Britain, Czechoslovakia and Spain. Part Three is concerned with the performance of such schemes, providing comparison with other systems of production. Part Four examines the developments in the formal economic theory of self-management, and the changes required in traditional economic theories.

Business Strategy:
Selected Readings

Edited by H. Igor Ansoff

Business Strategy introduces the reader to the explicit formulation of the strategy of a firm. Part One looks at the ways in which changes of policy come about. Part Two takes a look at the effect the future will have on the firm and the individuals in it; while Part Three compares two different approaches to the formulation of strategy. The determination of the goals of the firm is discussed in Part Four in a fascinating mixture of description (Galbraith), prescription (Rayek) and cool analysis (Simon). Parts Five and Six are devoted to case histories from Britain, France and the United States of firms that needed to find a strategy to ensure their success.

'Catholic, exhaustive and commendably eclectic'
The Times Literary Supplement

Management is an international science whose boundaries are as wide as the work men do and the organizations they work in. Penguin Modern Management Readings bring together leading articles and extracts, edited by distinguished authorities from every field of management work and education.